Notes from a Colored Girl

~ *Notes from a Colored Girl* ~

THE CIVIL WAR POCKET DIARIES OF
EMILIE FRANCES DAVIS

Karsonya Wise Whitehead

The University of South Carolina Press

© 2014 Karsonya Wise Whitehead

Published by the University of South Carolina Press
Columbia, South Carolina 29208

www.sc.edu/uscpress

Manufactured in the United States of America

23 22 21 20 19 18 17 16 15 14   10 9 8 7 6 5 4 3 2 1

Library of Congress Cataloging-in-Publication Data

Whitehead, Karsonya Wise.
  Notes from a colored girl : the Civil War pocket diaries of Emilie Frances Davis /
Karsonya Wise Whitehead.
    pages cm.
  Includes bibliographical references and index.
  ISBN 978-1-61117-352-9 (hardback) — ISBN 978-1-61117-353-6 (ebook) 1. Davis, Emilie
Frances, 1838–1899—Diaries. 2. African Americans—Pennsylvania—Philadelphia—
Biography. 3. African Americans—Pennsylvania—Philadelphia—History—19th century.
4. Philadelphia (Pa.)—Race relations—History—19th century. 5. Philadelphia (Pa.)—Social
conditions—19th century. 6. Philadelphia (Pa.)—History—Civil War, 1861–1865. I. Davis,
Emilie Frances, 1838–1899. Diaries. II. Title.
  F158.44.W55 2014
  974.8'1103092—dc23
  [B]

                                                                    2013036697

This book was printed on recycled paper with 30 percent postconsumer waste content.

For my two favorite men:
my father, Carson Eugene Wise Sr.,
and my husband, Johnnie

The myopic sight of the darkened eye can only be restored when the
full range of the black woman's voice, with its own special timbres and
shadings, remains mute no longer.

Henry Louis Gates Jr., The Journals of Charlotte Forten Grimké

Emilie's story is an American story because what's more American than wanting to be
heard, wanting to be remembered, and wanting to be the type of change that you want to
see in the world. At a time when black people were not allowed to read and write,
she picked up a pen, bought a diary, and recorded her life, in her own words. If that
isn't a quintessential American story, then what is?

Dorothy Bamberg

CONTENTS

ILLUSTRATIONS

ACKNOWLEDGMENTS

This book has been written and rewritten a dozen times in my mind, and it exists on paper only because of the wonderful people who believed in me, challenged me, and pushed me to succeed. They never failed to remind me of how important it was for Emilie's story to be told and for me to tell it. I owe them more than I could ever begin to repay.

Emilie's diaries would have gone unnoticed by me (and others) had it not been for Fayetta Martin, who thought that they were interesting enough to make copies of them and mail them to me. Although we did not work on the project together, her contributions in the very early stages were an invaluable part of the process.

I am grateful to both the Historical Society of Pennsylvania for the care they have taken with storing and preserving the Emilie Davis diaries and for granting me permission to use the documents and the Library Company of Philadelphia for providing me with an office space and ongoing support. Mathew Lyons, Lauri Cielo, Dana Lamparello, Hillary Kativa, and James Green were extremely helpful and patient with me. The weekly visits (many times arranged at the last minute) and the summers that I spent in residence as an Albert Greenfield Fellow were instrumental in helping me to finish the transcriptions and my research. Matt Gallman, Judy Giesberg, Tamara Gaskell, Andrew Jewell, Amanda Gailey, Beth Luey, and Polina Vinogradova helped me to understand how to place Emilie in a broader context. Their various comments on my articles were both insightful and challenging. Paper presentations and discussions at the National Women's Studies Association (NWSA), the Association for the Study of African American Life and History (ASALH), Camp Edit, the Dissertation Writing House, and on two faculty retreats: Collegium and the Ignatian Pilgrimage, which provided me with forums to talk through my work and my ideas.

This book comes directly from my dissertation, and at every critical step and moment, my committee supported and believed in me. Theirs are the shoulders on which I stand as both a scholar and a teacher. I am thankful for all that they have done and, in some cases, continue to do. My cochairs, Christine Mallinson and Kriste Lindenmeyer, and my committee, Michelle Scott, Christel Temple, and Debra Newman Ham, read through countless drafts of my work and helped me to define and shape the project from the beginning until the end. Other scholars who supported me and provided me with invaluable criticism, suggestions, and ideas include Ira Berlin (a genius and a trailblazer); Kelly Gray and the Baltimore History Writing Group; Renetta Tull and Wendy Carter from the (amazing!) UMBC Promise Group; Daniel Biddle and Murray Dubin, my Philadelphia scholar support team; Sylvia Cyrus, Daryl Michael Scott, and the Association for the Study of African American History (ASALH); and my mentors La Vonne Neal and Martha Wharton, who never failed to light the path and point the way. I must also thank my unofficial team of editors who read through all of my copyedits and offered guidance, support, corrections, and encouragement: Toya Corbett, Christy Dupeé, Ronald Harrison, Jr. (who went above and beyond the call of duty!), and David Leonard.

In addition to Suzanne Keilson, whose unique insight into Emilie's life and her story forced me to rewrite quite a few paragraphs, several of my colleagues at Loyola University Maryland have offered support and encouragement: Neil Alperstein, Stacey Bass, Father Tim Brown, Russell Cook (and his wonderful wife, Carol), Stephanie Florish-Kholish, Celia Goldsmith (who also went above and beyond the call of duty), Elliot King, Jonathan Lillie, Cheryl Moore-Thomas, Brian Mulchahy, Brian Norman (whose weekly Friday coffees provided me with a safe space to talk through my work), Peggy O'Neill, Mili Shah, and Amanda Thomas. My research assistant, Megan Fisher, was diligent and tenacious in tracking down primary sources, reading through articles, and looking over my transcriptions. Her help was invaluable. Dean James Miracky and the Center for the Humanities provided me with summer funding, travel monies, research assistants, and a much-needed junior sabbatical to complete the final edits on the manuscript.

Outside of Loyola, this project was supported by summer faculty fellowships and funding from a number of sources, including a Summer Stipend from the National Endowment for the Humanities, two Lord Baltimore Fellowships from the Maryland Historical Society, an Albert M. Greenfield Foundation Fellowship in African-American History from the Library Company of Philadelphia, a Southern Regional Education Board fellowship, and a summer research fellowship from the Gilder Lehrman Institute for American History. This project would never have been finished if it were not for the gentle encouragement and support of my editor, Alexander Moore; he was a rock, a hand-holder, and a very stable presence in the midst of my writing storms. This project would never have been finished in style if it were not for my copyeditor, Elizabeth Jones, whose careful eye and red pen caught and silently corrected every errant mistake.

And then there are the folks who knew me before I started on this path and who have supported me throughout this process with kind words, warm cups of coffee, and homemade gooey delicious snacks: Ameerah Almateen, Anne Angeles, Wendy Barton, Michele Berger, Kevin Carr, Yvette and Clive Davis, Christy Dupeé, Lajuanna and O'Neal Johnson, Johanne Rodriguez, Monica Stewart,

Jeanine Williams, and the Happy Hairstons: Brother Thom and Sister Olivia and their daughters Dorna, Yvette, and Tody. I owe special thanks to my in-laws, Luther and Florence Huzzey, who have always provided support and encouragement. I was blessed to receive guidance and instruction from two beautiful, classy women: my dear sweet grandmothers, Maria Anderson and Dorothy Bamberg (when I grow up I want to be just like them!). I also thank all of my extended family, particularly my favorite uncles: Henry Anderson, Bishop Billy Bamberg, and Ronnie Griffin; and my "adopted" son Jack Jack Cho. I am grateful to my siblings: Robyn, Labonnie, Carson (and Rosie Pearl); and particularly grateful to my parents, Reverend Dr. Carson and Bonnie Wise, who believed in me even on days when I was unable to believe in myself.

This project, in so many ways, consumed my family more than I ever could have imagined. Emilie Davis was the invisible fourth child who joined us on every summer vacation and every Saturday outing. My family welcomed her and was patient and kind while I spent more time with her than with them. My children—Mercedes Alexandria, Kofi Elijah, and Amir Elisha—cheered me up and cheered me on, on the days when the needs of the book took precedence over the needs of the home. Finally, and perhaps most important, I am grateful to my husband, my soul mate, and my best friend, Johnnie Whitehead—he blesses me beyond measure, and for that and so much more . . . this one is for him!

EDITORIAL METHODS

My research into the life of Emilie Davis actually began about six years ago when I received photocopies of her pocket diaries and began the painstaking process of transcribing and annotating her entries. Since Emilie's diary pages and a different transcription can now be found online, my goal was to present a heavily annotated reader-friendly version while still preserving her intent and style.[1] Transcribing the diaries was both time consuming and difficult, owing to Emilie's handwriting, the ink smudges, and the faded pages; therefore, the process of transcription entailed many methodological decisions on my part as a researcher. I worked directly on paper copies made from the original diaries and spent a considerable amount of time learning Emilie's writing. Many times I used a pencil to trace over her words in an effort to try and understand what she was writing. Since she took both French and German, there were times when I believed that she was attempting to use these words (sometimes incorrectly) in her entries. In those cases, I translated the word to the best of my ability and then provided the meaning. Thus, with "Yesterday, quite a remarkable *au courant* [my emphasis] meeting at Mrs. Rivers," I am guessing that she meant "au courant," which is French for "aware." She also could have meant "a current" meeting, writing "au" for "a" and misspelling "current." Because Emilie wrote for herself and did not revise her entries, there are a number of grammatical and spelling errors, as well as mistakes in capitalization and punctuation. I completed three drafts of the transcriptions constantly checking them against the original diaries; my research assistant then completed an additional transcription once the initial corrections had been made.

Along the way, I made various corrections and edits to the text, using the following guidelines to help organize my work:

Emily, Emilie, or Emlie

In the 1850 and 1860 U.S. Census, in the 1863 Report of the Ladies' Union Association of Philadelphia, and on both her death and marriage certificates Emilie Davis's name is spelled using the English spelling: Emily; at the Historical Society of Pennsylvania and in the front of her 1863 and 1864 pocket diaries, her name is spelled using the French spelling of her name: Emilie; and, in the front of her 1863 pocket diary, where she wrote her name in ink and in cursive, she spelled it Emlie: three different spellings. Thus far, I have been unable to locate a birth certificate for her; therefore, in this book, I have elected to use the French spelling of her name—as it seems to be the spelling she preferred in 1864 and 1865 (as well as the spelling of her daughter's name). Unfortunately no pictures of her or her family have been found.

Colored, Black, or Mulatto

In 1831, William Lloyd Garrison's abolitionist newspaper, the *Liberator,* published a series of opinion editorials from the free black community that documented their attempts to find a term to describe themselves that everyone could agree on. This discussion included a number of choices, including *Afric-Americans, Africans, Africanamericans, Americans, Colored, Colored Americans, Negroes,* and *Niger.*[2] The newspaper does not indicate that an agreement was ever reached, and in many ways, since then, there has been an ongoing debate about what is the most appropriate term to call African people who were involuntarily bought to America and have since become an integral part of the fabric of this country. In the 1850 and 1860 U.S. Census, Emilie is classified as mulatto, but, in her diary, in the two places where she racially self-identified, she called herself "colored." During the mid-nineteenth century, the term *mulatto* was used to describe free blacks that had lighter skin and Caucasian features; and the term *black* was used to indicate either an enslaved person or a free person who had darker skin and African features. At times the racial classifications were randomly applied to family members. For example, in 1850 and 1860, Emilie's mother, sister, and younger brother were classified as mulatto, while her father and older brother were classified as black. The term *colored* was actually a social term used interchangeably with the terms *black* and *mulatto.* Later sections will describe the politics around the use of these terms, and in an effort to narrow the scope of the discussion, I actively employed a black feminist perspective and decided to use the term *black,* since it is used today and it is less politically and historically charged than the terms *colored* or *negro* (I am thinking in particular of W. E. B. Du Bois's use of the term *negro* in his 1896 social study of the negro problems documented in *The Philadelphia Negro*).[3]

In addition the term *black* will be applied only to black Americans of African descent and not Africans who have willingly migrated to this country, Africans who were born here but whose parents are immigrants, or Africans who have dual citizenship. The term *mulatto* will be used only when I am comparing the political, social, and economic conditions of the black (that is formerly enslaved or those possessing darker skin) with the mulatto communities.

I also grappled with whether or not to capitalize the term *black.* I am aware of the contention around the use of this term as a form of both empowerment and denigration. Although I agree with W. E. B. Du Bois, who argued that people who have a history deserve to have their name capitalized, in the end I decided that the term *black,* like *white* and *colored* and *mulatto,* would not be capitalized. I know that everything racial is political and that every decision I make frames Emilie and my story in a certain way, but I stand by these decisions and simply note that I hope we get to a point where labels are not political, equality is simply how things are, and people are judged for who they are and not for what they look like—concepts that are not new but have not yet become the norm.

Spelling

As much as possible, I have left all of Emilie's original spellings intact, and in instances in which I was unable to understand what was written, I made an educated guess, placing the word that I thought it was within brackets. In instances in which she wrote the wrong word, the spelling is hard to discern, or she left out a word, I made a decision based on context clues and placed the word within parentheses. I removed random capital letters and I added capitals at the beginning of proper names and places, and at the beginning of what I felt were sentences. Illegible or obscured words that can be inferred from the text are included. In instances in which I was unable to understand or guess what Emilie meant, I included an ellipsis; in those few cases where I was not one hundred percent sure, I added my best guess with a question mark at the end. Finally, any words that she struck out but that I felt were relevant to the text have been included with a line through the words, and obvious spelling errors were silently corrected.

Punctuation

With regard to punctuation, I limited my edits to the period unless Emilie used the words *who, what, when, where, why,* or *how* at the beginning of the sentence, in which cases I added a question mark. I also added commas within run-on sentences when I was not sure if the excerpt was supposed to contain two separate sentences or express one full thought.

Proper Names

I made the spelling of proper names consistent. In her entries Emilie frequently changed the spelling of people's names. To add clarity I kept the first spelling she used and then kept the correction and the full name in parentheses. In instances in which there could be confusion about who was being referenced, I used the name that was most frequently used, for instance *Sue* for references to Sally Sue Jones, Sally Sue J., and Sue. I added clarifying and background information in the annotations, including last names, titles, and affiliations, wherever I could to provide further insight into the people and places that Emilie mentioned. So, "Beautiful day Nellie was up and spent part of the day reading was here Nellie had and engagement and had to go hom i stoped home a few minutes the girls were all there" with edits now reads, "Beautiful day. Nellie was up and spent part of the day. Reading (Redding B. Jones) was here. Nellie had an engagement and had to go home. I stoped home a few minutes. The girls were all there";[4] and a footnoted annotation provides the background information: "Emilie's 'girls' (her closest female friends) consisted of Nellie, Ellen Black, and Rachel Turner—all of whom lived in the lower section of the Seventh Ward—and Sue, who appears to have lived outside of the city; prior to being unanimously elected and serving as the pastor of First African Presbyterian Church 1873–79, Reverend Redding B. Jones worked as a community pastor in the Seventh Ward. Although he was very popular with his congregants, Redding was asked to leave the church because the Elders were concerned that he was becoming too involved with the "holiness" fad."

A more detailed biography is located in the Who's Who section at the end of the book. As much as possible, I tried to identify all of the people in Emilie's life, but there were instances when her notes either provided an unclear path or obscured it greatly. The path was most clear when she provided last names, as in the case of Mary Adger, Mary Alfred, Mary Brown, Mary Douglass, Mary Grew, Mary Jones, Mary Pierce, and Mary Proyer; and it was completely obscured when she did not, as was the case with Nellie, mentioned 504 times; Vincent, mentioned 213 times; and Cristy, mentioned 38 times. Other than her father, her brother, and her friend Sue, these three were frequently mentioned in her entries, but since she chose not to provide a last name or any identifying information about them, they are completely lost in the annals of history. The question that begs to be answered is, was Emilie writing for herself or the world? In these cases, it would seem she was doing both; but, as a result of this duality, the people who most shaped her life and with whom she spent a majority of her time are some of the few people whose story I cannot tell.

Dates

Although Emilie's entries are written in a datebook, she did not separate the days. Since she usually began the day by commenting on the weather, I used that as a natural starting place to organize her entries. When she chose not to record the weather, it was often difficult to separate the days; in those cases, I would use her weekly schedule. Emilie attended church almost every Sunday, had school on Monday evenings, club meetings on Tuesday evening, would often attend concerts or lectures on Thursday and Friday evenings, and would try to visit with her father on Saturday afternoons. At first glance, Emilie's simple organizing system is easy to overlook, but after reading her diary and understanding her daily procedure, I began to realize that Emilie recorded the weather because her movements were closely connected to it. Emilie did not own a carriage, so she either walked or caught a streetcar. She was often sick during the winter and would choose to stay in if it looked like rain or snow. Emilie was a social person who seems to have enjoyed being in the company of others at all times, and when she could not visit or did not have visitors, it really upset her. She would lament for days and complain about both the weather and her fair-weather friends.

I also made some minor clarifications to the Memoranda (or Miscellaneous section for the 1865 diary) sections located at the back of the pocket diaries and attempted to connect them to her daily entries. It appears as if she did not write in the Memoranda section until the end of the year, when she reflected on some of the major events that happened either in the world or in her life. Here, at the end of her 1863 diary, she wrote, "The riot in New York commenced on Monday the 13th, burning for days. The colored people suferd most from the mob." Because Emilie lived in Philadelphia, she was well aware of the major events that were happening around the country, usually mentioning them in her journal within a day or two (news traveled quickly but not instantaneously). The Draft Riots had broken out in several northern cities over the issue of conscription. In New York, in particular, an angry crowd looted and rioted throughout the city, terrorizing black people and burning black businesses and homes to the ground. By the end of the three days, over twelve hundred people had been killed. In contrast to her note in the Memoranda section, Emilie's July 13, 1863, daily entry briefly states, "Very busiy all day, Nellie stoped a little while. I went to see about a situation, (a live-in domestic job) didn't get it."[5] In places where she did not connect to larger events, I added that information to provide a context for her experiences. Although Emilie mostly kept her world small, in neatly defined parameters, I felt it was important to place her life within the broader context.

Reading the Diaries

In many ways reading someone's diary greatly blurs the lines between private thoughts and public information. The reader is unaware of the hidden meaning or intent behind the entry, and for this reason, parts of a diary—unless the writer is there to explain them—will always remain closed. It is much too complicated (in some instances, impossible) to catch up on what was written or what actually happened before beginning reading. In those cases, it is best to simply join the conversation as if it has just begun. Emilie's pocket diaries begin on January 1, 1863, the Day of Jubilee—for us it is the beginning; but for her, it is the continuation of a life already in motion. Her story began long before she started keeping her 1863 diary and continued long after she wrote her final entry in 1865, and with that knowledge in mind, we simply join her for three years on a stage that has already been set and a life that is already in progress.

Introduction

A WORLD DISCOVERED

The history of how the free and enslaved black communities were able to both survive and prosper within a slave society is both engaging and fraught with confusion, half-truths, and in some cases, unsubstantiated claims. Sifting through the history is particularly difficult for anyone who is attempting to understand how the social and political climatic shift that occurred in the nation on January 1, 1863, affected both of these communities. We now know that for a variety of reasons "freedom" for some did not actually mean freedom for all; and in both cases, there was not a clear definition of what freedom meant, how it could be negotiated, and how it translated into tangible rewards. Though there have been a number of books and articles that have attempted to answer these questions, many remain, and more research still needs to be done. Slavery and freedom are complicated terms that involve an understanding of how race, class, and gender were socially constructed in this country and how this social construction still continues to inform how these issues are viewed today.

This book cannot possibly answer all these questions and instead seeks only to tell the narrow story of one woman's life through an intensive reading of her pocket diaries from 1863 to 1865. It is easy to overlook the life of Emilie F. Davis, a freeborn woman who worked as both a domestic and a *modiste* (a dressmaker), as her name is unknown; her contributions to history are undetermined; and outside of her pocket diaries the details of her life would not exist. What sets Emilie apart is that her pocket diaries are one of only a few primary sources written by a black woman during this time period. Her ordinary has been rendered extraordinary simply because it has survived; and therein lies the dilemma and, of course, the interest. Because of Emilie's choice to keep a personal diary—her conscious act of identity assertion—she has moved from invisibility to visibility and been added to the literature on everyday, working-class free black American women.[1] Since her handwriting is difficult to read and her story had to be reconstructed, I viewed her diaries as a code that needed to be broken so that I could discover who she was.

Code Breaking

My earliest experience with code breaking happened when I was eight years old and I stumbled upon my father's fraternal ritual books. They were written in a coded language, and though I knew it was forbidden (family members were not allowed to touch or read the sacred books), I committed myself to finding a way to break the code. I remember holding the books and slowly looking through the pages hoping that the letters would right themselves and become the words that I was familiar with. I would sit for hours studying the words, writing them over and over again. There were days when I would just open up the book and lay it across my forehead thinking that the meaning would simply come to me. I wanted to know (I had to, really) what was hidden behind the code. I remember how excited and satisfied and pleased I felt when I had finally broken it. It was that moment, that feeling of being inside rather than outside of the text, which has informed my research. Since then I have had an ongoing desire to break codes in an effort to try to understand the writer's meaning behind the text.

Writing, even in a diary, is not a private act. It is a public act, where the writer is attempting to share himself or herself with others. It is part of a larger discourse that shapes how and what we remember. Writing our memories down separates the chaff of our emotional experience from the wheat of the actual experience by informing how and what we remember. The moment you record something on paper; that record has the potential to find its way into the hands of others—even if it takes years to get there.

The pocket diaries of Emilie F. Davis are over 150 years old, and it is not known why or how her diaries (her memories) have been preserved. Perhaps they were passed from one family member to another as a way of maintaining the family's story, or perhaps they were packed away in an heirloom box that sat for years in someone's attic. That the diaries exist at all, that they have not disintegrated or been destroyed, and that years after Emilie penned her first entry they have ended up in my hands, is remarkable. Even though the diaries are tattered and fragile, her words have not faded, and her story stands as an intact finished product. Through the process of intensively reading Emilie's diaries—that is, by carefully examining every word that she wrote for meaning, context, and historical information—Emilie's written lines can be interpreted in a broader context.[2] This intensive reading of her pocket diaries situates Emile as an active agent telling her own story; gives a shape and a form to her personhood; and reveals how she interacted within her environment, her circumstances, and her life experiences.

The Emilie Davis Pocket Diaries

The process of editing a diary demands that the researcher be "deliberately articulate." This becomes even more important when one is editing and interpreting a diary like Emilie's. Transcribing her pocket diaries, along with reconstructing her life, is vitally important in black cultural mythology as researchers and historians continue their work to find, rescue, and preserve black history. Since diaries of black people from this time are so rare, Emilie's daily recordings of her mundane, everyday events get repositioned as a lens through which one can view the black community at this time. At the same time, by repositioning *Emilie* as the lens, her experiences and her life become more important and significant than she or they actually may have been at that time. She becomes—simply because there are so few other voices—the democratic catechism of the free black community.[3] Her private space has become a public forum and a starting place for discussion and analysis. Her story, as it stands, is an ongoing dialectic that provides insight into the relationship between the mulatto and the black communities, the elite and the enslaved; and into the different lived experiences of freeborn black men and women. Emilie both negotiated her freedom and expanded the definition of it based on how she chose to spend her time. Her diary was a place where she could be herself and share her thoughts. She was a constant and consistent diarist who seemed to have written despite what was going on around her.[4] Her entries provide insight into what was happening on the ground in the free black communities and how free black people lived their lives every day in the midst of the Civil War. As it stands now, this war is one of the most researched areas in American history, and the huge volume of books, movies, articles, and other materials that have been produced and are being produced about it are designed to pull the reader/viewer from the outside of the story to the inside of it.[5] Emilie's pocket diaries do the opposite: they allow the reader to view the Civil War from the perspective of someone who was living during the time of the war but who was not a participant or a discussant.

Before my work with Emilie, free black Philadelphia was not the focus of my research. I was more interested in doing a comparative study of the lives of free and enslaved women in Virginia and Maryland. But ever since I started working with the diaries, Emilie's story has become my own. I recognize that I am in a unique position to tell her story, standing as I do on the shoulders of black women—writers, artists, activists, archivists—who have come before me. Writing Emilie's story has helped me to appreciate (and in some ways, understand) how black women negotiated space and time within a free environment. This work has also helped me to understand how the tenuous strains of nineteenth-century freedom, the malleable societal roles, and the different definitions of elite and privilege have shaped and informed the black communities. In doing so, I slowly began to realize how Emilie's situations, friendships, beauty rituals, and relationship struggles were very similar to my own everyday experiences. I knew that I was working on telling Emilie's story from my position as both an "outsider," from another time and place, who is squinting at her life through a telescopic long view of history, and as a loosely connected "insider." At the same time, since I am from South Carolina and am only five generations removed from, I do believe that as Emilie worked in the North to raise monies for the freedman in Charleston and to help end enslavement, it benefitted my family in the South. I am living the future—with a black president, the legacy of the civil rights movement, and the impact of the Reconstruction Amendments—that she worked for but probably never could have completely imagined.

Emilie occupies a unique space that has not been fully researched or studied. In reviewing and framing her work, I actively applied the theories of immortality (since Emilie's story, in her own words, has survived) and the deconstruction of Emilie's literary form (that is, her consistent use of and practice with pocket diaries) to provide a narrative framework to properly reconstruct a narrative of her life.[6] My goal was to present Emilie without distortions, limitations, or prejudices; therefore, I committed to working every day, starting without judgment, at the place where I stood. I worked as a "forensic herstorical investigator," using a black feminist lens to analyze her life from three different perspectives while working across multiple disciplinary fields: as a historian, I was doing a herstorical reconstruction of her life using primary and secondary sources to both support and confirm her experiences; as a journalist, I was piecing together her entries to reconstruct her daily life, particularly during the moments when I could not find corroborating information (the times when I had to trust that events happened exactly as she recorded them); and, as a documents editor, I was doing a word-for-word transcription and annotation of her pocket diary entries. Her diaries in and of themselves are historical artifacts, and I was looking for ways to analyze how they conveyed information about the world as it existed outside the imagination and the interpretation of the diarist.

Emilie's life story was written as it progressed cumulatively, meaning that new information, as it was found, was always analyzed and included. In addition, I explored all of the contradictions that existed in Emilie's life. On the one hand, Emilie possessed cultural capital as a lighter-skinned woman who had unearned color-based social privileges along with a very powerful political and social network of relatives and friends, and out of this small number of women, some of their words and experiences have survived.[7] On the other hand, Emilie was a part of the unknown masses whose stories, under normal circumstances, have never been retold.

From the beginning of my research, I decided that everything about Emilie's life was important and significant because it provided an understanding of how she lived and interpreted her life. I was also aware that Emilie's survival, in the words of Audre Lorde, "was a learned skill and not an academic one," meaning that the fact that her words have been preserved is just as important as the fact that she chose to record them.[8] I ensured that as I wrote about Emilie a constructed analysis of her diary entries would always accompany my narrative of her life. I knew that in interpreting Emilie's diary, it was just as important to interpret and determine what she left out as it was to analyze what she left (or chose to include) in her diary. I also aimed to maintain a balance between self-reflection and scholarly analysis by allowing Emilie's story to speak for itself.

At the same time, however, I sought to remain engaged in Emilie's life and story as an active participant who had decided to write into her life and consciously create and build out her narrative. I was honest about the fact that the personal is and was always political—both hers and mine; even my decision to refer to her by her first name rather than her last was a conscious decision on my part to acknowledge and recognize her identity. I wanted to personalize her, to make her into my familiar. She became real to me, and at some point her story and mine merged, and though I tried, it was very difficult for me to have (and maintain) a bird's-eye view as I was pulled into her story. Diaries have a way of doing that to you. They pull you in and force you to see the world through the eyes of the writer. There were times when this immersion limited my ability to critically analyze *the* world and not just *her* world, which on all accounts were never the same. Emilie, like most diarists, constructed her world, and she existed in a space that needed to be examined. In this regard I was careful to balance the fact that I care about Emilie's story with the realities of the fact that I had chosen to invade and interpret her life. Although Emilie was not writing for me or anyone else, I was taking a certain amount of liberty as a black feminist in telling her story and in using an interdisciplinary framework in interpreting her life. I recognized that Emilie had a story to tell and that it was my job—as a fellow diarist and sister—to tell it, following a long tradition of other scholars who have come before me. I will never know why Emilie chose to record her life in the way that she did: perhaps, she engaged in close writing, where each word was nurtured and tested before it was written; or maybe she spoke out loud as she wrote, tasting each word to make sure it was satisfactory to her; or maybe what seems to me to be a random collection of daily activities was for her a very complex system of organizing her day and her life. This process—of reading her diary and then researching, interpreting, and analyzing her life—is why forensic herstorical investigation is so interesting because there are some questions that will never be answered. Emilie wrote just about every day, and her act of actively recording her life as she lived it is both impressive and daunting.[9]

The Pocket Diaries

Emilie's three pocket diaries are currently housed at the Historical Society of Pennsylvania, and the provenance is unknown. The pocket diaries are small books, bound in soft brown leather, with beige paper embossed on the edge with a gold-colored finish. On the outside front cover, there is a sliding loop used to keep the pocket diary closed as well as a ring into which Emilie could insert a small pencil or pen. The diaries are small, ranging in length from ten to twelve centimeters, and are approximately six to eight centimeters wide, which means that they are small enough to have fit under her pillow, in her pocket, or in her tote bag so that she could jot notes and record her activities throughout the day. Emilie probably kept hers in her pocket. During the seventeenth and eighteenth centuries, pockets were small bags that were tied either around the waist and hung behind a ladies pannier hoop skirt or around the neck.[10] Pockets were designed to hold small things that were both "easily lost yet precious" and were usually made at home. Emilie, as a dressmaker, probably designed and made her own.[11]

Her pocket diaries have close to one hundred pages each: there are three days per page and a section of lined pages at the end of the book. Because of their size, pocket diaries were intended for brevity of words and mobility. They were primarily designed as record-keeping tools in which the author documented the weather, noted visitors, and jotted down daily activities.[12] Prior to 1860 pocket diaries were generally considered to be public artifacts, used to record events from everyday life for posterity. With the introduction of flaps and locks, however, which allowed diaries to be kept closed, pocket diaries assumed a more private form. Emilie's entries, which contain frequent disparaging and humorous comments about her family, friends, and fellow church members, suggest that she viewed her pocket diary as a private space in which to record her personal emotions.

On the first page of her 1864 and 1865 pocket diaries, Emilie inscribed her full name, *Emilie F. Davis*, in black ink. In 1863 she simply wrote *Emlies* above the commercially printed words "Pocket Diary for 1863 containing A Blank Space for Every Day." She wrote in cursive, and her penmanship consisted of small letters, open *a*'s and *o*'s, uncrossed *t*'s and lower- and uppercase single *I*'s. Her letters are slanted slighted to the right, and there is very little space between the words. Her *a*'s and *o*'s are similar to each other, as are her *t*'s and *f*'s. Emilie did not waste any space on the page, filling every inch of it by crowding the words together, writing smaller at the bottom of the page, writing into the creases of the pages, and sometimes writing words on top of each other. Her text is illegible in some places, particularly on the days when she wrote in pencil. Emilie's daily diary entries were short, generally about twenty to forty words each, and she rarely discussed any event or activity in detail. On most days she began by recording the weather, which was a necessary part of the salutatory discipline. In William Cobbett's 1830 manual, which was designed to teach young boys and girls how to keep a diary, instructions included "putting down something against every day of the year, if it be merely a description of the weather" because "tested it disburdens the mind of the many things to be recollected; it is amusing and useful, and ought by no means to be neglected."[13] When Emilie did not start the day's entry by writing about the weather, it is difficult to tell when one day ends and another one begins. On those days Emilie's pocket diary is like a kaleidoscope of fluctuating points that must be linked together to form a story.

Within her private and public spheres, Emilie interacted with many different people: some are mentioned by their last name, others by their first or by a nickname, and still others by their entire name. There are some familiar characters, like Emilie's brother, Alfred, and his wife, Mary; her father, Charles; her best friend, Nellie; "the girls" (Ellen, Rachel, and Sue); and "the boys" (Vincent, Cristy, George, and Barker) and some well-known public figures, like William Still, the Whites

Diaries of Emilie Davis, 1863–1865.
Courtesy of Archives of the Historical Society of Pennsylvania.

(Jacob Sr., George Bustill, and Jake), the Cattos (William and Octavius), the Douglass family (William, Sarah Mapps, and Sarah), and Jonathan Gibbs with whom she had regular (and sometimes weekly) contact. In any given week, Emilie made eight to ten home visits and had anywhere from ten to fifteen visitors. Her life was full and busy, and her diary was a place where she attempted to record some of her movements.

That Emilie possessed a leather-bound pocket diary and wrote most of her entries in ink suggests that she had some economic privilege. Since fountain pens and lead pencils were costly, Emilie's ability to regularly purchase writing instruments provides further insight into her economic status.[14] Only authors who had the means to record their thoughts in a permanent form left tangible archives such as these pocket diaries to be available for examination today. Emilie's entries are not detailed portraits of her life or highlights of the events that were happening throughout the city; they are, instead, brief three-to-five-sentence daily snapshots. In this way Emilie Davis was not an annalist of nineteenth-century history but rather a keeper of her personal records. Nevertheless, from the daily snapshots recorded in her pocket diary, we gain a rare insight that helps us to illuminate, analyze, and understand the free black woman's everyday experience.

Reconstructed

In 1863, on the first day of the year, Emilie Frances Davis sat in her room in Philadelphia, Pennsylvania, pulled out her pocket diary, wrote her name in ink and in cursive on the first page, and proceeded to describe her day. The day was historic: it was Jubilee Day, the moment when the "throat of slavery" intersected with the "keen knife of liberty" as the nation began its slow march toward liberty.[15] It was a day of celebration, the one that free and enslaved black people in America had been hoping, working, and praying for since permanent slavery became the law of the land and since states (starting with Virginia's House of Burgess) shifted a child's inherited status from the father to the mother.[16] It was also a day of marked contradictions. While some enslaved people were dancing, singing, and working hard spreading the good news, some former plantation owners were crying, mourning, and working hard to circumvent the spreading of the news and the planned migrations of their enslaved community. On one Virginia plantation, an enslaved person reported that when they heard the news, the former slaves "didn't care nothing 'bout Missus—was going to the Union lines. An all dat night de niggers danced an' sang right out on de cold."[17] Up North, in the Seventh Ward of Philadelphia, the mood was both somber and joyous. Emilie Davis, in writing about the day, noted that many were celebrating and reflecting as "the day was religiously observed," "all the churches were open," and the community enjoyed "quite a Jubilee."[18] Emilie's Jubilee Day experience as a northern freeborn black woman was obviously much different from the experience of a southern enslaved woman. As a freeborn resident of Philadelphia, a well-known hotbed of antislavery activism, Emilie viewed enslavement from the outside in. She was familiar with the intricacies of enslavement, but she had not personally experienced it. As a result she celebrated Jubilee, but it did not change her legal status. The Jubilee Day celebrations may also have prompted Emilie's decision to keep a pocket diary. It was a historic time, and perhaps Emilie felt that her voice and her experiences were significant enough to be recorded in the annals of history.

The Seventh Ward, which had the largest concentration of black wealth on the East Coast and where twelve percent of its population was black, was a close-knit community that had actively been working for the abolition of slavery for over one hundred years through the resident churches, benevolent societies, and fraternal organizations. It was a large community with boundaries to the east and west from Seventh to Twenty-fifth Streets and to the north and south from Spruce to South Streets. Walking down the streets of the Seventh Ward, it is easy to get a sense of what Emilie may have encountered when she stepped outside of her door onto the wide cobblestone streets. She would have seen both the omnibus and the horse-drawn streetcars, pulled over iron rails. Designed for speed and efficiency, the horse-drawn streetcars seated twenty to twenty-five people, moved at a speed of six to eight miles per hour over the rails, and cost about five cents per ride. In contrast, the omnibus was slow, sat only ten to twelve passengers, traveled directly on the cobblestones and in the mud, and catered primarily to businessmen and wealthy merchants. Streetcars changed the face of the Seventh Ward as areas that were previously inaccessible were pulled into the heart of the city. Even though Philadelphia had a bustling and thriving black community, there were still some areas that remained closed. Long before Jim Crow, Philadelphia had one set of streetcars for white and one for black passengers. Black people had two choices: either wait for a streetcar for people that looked like them so they could sit and ride in peace, or catch one for whites and stand outside, on an iron and wood platform, near the horses, gripping the side windows.

On any given weekday, nearly forty-six thousand people moved in and out of the center of the city, which bordered the Seventh Ward, on their way into and out of Philadelphia. During the summer, traffic was constantly held up as horses, exhausted from the work and overheated, frequently dropped dead in the streets.[19] During the winter, wood fires were lit during the early morning hours and burned throughout the day. The blocks were lined with a variety of buildings, Victorian-style brick houses with large windows, columns, and wide steps, sitting next to confectionary and bazaar shops and crowded wood-frame houses.

Depending on the direction that Emilie walked, she would have encountered everything from a middle-class and workingmen's section to the south, a low-income section to the east, the river and an industrial section to the west, or an upper-middle-class residential and business district to the north.[20] The sidewalks were narrow, and people moved in close contact with one another. The dress was conservative: the men wore dress pants, long coats, and top hats, while the women wore dresses with pannier hoop skirts, long sleeves, high collars, and pockets tied around their waist or worn around their necks. The crowds shared the streets with chickens, pigs, and goats being pulled along by their owners or sitting in pens waiting to be bought and sold. Street vendors were set up on the corners selling jelly donuts, crabs, herbs, and bowls of pepper pot—a spicy soup made with vegetables, tripe, ox feet, and cheap meat—for a few pennies. Musicians set up shop next to the vendors and would play music by request on their fiddles or banjos.[21]

The neighborhood was alive and full of intelligent, bright, and forward thinking black men and women. They were educated, attending one of the free black schools or they had private tutors; cultured, speaking French, German, Latin, and in some cases Spanish; rooted to their churches, which were hotspots for activism and activity; and they believed that they had carved out a safe space for themselves and their children. This was the world of the nineteenth-century black glitterati, a place where the feelings of tradition, hope, wealth, and privilege ran deep. With the animals and the smoke, the music and the pepper pot, the street vendors and the beautiful black people, there were an amalgam of sounds, sights, and smells that Emilie encountered and absorbed in and around her neighborhood on a daily basis.

Emilie was born on February 18, 1838 in Harrisburg, Pennsylvania and was raised in Roxbury, Philadelphia, near the shipyards, where she attended a local public school. Growing up, she lived with her parents, Charles and Helena, her younger sister Elizabeth, and her two brothers, Alfred and Thomas. In the 1850 U.S. Census, there are two other family members mentioned, Elwood (five) and William (eighteen), neither of whom are mentioned in the 1860 U.S. Census or in Emilie's pocket diaries. By 1860 Emilie had moved in with her uncle, Elijah Joshua (E.J.) Davis, his wife, Sarah, and their son, Elwood, at 916 Rodman Street, between South and Lombard.[22] They lived within walking distance of First African Presbyterian Church, the Institute for Colored Youth, Pennsylvania Hospital, and the Ronaldson Cemetery.

At some point between the end of 1860 and 1863, Emilie moved to the upper section of the Seventh Ward, either to an established boardinghouse or to a private home that took in boarders. There she attended the Institute and made a living as both a domestic and a dressmaker. Although Emilie made dresses for family and friends, she did not derive her entire income from dressmaking. Her pocket diary entries do not state or suggest that she was either a milliner, which was a highly valued and lucrative skill, or that she was just a seamstress, in which she would have been able to stitch but not cut out the fabric for the dresses. Milliners usually had shops and were skilled in transforming raw materials into decorative, distinctive, and stylish hats and bonnets.[23] Emilie would actually be classified as a *modiste* because she was able to fit and cut the fabric to the body of her customers, copy patterns, and stitch the fabric. Here she wrote, "Nellie and I went out shopping. She bought a dress and I cut it out for her"; and "Mary A. was up here in all the rain. I cut her dress, finally"; and "Quite a fine day. Nellie stoped here as she went up town this morning. In the evening, went to the milliners for my bonnet." Being a dressmaker, a *modiste*, was a valued skill, a status symbol of sorts because it set the elite apart from the "puckered, gaping, and baggy masses."[24]

In contrast, working as a domestic was a devalued skill within the free black community.[25] That domestic work was both devalued and primarily a woman's job was not a new occurrence in free black Philadelphia; the "patterns of oppression of black women" in their occupations, lives, and experiences were designed during the eighteenth century and actively maintained up until the twentieth.[26] As a member of two economic classes, Emilie was part of a subset of free black women who were able to effectively cross class boundaries. At this time in her life, Emilie was an independent, literate, skilled, urban woman, moving and interacting in free black Philadelphia in a way that was unique to her life and to her experiences.

SCHEDULE 1.—Free Inhabitants in 7th Ward City of Philadelphia in the County of Philadelphia State of Pennsylvania enumerated by me, on the 11th day of June 1860. Evan O. Jackson Ass't Marshal.

Post Office Philadelphia .

			Descriptive.				Value of Estate Owned.						
Dwelling-houses numbered in the order of visitation.	Families numbered in the order of visitation.	The name of every person whose usual place of abode on the first day of June, 1860, was in this family.	Age.	Sex.	Color—White, black, or mulatto.	Profession, Occupation, or Trade of each person, male and female, over 15 years of age.	Value of Real Estate.	Value of Personal Estate.	Place of Birth, Naming the State, Territory, or Country.	Married within the year.	Attended School within the year.	Persons over 20 y'rs who cannot read and write.	Whether deaf and dumb, blind, insane, idiotic, pauper, or convict.
1	2	3	4	5	6	7	8	9	10	11	12	13	14
367	480	Mary Guffens	30	F				✓	Ireland				
		James "	6/12	M					Pennsylvania				
368	481	Isaac Chase	22	M	M	Musician		✓	do				
		Sarah "	20	F	M				do				
		Isaac "	2	M	M				do				
		Rachel "	1	F	M				do				
		Rachel "	54	F	M	Cook		✓	Maryland			1	
		Flora Maris	40	F	M	do		✓	do				
		Ann Reede	45	F	M	do		✓	do				
		George "	21	M	M	Waiter		✓	Pennsylvania				
	482	John H. Turner	24	M	M	do		✓	Virginia			1	
		Mary "	38	F	M				New Jersey				
		George "	2	M	M				Pennsylvania				
369	483	Major Johnson	49	M	M	Restaurant	1000	2000	Maryland				
		Lydia "	45	F	M				Pennsylvania				
		Mary Hageborn	27	F	M				do				
		James Johnson	23	M	M	Restaurant			do				
		Josephine "	21	F	M				do				
		George "	14	M	M				do		1		
		Howard "	7	M	M				do		1		
		Mary "	8	M	M				do		1		
		William Hageborn	6	M	M				do		1		
		Aurelia "	4	F	M				do		1		
370	484	Elijah Davis	40	M	M	Waiter		✓	Maryland				
		Sarah "	35	F	M				Pennsylvania				
		Elizabeth "	10	F	M	Semstress		✓	do				
		Thomas "	13	M	M				do		1		
		Oliverdo "	1	M	M				do				
		Emily "	41	F	M	Servant		✓	do				
	485	David Warren	40	M	M	Boot maker		✓	do				
371	486	John R. Vening	50	M	M	Carpenter	3000	200	South Carolina				
		Mary "	49	F	M				do				
		Adeline Cooper	24	F	M	Dress-maker		✓	Pennsylvania				
		Joseph Vening	38	M	M	Restaurant keeper			South Carolina				
		Thaddeus Jaspertes	11	M	M				do		1		
		Ellen Cooper	4	F	M				Pennsylvania		1		
		Harriet "	5	F	M				do		1		
		Sally Jones	40	F	M	Cook		✓	Delaware			1	
		Mary "	30	F	M	Waiter		✓	do			1	
		Lucy Thomas	38	F	M	Washer			New Jersey				

No. white males, 1 No. colored males, 18 No. foreign born, 1 No. blind,____ 4000 2,200 No. idiotic,____

No. white females, 1 No. colored females, 20 No. deaf and dumb,____ No. insane,____ No. pauper,____ No. convicts,____

1860 United States Census.

In the days leading up to January 1, 1863, Emilie was aware of the sense of excitement and hesitancy in the air, since some blacks were nervous that President Abraham Lincoln would not "release" the Emancipation Proclamation. On the evening of December 31, 1862, the community's churches, libraries, and schools stayed open all night as residents waited for the news to come across the wire that Lincoln had kept his promise and had issued the long-awaited document. Although Emilie's background does not reflect that she had any firsthand experience with slavery, she was fully aware of the significance of this moment in the struggle for freedom.

How Emilie spent the "Watch Night" is unknown, because she recorded her story on the first day of the New Year without commenting on anything that took place leading up to the historic moment. As a faithful church member (she rarely missed a Sunday service or Bible study class), Emilie probably attended the Watchtower services at First African Presbyterian along with her family and friends. Her short entry about her activities on Jubilee Day is indicative of how she usually wrote in her diary. They were typically short, but they provided insight into the type of community in which she lived, the people she spent time with, and the activities that were important to her as a twenty-five-year-old single woman. Since she worked, she was able to control both her mobility and her finances, and this control was a critical dimension of her life. For enslaved women, it aided the small number of women who were brave enough to either flee their situations or run a small business (on larger plantations some would grow and sell vegetables); and for free women, it gave them more control over their lives.[27] Emilie was mobile, influencing the way that she interacted and responded to events happening in Philadelphia, within both the black and white community.

Her pocket diary entries are a lens into the free black community, a "port of entry," through which we can examine her place within the free black community, her worldviews and her politics, her perceptions of both public and private events, and her personal relationships. Her diary entries are used as a starting point to investigate, explore, and reconstruct a narrative of her life. Throughout the process of analyzing her entries, it has become evident that Emilie's pocket diaries make a significant contribution to nineteenth-century history. From 1863 to 1865, throughout the latter half of the Civil War, Emilie wrote and recorded her feelings and experiences: on the days when black men were drafted, ward by ward, into the armed services; when confederate soldiers invaded Vicksburg, Pennsylvania; when General Robert E. Lee surrendered; when President Lincoln was assassinated; and when the Thirteenth Amendment was ratified. Emilie mentioned all of these events in her pocket diary along with her personal joys and pains, including her father's ongoing illness, her pastor's very public and messy divorce, her trips in and around the city, and the deaths of friends, church members, her sister-in-law, her nephew, and finally, her brother. Emilie wrote just about every day, at least for the 1,095 days that have survived into the present, and perhaps even longer than we know. In the process she wrote herself into America's history.

The Nineteenth-Century Black Woman's Continuum

Although Emilie's entries are sparse, brief snapshots of her life, she has given us a tool to analyze the background and history of her worldview in the larger context of nineteenth-century black American life. Through an analytical lens, Emilie can be situated in a historical and literary context adding to the study of the nineteenth-century black American women's experiences and filling a void in scholarly documentation of women who dwell in spaces between those who were considered elite and those who were enslaved. As it stands now, the majority of literature about nineteenth-century black American women tends to focus either on documenting the lives of individual elite women or discussing the lives and conditions of enslaved women, usually as a group rather than individually.

In this study a free black woman is defined as "elite" based upon the following characteristics: her ability to hold a public high-profile position, the socioeconomic status of her family, her unrestricted access to education, and her ability to travel nationally and internationally. Additionally, and perhaps most importantly for this study, elite also refers to the fact that information written by and about these women has survived and has been preserved and discussed in the canon of black women's archival history. By this definition, Emilie would not be categorized as elite within the free black community, though she was nevertheless exceptional because she recorded her life in pocket diaries that have been preserved.

At the same time, it is also not sufficient to define Emilie as elite based on her employment, since most elite women also held jobs outside of the home. During the nineteenth century, upper-class black families were often elite in status but working-class in income. Unlike elite white families, people of high social status in the free black community generally had to sell their labor and work for a living. Thus, being black or mulatto and free was far from being white and free.[28]

To some extent, Emilie could be defined as "ordinary," a term used by Kriste Lindenmeyer to refer to women who are not featured in mainstream history but who have led lives that provide insight into that time period. Defining a nineteenth-century woman as ordinary, Lindenmeyer writes, "does not mean lesser, does not denote class, ethnicity or age."[29] In this regard, even though Emilie's life is not discussed in mainstream history, it does provide an insight into ordinary life during that time period. Yet, Emilie was in many ways privileged by virtue of being a literate, freeborn, lighter-skinned black woman. She grew up in a black middle-class community and had connections to the elite black community through both her family and her friends.

In sum, since none of the above statuses—elite, working-class, or ordinary—best describe and capture Emilie Davis's life, she might be more aptly defined as "everyday." Her experiences were exceptional, but they were not exclusive to her. What sets Emilie apart is that her words have survived and have been preserved. At the same time, there are some difficulties in trying to ascribe just one label to Emilie (or to anybody) and her experiences. Because of the contradictory elements of her life, Emilie can almost be placed in a category by herself: she is more than ordinary but not quite elite; she is both a *modiste* and a short-term live-in domestic; she worried about money, yet she purchased leather-bound diaries and ink, took private guitar lessons, and bought a new sewing machine; and, while she did not live an extraordinary life, her story, in her own words, has nevertheless survived. With these contradictions in mind, Emilie does not completely fit into the neatly defined historical categories that currently exist for nineteenth-century black American women.

Emilie was an active agent in recording her history. By putting her words on paper, at a time when her status as a black woman meant that she was in many regards directly controlled by the white male hegemony, she claimed her voice and her space. Emilie was both a "reading" woman and a "learned" woman who wrote letters, kept pocket diaries, attended lectures, and created and maintained friendship albums. She actively used the page as a place to explore who she was. As a result Emilie's life and experiences require the creation of another historical category altogether. In *Poetry Is Not a Luxury*, Audre Lorde compellingly presents the idea that the guiding principle for the white American forefathers was "I think; therefore, I am," and black American mothers were guided by the principle "I feel; therefore, I am."[30] For Emilie Davis, her guiding principle seems to have been "I write; therefore, I exist and feel and, therefore, I am." For her to claim the space to write, it also means that she had the leisure, the money, and the space to do it. Adding to that, as signaled by her self-assured use of language in her diary entries combined with the consistency of her diary writing practice, Emilie also possessed the confidence that her life and her experiences were important enough to be recorded and preserved.

Free Black Women

In 1860, there were approximately 1,111,000 enslaved women and 250,000 free black women living in America. These numbers had significantly increased from 750,000 and 121,000, respectively, since 1820.[31] Of the number of free black American women, less than one percent was part of the elite class and occupied key public leadership positions. Because elite women often wrote, spoke publicly, and published, a number of their public primary sources (speeches, books, editorials, public letters) have survived and are available for research and study. This attention paid to the lives of elite free black American women has not gone unnoticed within the literary and historical canon. Henry Louis Gates Jr. writes that the historian's focus must extend past the elite that are "humanized through the eyes of the white bour-geois" to highlight the experiences of "everyday" black women.[32]

The lives and experiences of everyday free black American women, told in their own words, are not typically featured in mainstream history because there are very few primary sources—pocket diaries, diaries, or journals—that document their daily experiences. This type of research goes beyond public artifacts such as speeches, editorials, poetry, or autobiographies to include private writings. By seek-ing out the private space within the continuum of the public and private experi-ences of nineteenth-century black women, an analysis of Emilie's pocket diaries provide a much-needed look into the mundane world of free black life.

Three of the known published diaries, which will be explored more in a later chapter, by nineteenth-century black women were written by Charlotte Forten, the granddaughter of sail maker and Revolutionary War veteran James Forten; Alice Dunbar Nelson, a nationally known writer who was born and came of age during Reconstruction and was married to poet Paul Laurence Dunbar; and Ida B. Wells-Barnett, who was born enslaved in 1862 and eventually became a national crusader against lynching and co-owner of a Memphis based newspaper, the *Memphis Free Speech and Headlight*. These women either occupied the elite class or had a high public profile, and their diaries document some of their experiences.[33] The diaries of these women were selected to serve as a point of comparison to Emilie's because these writers shared similar experiences that paralleled her life. Forten, like Emilie, grew up in free black Philadelphia during the 1840s; Nelson, Forten, and Emilie were lighter-skinned mulattoes; and Wells, Forten, and Emilie all kept their diaries while they were single and in their early twenties. At the same time, unlike the published well-known diaries of Forten, Nelson, and Wells, Emilie's pocket diaries provide insight into the experiences of unremembered women and highlight the type of accomplishments that history has generally failed to record or discuss.

The diaries of Forten, Nelson, and Wells are also part of the more general canon of literature about freeborn black American women and their particular ex-periences. There are only a few primary sources, and it stands to reason that the material from this small cadre of women would be analyzed and examined re-peatedly. The freeborn and enslaved black American women who have been most frequently studied in history were typically literate, elite, or held a high-profile po-sition, and, editorials, and diaries have survived.

Enslaved Women

At the other end of the continuum from elite or high-profile black American women are the amorphously defined "enslaved women," who are typically researched and discussed as a group, rather than as individuals, and are viewed as "generic" women. They are akin to Richard Henry Tawney's description of the "ambiguous mass" that are "seen and probed from different angles."[34] But within this mass, there were some distinct differences. Tera Hunter points out that although ninety-five percent of the enslaved population in 1860 was illiterate (it was illegal to teach an enslaved person how to read and write), five percent of them defied the law by organizing secret schools and learning how to read and write. They actively created a "culture of dissemblance," by consciously masking their literacy (and by extension, their growing desire to become more literate) behind a cloak of ignorance.[35] With few surviving primary sources, historiographies about enslaved women tend to rely on the collected oral histories from the Federal Writers' Project of the Works Progress Administration (WPA). Beginning in 1936 student researchers, including noted black anthropologist Zora Neale Hurston and historian Dorothy Sterling, were hired and sent to seventeen states including Georgia, Florida, South Carolina, and Virginia (states that had the largest enslaved populations) to interview formerly enslaved men and women, in an effort to capture the memories and experiences of slavery from those who had firsthand knowledge about it. Since then, these interviews—close to two thousand were recorded—have been used as primary source material in literature about the enslaved.

Yet John Blassingame, among many other scholars, has contended that the WPA interviews cannot be properly substantiated for a number of reasons: the interviews were conducted by mostly white researchers who were asking black people to vividly recollect sensitive and emotional events that had happened to them over sixty-five years ago; some of the white interviewers were closely identified or related to the ancien régime (meaning that some of the interviewers were direct descendants of slaveholding families); the formerly enslaved, who still relied on whites to help them receive their pensions, were understandably cautious in truthfully and authentically answering interview questions about their enslaved experiences; the questions were written in such a way that it was hard to distinguish between past and present-day race relations; the interviewers had not been properly trained in the methods of interviewing; interviewers referred to the formerly enslaved in terms that were reminiscent of slavery, such as *darkeys*, *niggers*, *aunteys*, *mammies*, and *uncles*; the formerly enslaved rarely mentioned anti-white sentiments, contrary to the ethos captured in other forms of enslaved expression, such as in the surviving music and stories; and the interviews were edited or revised by staff members before they were typed and catalogued.[36] Additionally some of the interviews have been problematized in both the fields of history and sociolinguistics because the transcribers were told to focus on telling the truth *in idiom* and not necessarily to use accurate pronunciation or phrasing, which likely compromised their reliability and validity as historical sources.[37]

At this time only two named enslaved women have been written about, taught, and researched extensively: Harriet Tubman, an enslaved woman from Maryland who helped more than seventy people escape to freedom, and Sojourner Truth, a freed Shaker from New York (state emancipation laws were enacted in 1827) who worked as a lecturer for both the antislavery and the women's movements. Because of the unique circumstances of their lives and experiences, defining these women according to traditional social class labels would be misleading. Neither woman could read or write nor were they limited by their legal status or defined by their familial ties; yet, in death, both have become transcendent historical figures whose images have been perpetuated by the black cultural mythology's tradition of a "survivalist hero dynamic." In addition to their work in the abolitionist movement, Tubman is known for her work as a nurse and a soldier during the Civil War, and Truth traveled and spoke for those "doubly oppressed by race and sex." Although other enslaved women have been researched and written about, none have been written about as much as Tubman and Truth, the so-called "twin mountains of the historic tradition of black women."[38]

It is this space, between the stories of elite and enslaved women, that the pocket diaries of Emilie Davis seek to help fill. Her story begins on January 1, 1863; the nation has gone through a climatic sociopolitical shift in thinking and in being. The albatross of slavery has finally been removed, and Emilie Frances Davis sits down to write.

~ I ~

Emilie Davis, 1863

"In the evening, we went to prayer meeting, had a spirited meeting.
Our party were the only colerd people.

Diaries, August 23, 1863

In the 1850 U.S. Census, when she was twelve years old, Emilie lived with her parents, her sister, and three of her four brothers in Roxbury, Philadelphia. (Her oldest brother, Alfred, either lived on his own or was not home when the census taker came to the house.) In the 1860 U.S. Census, Emilie and two of her siblings (Elizabeth and Thomas) had moved in with her uncle, Elijah J., and his family at 916 Rodman Street, between South and Lombard. Sometime between 1860 and 1863, Emilie moved to a home within walking distance of her family, her church, and her school. She was enrolled in evening classes at the Institute for Colored Youth, worked as a live-in domestic for four families, and supplemented her income by working as a dressmaker. The country was in the midst of the second year of a brutal "white man's War" that had already claimed hundreds of thousands of lives and did not seem to have an end in sight.[1] The year opened with a dramatic shift in the social, political, and emotional climate as President Abraham Lincoln made a bold and rather calculated move to redefine the Civil War and transform the country from a slave nation to a nation with free black and white citizens. With the issue of the Emancipation Proclamation and the eventual decision to allow black men to enlist in the military, the country was in the midst of a cataclysmic shift in focus and direction. At this time in history, there were no indications that the country was ever going to be united as one nation, but the free black community was invested, involved, and greatly concerned about the direction of the country. Emilie, as a freeborn black woman, had a voice, a pocket diary, and a pen.

January 1863

THURSDAY, JANUARY 1, 1863

To day has bin a memorable day. I thank God I have bin here to see it. The day was religiously observed, all the churches were open. We had quite a Jubilee in the evening. I went to Joness to a party, had a very blessest time.

Emilie was a member of First African Presbyterian Church, the first and only black Presbyterian church in the country and the fifth black church in the city. It sat at the corner of Seventh and Shippen (now Bainbridge) Streets, which was four blocks from Emilie's 1860 address.

FRIDAY, JANUARY 2, 1863

Beautiful day, Nellie was up and spent part of the day. Reading (Redding B. Jones) was here. Nellie had an engagement and had to go home. I stoped home a few minutes. The girls were all there.

Emilie's "girls" (her closest female friends) consisted of Nellie, Ellen Black, and Rachel Turner—all of whom lived in the lower section of the Seventh Ward—and Sue, who lived in Germantown, Pennsylvania. Prior to being unanimously elected and serving as the pastor of First African Presbyterian Church 1873–79, Reverend Redding B. Jones worked as a community pastor in the Seventh Ward.

SATURDAY, JANUARY 3, 1863

Very pleasant this morning, buisy all day. Redding on his wer (way) here to service. I went down home to see if Father (Charles Davis) had come, and was hurrying away when he came. I was delighted to see him.

In 1863 Charles Davis lived in the lower section of the Seventh Ward, within walking distance of Emilie.

SUNDAY, JANUARY 4, 1863

I did not go to church in the morning. Very good discours in the afternoon. Dave (DeClones) was down. We had a full choir bible class at Gertrudes, very interesting.

MONDAY, JANUARY 5, 1863

Quite pleasant to day, Nellie was up a little while. Redding went away this morning. Siminy [seminary] school begins tonight, we all went down. Several strangers were there, I was quite mortified to see so few out. We did not do any business.

The Institute for Colored Youth (now Cheney University) was located at 915 Bainbridge on Seventh and Lombard Streets, two blocks from Emilie's 1860 address. Classes were held every Monday night until May 25, 1863.

TUESDAY, JANUARY 6, 1863

Very dull to day, raining in the afternoon. I went down home. Heard some good news, Tomy (Thomas Davis) is here. I went to meeting, very few out, but we had a good meeting.

Thomas (Tomy) was Emilie's younger brother.

WEDNESDAY, JANUARY 7, 1863

The girls called to see me to day. I saw Alfred (Davis) last night, he did not say he sent me the album, but I know he did. Nellie and Sue were up here to night.

Alfred was Emilie's older brother. He worked as a hotel waiter and lived in Pottsville in the northwest ward, with his wife, Mary, and his seven-year-old son, Francis

(Frank). In addition to her pocket diaries, Emilie also kept friendship and photography albums.

THURSDAY, JANUARY 8, 1863

Very stormy to day, did not go any were but home and Marys. Liz (Elizabeth Harriet Stevens Bowser) and Stefan at Mrs. Joneses. Nellie bought the long, talked of gloves for Cristy. I spent the evening hour with Father.

Elizabeth (Liz) Harriet Stevens Gray Bowser was a seamstress and a member of the Ladies' Union Association of Philadelphia, along with Emilie. Bowser was married to David Bustill Bowser, the grandson of Cyrus Bustill—one of the founders of Philadelphia's Free African Society.

FRIDAY, JANUARY 9, 1863

Very dull. I had a letter from Lile to day. Liz Williams brought it up. Vincent was up here this evening, he bought me a hansome album from a Philadelo (Philadelphia) present. I am delighted with it.

Vincent was Emilie's suitor 1863–65.

SATURDAY, JANUARY 10, 1863

It rained so I did not go out. I was very buisy with my dress. I cut the body out.

Cutting out the body of the dress was extremely laborious and usually took a full day to complete. It had to be done before the corsets or stays were designed.

SUNDAY, JANUARY 11, 1863

Very pleasant, most too much so for this time of year. I went to church in the morning. Mr. (Jonathan) Gibbs was not there. Mr. (Alexander "Pop") Guy spoke, his remarkes were very good. After church, we went to see Nellie's Grandma Ana.

Reverend Jonathan Gibbs was the fourth pastor of First African and served from 1860–65. Alexander "Pop" Guy served as both an elected elder and a trustee of First African.

MONDAY, JANUARY 12, 1863

Father spent this day with Alfred. I spent the afternoon and evening in reading and singing. No one com up to see me.

TUESDAY, JANUARY 13, 1863

I went down to school last night. We had a very nice school. We elected officers for this year. Dave was down. Nellie stoped to go to meeting. Mary G(rew), and her son were here. How glad I was to see them, he is a fine boy.

Elections were held at the Banneker Institute of Philadelphia: Jake White was elected president, Joel Selsey as vice president, St. George R. Taylor as recording secretary, Octavius V. Catto as correspondent, and William H. Minton as treasurer. Mary Grew was a member of the Philadelphia Female Anti-Slavery Society.

Nellie was up here this afternoon. She is afraid to com up at night.

Mary and I went out shopping. Mary Simson (Simpson) was married this morning at 8 o'clock, stoped at our hous for dinner, then when home to Briasbury. Mary Caris (Cares) was brides maid. Last night I spent a very agreeable evening at Aguste's (Auguste) with Nellie, Cristy, and Mary, all my favorite.

Mary Cornelia Simpson married Gideon H. Pierce of Bridgeton, N.J.

Nellie did not get up here to day. I have not bin out all day.

Very stormy yesterday morning. In the afternoon, Father whent out to Mr. Cares. Sue was up here this evening. Very cold, I stoped down hom and at Nellie, she was quite sick.

Clear and cold this morning. I did not go to church in the morning. In the afternoon, I went out with Father to Cares. We had a missionary to preach for us in the afternoon. In the evening, we had a very nice bible class. Great many out.

I wrote two letters yester morning, quite cold. Sue and Nellie were up here. I went down to school. We had no teacer, but will have one next Mondy night. Vincent come home with me.

I was down hom this morning, father was well. I went to meeting, we had a very nice meeting. Lizzie Brown was up here yesterday.

In 1865, Lizzie Brown served as the secretary of the Ladies' Union Association.

Very stormy all day. Bin in the house all day. Nellie did not get up here this evening.

Very dull. Nellie and I went out shopping. She bought a dress and I cut it out for her. Lizzie stoped at our house, and staid untill it was time to go to the lecture. We went to the lecture, it was very good, not many out owing to the weather.

Lectures were held throughout the week in churches and meeting halls throughout the city. First African usually held their lectures on Friday night, and both the Banneker Institute and the Lombard Street Central Presbyterian Church held their lectures on Thursday night.

Very pleasant to day. I stopped at Meals this morning, my friend was better. Nellie was up spent the evening. Cristy was up, he was not well.

Very cloudy to day, Sue was up her this evening, Went down home, had quite a plesant chat with Father. Stoped at Nells (Nellie) a little while, she was buisy fineshing her dress.

Cloudy in the morning, clear in the afternoon. We had an excelent sermon this morning. Mr. Gibbs was very impressive. I went down to hear the children pratice in the afternoon. Mary was up to see me in the evening, Sue and Mr. Cooper called.

Very cold morning. Lizzie come up and spent the afternoon with me and staid to tea. We went down to school together. Nellie was here a little while. Very poor school. No teacher, Dave DeClones teaching us again.

Meeting at Johnnies. We had a happy time, it was good to be there.

Poor Tomy had to go to the gard house yesterday. He did not want to go. Very heavy storm to day, snowing all day and night. Nellie was the teacher.

Storming a little, Sue spent the morning with me. I spent a very agreeable time at home to day. Dave was married tonight, I had to march in. Jon (John Simpson), Gorge (George Bustill White), and Jake (Jacob C. White Jr.) were at the wedding.

Both Jake and George graduated from the Institute and were the sons of Jacob White Sr. (In 1866, George and Emilie were married.)

Lizzie was here to day, poor girle, I feel sorry for her.

Sue stoped here to night and we went out together. She goes to Waistery on Monday. I went in home, had quite a pleasant visit. Stoped in to see Nellie, she was rather dry.

February 1863

Rather cloudy to day, I did not go to church in the morning. In the afternoon, we had an excelent sermon. Bible class at Clogs. Very rainy. George and I called on the bride. Nellie treated Sue very shabby yesterday, with out a cause. We had very interesting class.

Very fine day, I had a letter from Johns (John Gloucester Jr.). I went down down to shool, it was quite encouraging. We had to open school our selves. Meeting at Holms, very few out.

Johns was probably Reverend John Gloucester Jr. who was a student at Ashmun Institute (now Lincoln University) and the son of Reverend John Gloucester Sr., the founder of First African.

Very cold and no fire. Nellie's lazy, could not go. Mr. Farbeau (Jacob Farbeaux) lead the meeting.

Jacob Farbeaux served as an elected elder of First African.

Bitter cold day. I have not ventured out to day. Nellie being lazy, she won't get up here. I have bin very buisy sewing all the evening.

Very cold, Mary was up here this morning. She went to Woodberry. I went home and did not get much further. In the evening I went to Virgil's lecture. He lectured well, very few there owing to the weather, it very unfavorable. It was raining very fast when I came hom. Egerton cam home with me.

The Banneker Institute typically held their lectures on Thursday nights. They were usually given by their members and ranged in cost from 25 to 75 cents.

I was home a few minutes this afternoon.

Emilie referred to her father's home in Philadelphia, his place in Harrisburg, and her current residence as "home."

It is a beautiful day, as warm as it was cold. Sarah (Davis), Mary (Alfred), and I went down to see Tomy this afternoon. We found him well, but ansious to get off.

Sarah was Emilie's aunt, Elijah J.'s wife. In 1865 she served as the treasurer of the Ladies' Union Association.

Very fine day. I went to church this morning, herd a good sermin. I spent the afternoon in reading. Mrs. Hunt and Sue stoped to see me. Nellie has not bin up here for sometime on a Sunday evening.

MONDAY, FEBRUARY 9, 1863

Very fine day, Nellie was up this afternoon an staid untill I went to school. No teacher yet, or any prospects of any. John and Sue hav made up again.

TUESDAY, FEBRUARY 10, 1863

I have bin sick all day and did not go to meeting. Poor Lizzie is sick. Nellie was here. I wrote to Redding, finally.

WEDNESDAY, FEBRUARY 11, 1863

Very pleasant this morning, Mary was up to see me. Father is not well. Nellie and Sue stoped. It has bin snowing.

THURSDAY, FEBRUARY 12, 1863

Very dull day, raining all the time. I was out, I did not go any place but home and in Nellies. I spent the best part of the evening with Father. I feel so glad I have this opportunity of spending an evening with him.

FRIDAY, FEBRUARY 13, 1863

Egerton came home with me last night. Sue and John have becom reconciled to each other. Sue was here and spent the evening, we had quite a nice time.

SATURDAY, FEBRUARY 14, 1863

It is a lovely day. To day it Valentines Day, and Nellie's birthday. How I would like to make her a present, but I am not able at present.

SUNDAY, FEBRUARY 15, 1863

Very dull day. I went to church in the afternoon. We had quite a military sermon. After church, we went to see Barker (Henry Barker Black) and Aunt Jane (Davis), she is quite sick. Bible class at Nellies; it was very nice, but we did not read enough, and let out too soon.

Henry Barker Black was a member of the Banneker Literary Group and appears to have been one of Emilie's closest male friends. Emilie's father, Charles, had two siblings, Jane and Isaac Davis, both are listed in the 1850 and 1860 U.S. Census.

MONDAY, FEBRUARY 16, 1863

Very beautiful day, we had no school. St. Tomas (Thomas) concert cam off to night, I did not go. Nellie take dinner with me.

St. Thomas African Episcopal Church, located on Adelphi and Fifth Streets, hosted a concert (with singing and instruments) and an exhibition. The church was founded by Absalom Jones in 1792 and was one of the oldest black churches in the city.

TUESDAY, FEBRUARY 17, 1863

Yesterday, quite a remarkable au courant meeting at Mrs. Rivers. Very stormy, snowing all day. Very few were there in beginning.

Emilie sometimes used French and German words in her entries; here she wrote au courant, cf. French meaning, "aware."

It is very unpleasant to day. It is my birthday. Nevertheless, I feel thankful I have bin spared so long; and if I should be spard in future, I will try and spend my time more profitable.

Very unpleasant day. Nellie and I went out shopping. Muslins are frightfuly dear. In the evening, we went to the lecture. After witch, we went over to Rachels, then up to Nellies. Jake had Nellie birthday presentats.

Muslin was a heavy, expensive, cotton fabric that came in various degrees of fineness and was often printed, woven, or had an embroidered pattern on it.

Very dull day, we expected Tomy, but he did not come. This afternoon I went up to see Celistene. She is much better.

Clear and cold to day. Nellie was up this morning. I went down to Rachels. Celistene and (Sally) Sue was home waiting for me when I got home. Father was not well yesterday.

Very stormy, I have not bin able to go to church all day. It snowed all day. Sue come here this evening through all this snow.

The snowstorm that Emile referred to affected a number of cities on the East Coast from Baltimore to Buffalo.

Very fine day. Sue and I went out shoping, stoped to see Celistene. In the evening, we went down to school. It was very cheerless. Liz was not down. Cristy tried to put on French. Dave cam down about 10.

In the free black communities, men and women would sometimes greet and talk with one another in either French or German. Emilie may have been describing this practice as "putting on the French."

Mrs. Boas died yesterday morning. I did not go to meeting. Spent part of the evening with Father.

Fine day. Nellie has not bin here to day. They had practising for the funeral this evening. I did not go. Sue and John stoped as they went home.

Very wet day. I went down to the church, very large funeral considering the wet day. Mr. Cato (Catto) was there. Mr. Gibbs spoke butiful. Dear old man, he live a

Cristien (Christian) life and he died like a Cristien (Christian). Oh, that I may be calm in my last moments and prepard.

From 1854 to 1859, Reverend William T. Catto served as the pastor of First African.

FRIDAY, FEBRUARY 27, 1863

Sue spent the evening with me. How I will miss her when she goes to Germantown.

SATURDAY, FEBRUARY 28, 1863

Very fine day. Mary, Gertrude, and I went down to see Tomy and had quite a pleasant visit. He is very ansious to com a shore.

Although Tomy was only fifteen years old, it appears as if he was a member of the U.S. Navy troops. (Approximately 29, 511 black men served in the U.S. Navy.)

March 1863

SUNDAY, MARCH 1, 1863

Raining in the morning. I went to church this afternoon. It was Communion. It was a very solomn servis. Bible class was at Mrs. Rivers. We had quite a nice class.

Congress approved the controversial Enrollment Act (Conscription Act), which required all American males ages 20–46 to report for duty in the Civil War. President Lincoln later signed it, and the passage of this bill later led to the New York City Draft Riots.

MONDAY, MARCH 2, 1863

Lovely day. Nellie and Sue were here. Mary and her friend Sue went out to Germantown to day. I went down to school to night, no teacher yet. The Fair comences to night.

TUESDAY, MARCH 3, 1863

John Simpson came home with me last night. Meeting, wit [went] to clases, very few out, quite a cold meeting. After meeting, I went to Nellies. Coming up home I met John, he came up with me.

WEDNESDAY, MARCH 4, 1863

Beautiful day, but quite marshy. Nellie did not come up, as usual. I stoped to see Lizzie Brown. John is quite sick.

THURSDAY, MARCH 5, 1863

The first clear Thursday we have had for some time. Sue was in this morning. I paid a visit to Joneses to day. Nellie (and) Sue stoped at Aunt Janes, then went to the lecture. After wich, I went to the Fair. Dave came home with me.

Colonel Thomas Wentworth Higginson along with the First and Second South Carolina Volunteers left on an expedition to Florida to take the news of the Emancipation Proclamation to the enslaved. They were told to occupy as much of the area as possible and to obtain enlistments from among the freedmen.

FRIDAY, MARCH 6, 1863

Lanind stoped to Sue, sent for John to com out. I droped a note to Cristy to tell him.

SATURDAY, MARCH 7, 1863

Very stormy. Nellie stoped here, she was very wet. Tomy got leave of absence to. He has to report on Mondy.

SUNDAY, MARCH 8, 1863

Very rainy day. I went to church in the morning. Mr. Gibbs was sick, consiquneely Mr. White held lecture. Very few out. Neither of the girls were out, there cousin died this morning. Tomy came up and spent the afternoon. I spent a very lonsome evening.

Jacob Clement White, Sr. served as First African's Sunday School superintendent (under Reverend William Catto) and was the first president of their board of trustees.

MONDAY, MARCH 9, 1863

Very fine day. Nellie was up, she did not go down to school. Cristy and I went down about half past 8, no one came down but George. After school, George and I went to the Fair. He was very gallant.

This was either George Bustill White or George Burrell. Both of them were members of the Banneker Institute.

TUESDAY, MARCH 10, 1863

Snowing, meeting up at Whites. I fear few were there, it being so stormy. Hannah Brown stoped to see me to day.

Hannah Brown was married to John Brown, and they had a seven-year-old daughter, Lizzie.

WEDNESDAY, MARCH 11, 1863

My side has bin very troublesom every since Mondy. The Hutchisons give a concert to night is one of morches [muches] and dozens more.

The Hutchinson Family Singers was a traveling singing group that specialized in four-part harmony and sang about slavery, women's rights, and temperance. The concert was hosted by the South Carolina Statistical Association of the Colored People of Pennsylvania and was held at the Sansom Street Hall.

THURSDAY, MARCH 12, 1863

One minute it is clear, the next it is snowing. Nellie and I went to have our photographes taken, but we did not succeed. We went to see Celestine. I was quite sick all the evening.

Although photography had been around since 1839, it became very popular during the late nineteenth century as the public became more interested in securing family photographs and cartes de visite (hand-size photographs that were used as calling cards). The popularity of photography is also explained by the practice of many drafted soldiers of having their "tintypes" (small inexpensive photographs) taken for their families before they left for the battlefield.

FRIDAY, MARCH 13, 1863

Nellie and I stood for our photographes this afternoon.

SATURDAY, MARCH 14, 1863

Clear to day. I went up to Lizzie White, spent quite a pleasant time with her. She is very deaf. Went down home to see Father. Sudden very cold.

SUNDAY, MARCH 15, 1863

Very fine morning snow. In the afternoon, we had an excelent sermon. This afternoon Doct Joneses preach, Mr. Gibbs is still sick. We had quite a nice class, not withstanding the storm. All the young were there, but Vincent.

MONDAY, MARCH 16, 1863

No school to night. We have decided not to go down until we have a teacher. Nellie and I went up to Lizzie.

TUESDAY, MARCH 17, 1863

Last evening Vincent looked perfectly staid. Went we went in Fred Duglass lectures. To night, meeting at Stills. Mr. Gibbs was down in the room, but did not take any part in the meeting.

The meeting was held at Mother Bethel African Methodist Episcopal Church, located at the corner of Sixth and Lombard Streets. The main speaker was Frederick Douglass, whose lecture was entitled "Men of Color, To Arms." William Still was a noted abolitionist who lived within walking distance of the church.

WEDNESDAY, MARCH 18, 1863

Barker cam up for Nellie. The Hutchinsons give a concert next Thusday night for the benefit of our church. I am quite disappointed Nellie did not come up.

THURSDAY, MARCH 19, 1863

I went up to Hannahs then over to see Aunt Lizzy, first sold 3 ticets. Sue was in town to day, com to the concert. No lecture. This is hardly not much to do with myself, had to march.

FRIDAY, MARCH 20, 1863

Sarah Thomas and Mr. Shim (William Shimm) and Coiry were at Nellies yesterday. Shimm is fine looking.

SATURDAY, MARCH 21, 1863

Nellie came up this afternoon and we had one of our old time talkes.

SUNDAY, MARCH 22, 1863

Very fine day. I went to church in the morning with Meal. Mr. Gibbs is still sick. Mr. Farbeaux exorted for us. I went down to hear the children practice. Very lonsom in the evening, no one cam up to see me.

Very fine day. I was up to see Celistine and Hannah rely is quite sick again. Nellie and I went down to school, we had a very nice school.

TUESDAY, MARCH 24, 1863
Meeting at Mr. Deeriss, I did not go. Very stormy. Nellie nor Liz was not there. Lizzie was here yesterday, but I did not see her.

WEDNESDAY, MARCH 25, 1863
Very fine day. I have bin very buisy trying to sell ticets for the concert. Alfred brought one. Nellie cam up this evening, we had nice time.

A meeting was held in Philadelphia to discuss the promotion of an all-black brigade to be commanded by Colonel William Angeroth and to be fully supported by the secretary of war.

THURSDAY, MARCH 26, 1863
Very stormy to day. I sold all my tickets. Nellie and Rachel over, went to the concert. It was good, every one seemed pleased. Barker cam home with me, and Vincent with Rachel and Ellen (Black). I felt quiet displeased with Vincent.

Ellen Black was one of Emilie's closest friends. They sang together on the Singing School Association choir at First African and were both members of the Ladies' Union Association. The Hutchinson Family concert was held at First African.

FRIDAY, MARCH 27, 1863
I have not seen Nellie to day. Mary Alfred (Davis) is here in Mrs. Clinton's place. She went to the concert. Sarah and Meal did not go.

Emilie often called a married woman by her first name, with the addition of the first name of her husband, as in Mary Alfred for her sister-in-law.

SATURDAY, MARCH 28, 1863
Meal expected to go to New York this morning. I went down to see her off, but she had a letter that Liz was very sick; she did not go.

SUNDAY, MARCH 29, 1863
Very fine day. Mr. Gibbs still sick, he didn't preached this afternoon. Bible class was postponed on account of confirmation. Nellie and (I) went, it was a perfect jure. Sue was in. Cristy gallanted us to church, but we had to march home. Nellie was furious.

Here Emilie wrote that it was a perfect "jure," cf. French jour, *meaning "day."*

MONDAY, MARCH 30, 1863
I went down to school, we were down there untill nine o clock before any one came. Cristy came down, Nellie run off from him.

Meeting at Bruces, quite a nice meeting. Mr. Hill lead. Liz was not doing well.

April 1863

Very fine day, for the first. I sent a letter to Sister (Elizabeth Davis) on Monday. I have not bin out to day, very busiy sewing. Father talkes of going home next week. Nellie and Alfred were up. We had a jolly time.

> *Elizabeth was Emilie's younger sister. Although Emilie never referred to her by name, she does mention visiting and writing to her.*

Quite stormy, Em McCrell paid me quite a long visit. I went up to see Mr. Gibbs, he is better. Spent the evening home with Father. Had to march, as usal. Althueu Crutiers com home with me.

Quite a spring day. I was out promenading, stoped at Rachels. Nellie and Anna was up here this morning. Meal expects to get off tomorrow.

Quite a large fire near us last night. Meal left at 6 this morning. Tomy sailed on Thursday for Port Ro(y)al. Very stormy to day, snowing and hailing furiously.

> *Port Royal (or Gideon's Bend), South Carolina, was located halfway between Savannah and Charleston. It was seized by the Union Army in 1862 and was utilized by formerly enslaved men and women, who successfully worked on the land. There were over ten thousand free people living there.*

Very disagreeable day, raining all the morning. Nellie is not well. I went down to church. Mr. Catto preached, very few out. I spent quite a pleasant evening, no one cam up to see me. I spent the evening in reading the history of Abraham.

Very dull day. Nellie came up, I went out to 6th and Arch with her. Mr. (Charles W.) Gardner's death was announced yesterday. Although we expected it, it was quite shock.

> *Charles W. Gardner's death certificate states that he died from dropsy (swelling of soft tissue due to the accumulation of excess fluid in the body—today it is more commonly known as edema). He was a teacher at the Institute for Colored Youth and a Presbyterian minister who was one of the seven black men who participated in the first meeting of the Pennsylvania Anti-Slavery Society. The other black participants were sailmaker James Forten; Robert Purvis, the first black person admitted to the Pennsylvania Society for Promoting the Abolition of Slavery; dentist James McCrummell;*

John C. Bowers; barber John Peck; and businessman Stephen Smith (who in 1847 owned property that was valued somewhere between $500 and $12,000). Lapsansky, Neighborhoods in Transition, *148–49.*

TUESDAY, APRIL 7, 1863

We had no school last night. We spent the evening at Rachels. The boyes are very carless about school.

The boys (Emilie's closest male friends) were Henry Barker Black, Cristy, and Vincent. Although she mentioned many male visitors (on average, she had 3–4 male visitors per week), these three were the most constant.

WEDNESDAY, APRIL 8, 1863

Mr. Gardner's body was rested in the church, as was his request. Nellie cam up and spent the evening. We had quite a nice time to our selves. Mary Alfred is still at our house.

THURSDAY, APRIL 9, 1863

Beautiful day, I went down to the funeral. Mr. Gardener looked very badly. He was so much swollen. He had quite a busiy funeral. Mr. Catto preached his funeral sermon. He spoke beautiful. Mr. Gibbs was not able to be there, I know he regretted it.

FRIDAY, APRIL 10, 1863

Nellie spent the evening with me.

SATURDAY, APRIL 11, 1863

Very fine day. Redding is in town. He was here this morning, and did paid one of his sosicble visits. I had bine quite sick all day. Stoped in home to Father.

SUNDAY, APRIL 12, 1863

Lovely morning, I was not out in the afternoon. The Intercommunion was out at (St.) Marys, the serviess very dry. Impressive bible class at Stills. I did not go. I was quite sick.

Founded ca. 1827, St. Mary's, the Episcopal church at Penn, was located at Fortieth and Locust Streets and was one of the first churches to get involved in the Oxford Movement to reincorporate Anglo-Saxon style worship into the Episcopal Church. The Intercommunion is a Eucharistic Intercommunion, where the sacrament is given to a baptized person who is not Catholic.

MONDAY, APRIL 13, 1863

Monday, not well, I did not go out. Nellie was here for me to go to down to school. School is very poorly attended.

TUESDAY, APRIL 14, 1863

Meeting at Mrs. Hill. Father talks of going home Saturday. We had a very good meeting. Father Guy was so happy. Nellie went to the lecture.

WEDNESDAY, APRIL 15, 1863

Stormy day. Little Frank (Frances Davis) is quite sick. Mary is still here. Nellie did not come up as.

Francis "Frank" Davis was Alfred and Mary's one-year-old son.

THURSDAY, APRIL 16, 1863

Very dull day. I was down to Nellie this morning. We went out shopping, she bout a dress and I did too. Egerton was up to see me. He did not go in to Nellie, I was supprised. He is quite friendly. I did not tell her he was in our house.

FRIDAY, APRIL 17, 1863

Father was quite sick last night. He is better to day.

SATURDAY, APRIL 18, 1863

Ran down to see Father, he is much better. Nellie was up here this morning. Jons was up to the house, I did not see him.

SUNDAY, APRIL 19, 1863

Very pleasant morning to day. Should be kept holy by everyone and I fear I do not observe it as much or I should. Mr. Gibbs spoke for us, it was like music to my ears to hear his voice again.

MONDAY, APRIL 20, 1863

Rachel and Lizzie spent the evening. Cristy came for them. We had quite a pleasant talk. No school to night, raining quite hard. Nellie was up here part of the evening. George is sick.

TUESDAY, APRIL 21, 1863

Very pleasant morning. Father is talking about going hom tomorrow. How I shall miss him. Meeting in Seventh St sulhr. I am ashamed to say I did not enjoy the meeting. Mr. Farbeaux lead. Mr. Guy seemed so happy.

WEDNESDAY, APRIL 22, 1863

Father went home this morning. I went up to the Depot to see him off. I felt so badly to see him go.

Although he had been in Philadelphia since January and Emilie frequently referred to wherever he was staying as home, it seems as if her father also had a home in Harrisburg.

THURSDAY, APRIL 23, 1863

Very disagreeable day. Mary, Nellie, and I all went out shopping. We meet Redding, he went along. I spent part of the evening at Marys and the other with Nellie. Redding cam to bid me good by. He has gone back to college.

FRIDAY, APRIL 24, 1863

Sue was in to day. It rained all the evening.

Fred Duglass lectured last night at National Hall. Stoped at Nells tonight and home. Then we went around to Marys. Barker promised me his photograph.

Douglass's speech was entitled "The Affairs of the Nation."

Very fine day, very windy. I went to church in the afternoon. Mr. Gibbs gave us very good sermon. Bible class at Mrs. Hills, very well attended. Mr. Guy did not get there.

We did not go down to school. The boyes went down. They did not like it because we will not come down.

Very pleasant meeting at Rachels. Nellie was here last night, we went around to Aunt Janes before meeting. Cristy came in write were (right where) Barker had steped out.

Very rainy all day. I have bin very busiy with my dress. Nellie did not com up. Gloster Levee came off tonight. Next Sunday, the long looked for meeting came off.

I finished wrighting William (Dorsey) to day. Another stormy day. To day is set apart as National Fast Day. I spent the evening home. No letter from Father yet.

William Dorsey was friends with both Jake White and Robert Adger Jr. He is listed as an artist in the Philadelphia city directory and was a custodian of the American Negro Historical Society. On March 20, Abraham Lincoln signed a proclamation declaring that April 30 was to be set aside as a day of fasting, prayer, clemency, and humiliation.

May 1863

Lovely day, very warm. Nellie cam up this afternoon, and bought her sewing. She spent the evening with Lanind. Stoped here on her way to the Cares.

Another lovely day. How I would like to go wagering. Hannah Brown stoped here to night to see what I had to say about Mr. Gibbs. I had nothing to say.

It is not clear if Jonathan Gibbs was still married to Anna Amelia Harris but they were having marital problems again. (She had publicly left him once before in 1852.)

SUNDAY, MAY 3, 1863

Very fine day for the wedding. Mr. Gibbs preached this morning. In the afternoon Doctor Ovaries delivered a beautiful discourse. After the sermon, the bridal parties came in and were married. I expected to hear some objection, bon, not a word. The bride looked lovely, the church was crowed.

Here Emilie wrote bon, *cf. French meaning, "good."*

MONDAY, MAY 4, 1863

No school, Nellie was up here a little while.

TUESDAY, MAY 5, 1863

Meeting at Deeris. Very few out, the groom was not there to night. The grand supper comes off (at) The Sons of St. Thomas.

The Sons of St. Thomas was an all black fraternal and mutual-aid society.

WEDNESDAY, MAY 6, 1863

Very stormy. Tomorrow is exsamination. Nellie has not bin up to day. Mary A was up here in all the rain. I cut her dress, finally.

Emilie is either referring to Mary Davis, Alfred's wife, or Mary Adger, Robert Adger's wife, who was a member of the Ladies' Union Association.

THURSDAY, MAY 7, 1863

Thursday morning I did not go in the morning to the school. Examination in the afternoon, it was very much crowed. Cristy had a special spelling class in the afternoon for our benefit.

The Institute for Colored Youth hosted a yearly written examination for all senior students testing under the direction of Professor Pliney E. Chase. Out of the five students who tested, two were women, Caroline (Carrie) Rebecca Le Count (who received the highest scores and served as the corresponding secretary of the Ladies' Union in 1865) and Rebecca J. Cole (who was the second black woman in the United States to receive a medical degree).

FRIDAY, MAY 8, 1863

The exercises this morning were very good. Sue came in this morning to see Wanfound. Nellie and Annie stoped as they were going.

SATURDAY, MAY 9, 1863

Quite a fine day. Nellie stoped here as she went up town this morning. In the evening, went to the milliners for my bonnet.

Although Emilie could trim a bonnet, it appears as if she was unable to cut or shape it.

SUNDAY, MAY 10, 1863

~~Bridal party came in. The bride looked beautiful, the ch~~ Very fine day, the groom did not preach to day. After church, we all in a body went to call on the bride. Bible class at Mary Joneses. Clear, I noticed the church looked thin in the afternoon.

Mary Jones was a washerwoman who lived at 511 South Tenth Street within walking distance of First African.

No school as usally. There is a gaddys wonder out about DJJG and his lady, allso about Mr. Gibbs because he thought he would take a wife to himself. There is great deal of dissatisfactoon in the church about it.

Dr. James J. Gould Bias was married to Eliza Anne and was a former slave and a Methodist preacher. By this time, Gibbs was probably seeing Elizabeth who would later become his wife.

Meeting last night at Bundys. Very few out, perhaps the rain prevented some. Mr. Gibbs was not there.

We have had another shower to day. Nellie spent the evening with me.

Another dull day. Called on Mrs. Harris and Craig from Prinston. The rain prevented me making several visits. I spent the best part of my time with Nellie.

Lovely day after the rain. I received a sweet little letter from Redding and his photog to day. I called on Nogil Bucone and Lizzie Brown this afternoon.

Very fine day. Nellie was here this morning. We had a nice little chat about matters and things. Mary stoped in the evening after work. I did not get down home to night.

It has bin quite showery all day. We had a very heavy thunder storm this afternoon. I have bin quite sick all day, havn't bin to church. Nellie stop after church this morning.

I answered Redding letter to day. No one came to see me yesterday but Nellie. I have not seen anything of her to day.

Very warm to day. Nellie stoped a minute to see if I was going to meeting. Meeting at Brother (Robert) Adgers, we had a happy time. Mr. Farbeaux lead meeting, quite a number out.

Installed in 1874, Robert J. Adger Sr. served as an elder at First African and was married to Mary Ann. He worked as a clerk and a purveyor of used furniture and served as an elder and a member of the board of trustees at First African Presbyterian Church. Mary was a member of the Ladies' Union Association along with Emilie.

WEDNESDAY, MAY 20, 1863

Cloudy all day. Nellie came up and spent the evening with me. She seems to be my only visiting friend.

THURSDAY, MAY 21, 1863

Very busiy all day. I did not get out until after four. I went home, then to Nellies. Went over Em McCrell and went down to Mrs. Potters with her in the evening.

FRIDAY, MAY 22, 1863

I went to Shiloh church seroy [service], beautiful day. Nellie and (I) went out shoping for Mrs. Potters.

SATURDAY, MAY 23, 1863

Very warm day. Very busiy all day. In the evening I went down to Mrs. Hills to take Sue's bonnet. Nellie went withe me. Mrs. Hill promise me one of her photographs.

SUNDAY, MAY 24, 1863

Lovely morning. Sue and here friend stoped here this morning. I do not like his looks. We had a very good service on this afternoon. The bible class was at church.

MONDAY, MAY 25, 1863

We went up to Whites to bible class. It was very late, this rain prevented us. Liz was ready to take us. We had a very interesting class.

TUESDAY, MAY 26, 1863

I ran down home a little while last night. Nellie was up here. Meeting at Brownes, very few males out. Very lively meeting, I was very drowsy, I am sorry to say it. After meeting, we went to Mrs. Palmer. Coming home, we met A. Jones. He came home with us.

WEDNESDAY, MAY 27, 1863

Nellie spent the evening with me.

THURSDAY, MAY 28, 1863

Lovely day, Liz and I went out visiting. We went to call on the Fralerne and Mrs. Read, then went down to the Proctoring. I went out to see Mrs. Harris, then went down to the concert. It came off very well.

Here Emilie wrote "fralerne," cf. German fräulein, *meaning "young woman."*

FRIDAY, MAY 29, 1863

I have not heard a word from Father. I fear they (the city of Harrisburg) have seceded. Very buisy all day. Have not seen Nellie. Mary went to the concert.

SATURDAY, MAY 30, 1863

I went down home, found no one there as usal. Stoped at Nellies, we had quite a long chat.

SUNDAY, MAY 31, 1863

Beautiful morning, I went down to church, great many out, considering. The sermon was very interesting. After church, we went to see Mrs. Colegates. I stoped to Aunt Janes in the afternoon. I spent this evening alone because I am reading the history of Abraham and Jacob, very interesting.

June 1863

MONDAY, JUNE 1, 1863

Lizzie Brown was to see me to day. I spent part of the last evening with Nellie.

TUESDAY, JUNE 2, 1863

Meeting at the Offerely, not many there. We met Vincent at the step. He came up home with me. Elijah J was not at meeting, has not bin for some time.

WEDNESDAY, JUNE 3, 1863

Beautiful day, Nellie and Miss Uhrmon called on the bride. Nellie stoped here in the after noon. She did not come up in the evening. Levina was here to day. Nellie did not get (here) this evening.

THURSDAY, JUNE 4, 1863

Very pleasant day. Nellie and I went out. It has been a long time sin(ce) we went shopping toge(ther). I went out to Germantown about 6'o, had a very pleasant time. Vincent came out for me, which was the pleasantis part of the evening.

FRIDAY, JUNE 5, 1863

Nellie has not bin up here to day. I taken Sues skirts off to furnes (finish).

SATURDAY, JUNE 6, 1863

Nellie stoped here this morning. Tomorrow is Communion. I, I will be prepared to partake of the Holy Sacrament. I stoped at Nellies.

SUNDAY, JUNE 7, 1863

Very cloudy all day. I went church in the afternoon. Nellie was sick and was not out. It was Communion. We had quite a happy time. Bible class at Mrs. Chases. Mr. Gibbs did come.

MONDAY, JUNE 8, 1863/TUESDAY JUNE 9, 1863

Very buisy all day getting ready for the wedding. Nellie stoped here a little to day. Vincent was here this evening. He wanted me to go to the Leeve, but I could not make up my mind to neglect my meeting. I felt much better sitting in meeting that I would have bin in the hall.

WEDNESDAY, JUNE 10, 1863

Very buisey all day. I have bin expecting Nellie all the evening. She came late, but had bin here early in the evening, but could not get in. I was quite disappointed.

THURSDAY, JUNE 11, 1863

Very pleasent morning. I had a very in teresting letter from Tomy on Monday. Nellie and I started out but it comenced raining. We had to run back home. Went out later.

FRIDAY, JUNE 12, 1863

Nellie was here this morning. I wrote to Redding this evening. Vincent came home with me last night. He seemed the same as ever.

SATURDAY, JUNE 13, 1863

Very warm to day. I stoped home, Sarah seem quite sociable. Nellie was not home. I staid until she came in.

SUNDAY, JUNE 14, 1863

Very pleasant in the morning. I went to church, herd a very good sermon. Mr. Gibbs was very earnest in his remarks. In the evening, Nellie and Jake cam up.

MONDAY, JUNE 15, 1863

I wrote a long letter to Tomy and sent it to the office by Cristy. I was out this afternoon and stoped at Nellie. I saw a company of colored recruits. They looked quite War like.

TUESDAY, JUNE 16, 1863

I was quite sick last night. Nellie was up. Meeting at Stroces. Very good meeting. Great many out. Mr. White frighten us by saying that a great many of his dear frien(d)s expeced to go to Ware (War) at 12 o'clock. After meeting, I asked who, he said all the boyes.

All the "boys" included institute teachers Octavius Catto and Jake White, and students Raymond Burn, Henry Boyer Jr., and Joseph G. Anderson Jr.

WEDNESDAY, JUNE 17, 1863

To day has bin the most exciting I ever witness. We went to see the boyes start for Harrisburg. I left home about 9 o'clock. It was almost 12 when I came home.

Governor Andrew Gregg Curtin issued "A Call to Arms," and a full company of ninety black soldiers (including teenage boys) was organized under Captain William Babe. They marched from City Arsenal on Broad Street to the Harrisburg station.

THURSDAY, JUNE 18, 1863

This morning, the first thing I heard was that the boyes had bin sent back. I feel glad and sorry.

Last night, they had quite a disloyal meeting about Mr. Gibbs. The Trustees were about to turn Mr. Gibbs right out of the church. The meeting was posphoned. It was almost 12'o when we left the church.

The Trustees included Jacob White Sr., Alexander Guy, Robert Adger Jr., and Jacob Farbeaux. A meeting was also held at Sansom Street Hall to constitute a general committee for raising black regiments. Both Anna Elizabeth Dickinson (antislavery and women's rights' lecturer), and Frederick Douglass spoke and helped to raise over $30,000 to support the troops.

SATURDAY, JUNE 20, 1863

The boyes are still talking about going to Ware (War).

Eight thousand rebel troops convened near Harrisburg, Pennsylvania.

SUNDAY, JUNE 21, 1863

Rather showery, I went to church in the afternoon. We had very good sermon. We all are so thankful that our boyes are all home again. Bible class closed this evening, the attendence was very large. We chosed to meet in October if we are spared.

The institute's school year usually began in October and continued until May.

MONDAY, JUNE 22, 1863

Sue stayed with me all the night, and went out (a)lone this morning. Nellie was up here a little while.

Lieutenant Colonel Louis Wagner (of the Eighty-Eighth Regiment, Pennsylvania Infantry) was appointed to command the soldiers at Camp William Penn.

TUESDAY, JUNE 23, 1863

I feel so worried about Father. We had a very happy meeting to night. Johns lead the meeting, every one seemed to enjoy it. Mrs. Gibbs was there awhile.

As the rebel troops began moving into Harrisburg, hundreds of free black people were kidnapped and sold into enslavement.

WEDNESDAY, JUNE 24, 1863

Very buisy to day. Nellie came up and staid until 10 o'clock go. We had a pleasant chat as usal, about Cristy.

THURSDAY, JUNE 25, 1863

Beautiful day. I went to Harris stoped at Douglasses an Gordanes, spent a little while with Nellie, then went down to Afforts to see Ellie Spence. I spent quite an agreeable time with the girls. Came home about 15 past nine.

FRIDAY, JUNE 26, 1863

Cristy came up with me. Redding spent the morning with me, his visit was pleasant.

The black volunteers, who had attempted to enroll on June 17, were drafted into service, including some of the boys (except for Catto who refused to re-enroll). They became Company A of the Third Regiment of the U.S. Regiments of Colored Troops and were the first company of colored troops from Philadelphia enrolled in the U.S. service.

SATURDAY, JUNE 27, 1863

Nellie had a letter from Reading and Sarah Thomas is married. It seems like a dream but it is reality. Nellie was up this morning, I spent there the afternoon. Rochel came in and staid a little while.

Sarah Thomas married William Shimm, a storekeeper from Reading, Pennsylvania.

SUNDAY, JUNE 28, 1863

Lovey day, I went to church. Johns preached for us, his sermon was very good. After church, went to Mrs. Colgate & Palmers & Mary Grews. I went around to Sunday school, and said to Mary to teach her class. I sent a letter to Father last night.

MONDAY, JUNE 29, 1863

To day has bin the exciting day. I have witness refuges are comin from all the towns this side of Harrisburg. The greetes excitements prevails.

There was a lot of excitement in the city as black men marched on Sixth Street in Philadelphia en route to Camp William Penn and black and white refugees came into the city in advance of General Lee's invasion of south central Pennsylvania.

TUESDAY, JUNE 30, 1863

I am all most sick wrossien (worrisome) about Father. The city is considered in dangue. Meeting at Mrs. O'Neils, very feeling, Mr. Guy lead. There seems to be a better sprit among our people. The excitement is not quite so great to day. Johns started for Reading (Pennsylvania).

July 1863

WEDNESDAY, JULY 1, 1863

To day, Vincent is perfectly wild with excitement. The boyes have all volentered. Nellie came up and spent quite a pleasant evening.

THURSDAY, JULY 2, 1863

I went down home, found things quite agreeable. In the afternoon I went to see Mrs. Burk. Spent the evening with Dave.

FRIDAY, JULY 3, 1863

Cristy did not come up last night. Vincent came home with me. What I would (do) if he was not about, I do not know. Kirbe came up this morning, he left about half past one for St. Louis.

SATURDAY, JULY 4, 1863

Colored soldiers has becom quite a matter of course. The fourth has bin very quiet up in our part of the city. I was down hom a little while, very few fire workes.

SUNDAY, JULY 5, 1863

Quite a rainy day. I went to church, very few out. We had very good sermon. After church, I spent part of the time home and the evening in Nellie house. How I miss bible class.

MONDAY, JULY 6, 1863

Vincent came home with me. Nellie was up here to day.

The Honorable William D. Kelley, Anna Elizabeth Dickinson, and Frederick Douglass held a mass recruitment meeting at the Philadelphia National Hall for the promotion of colored enlistments. Octavius V. Catto, Jake White, and Ebenezer Bassett acted as recording secretaries and the vice presidents were Reverend William Johnson Alston, David Bustill Bowser, and Robert Adger Sr.

TUESDAY, JULY 7, 1863

Very dull day. Meeting at Mrs. Walkins, very few out. Great rejoicing where the surrender of Vicksburge. Tonight, Mr. Gibbs over (he is) looking to come up to Nellies after meeting. Mrs. Bagard left for Cape May.

In recognition of the unconditional surrender of the Confederate bastion of Vicksburg, Mississippi, the city hosted a fireworks display downtown, near the Union League building.

WEDNESDAY, JULY 8, 1863

This morning, very heavy storm, it rained in torrents all day.

THURSDAY, JULY 9, 1963

Very dull day, it rained, rained hard. Soon after, I went out. I received a leter from Father to day. I went around to Maryes. I spent the evening with Nellie.

FRIDAY, JULY 10, 1863

Cristy did not come, I had a letter from Tomy. Cristy and St are began to past with recruits. Sue was in to night, she looked lovely. John stoped for her.

SATURDAY, JULY 11, 1863

Very buisy, getting the folks ready to go away. I went down hom. Sarah was quite talkative.

The "folks" that Emilie referred to were the Powell family, one of the families that she worked with either as a day worker or a live-in domestic.

SUNDAY, JULY 12, 1863

Quite pleasant this morning, I went down to church. Mr. Colken preached for us, he gave us quite a military discourse. I went down to Sunday school. Vincent came up to see me in the evening. He paid quite a pleasant visit.

MONDAY, JULY 13, 1863

Very busiy all day, Nellie stoped a little while. I went to see about a situation, didn't get it.

Emilie's "situation" was either a job as a live-in domestic or as a day worker. Draft riots broke out in several Northern cities over the issue of conscription and lasted from July 13–17, with several black business and homes being burned to the ground and over twelve hundred people killed.

TUESDAY, JULY 14, 1863

Very dull morning, Mrs. Powell did not get off at all. Went to help her and sent him some money. Meeting at (Samuel and Amanda) Stewards, very few out, even Vincent was not there.

WEDNESDAY, JULY 15, 1863

This has been fine. Its a holiday. I have not seen Nellie to day. I do not like the prospect of having no work all summer.

THURSDAY, JULY 16, 1863

Very fine morning, the folks got off. I am happy to say I staid untill most nine o'clock. I staid in Nellies all night.

FRIDAY, JULY 17, 1863

I am all most tired of doing nothing everyday. I went up to Lizzies with some things. Lizzie gave me som lunch, witch was very nice.

SATURDAY, JULY 18, 1863

It rained so hard last night. I did not go to meeting to day. Have been buisy helping to clean up. I do not feel so well.

One week after the Union failed to seize Fort Wagner, the Fifty-fourth Massachusetts heroically (but ultimately unsuccessfully) led the Union troops into the Second Battle of Fort Wagner. Two of Frederick Douglass's sons were members of the Fifty-fourth.

SUNDAY, JULY 19, 1863

I went to church in the morning. Very few out. In the afternoon, I went to Sunday school. I taught Liz and Nellie's classes. After church, Mary and I went down to Offenses. Gertrude (Offit) and (her) mother both sick. In the evening, Sarah Duglass (Douglass) and I went down to Cristy.

M. Gertrude Offit was an 1864 graduate of the institute. Sarah Douglass was a teacher at the Institute for Colored Youth and a member of the Philadelphia Female Anti-Slavery Society.

MONDAY, JULY 20, 1863

Has bin a lovely day. I have bin buisy sewing all day.

TUESDAY, JULY 21, 1863

This morning it rained quite hard, clear in the afternoon. Meeting was at our house. Very good meeting. Pop Steward is seriously impressed. Nellie was not out all day Sunday.

Although Emilie wrote about the meeting on July 21, the official records of the Ladies' Union Association of Philadelphia state that the organization was founded on July 20.

WEDNESDAY, JULY 22, 1863

Very busy all day. Went aroun to Marys. After, stoped at Nellies.

THURSDAY, JULY 23, 1863

Very warm. Nellie and I went out shoping. Stoped to see Lizzie at 16st and Walnut. Very buisy sewing part of the evening.

FRIDAY, JULY 24, 1863

Very pleasant day. I stopped to visit Nellie, then spent the afternoon at 16th & Walnut. About five, Nellie and I went up to Whites and staid until meeting time. I spent quite a pleasant visit. I had the pleasure of meeting some rebels that were opisite.

SATURDAY, JULY 25, 1863

Home all day, not very well.

SUNDAY, JULY 26, 1863

Very pleasant, I went to church all day. Had a stranger to preach for us in the afternoon. In the evening, Nellie, Cristy, and I went to Sues. Spent a very pleasant evening.

MONDAY, JULY 27, 1863

I spent part of the morning at Marys, she is better. After super, Nellie and (I) went out to Duglassess (Douglasses). I went to see the soldiers come home.

William Douglass was the rector of St. Thomas Protestant Episcopal Church, and he and his wife Elizabeth had twelve children before she died in 1862. In 1863 (shortly after he married Sarah Mapps), there were at least eight children, including his daughter Sarah, living in the home.

TUESDAY, JULY 28, 1863

Meeting at Nellies. Quite a sudden death, Mrs. (Amanda) Steward died this afternoon. I can hardly reorlize it. Very nice meeting. I received a letter from Father to day.

According to her death certificate, Amanda Steward died of a heart infection.

WEDNESDAY, JULY 29, 1863

To day is the great day out at the Cogs. I did not go. I had a letter from Alfred. I was to go to Gertrudes, but the rain prevented us.

THURSDAY, JULY 30, 1863

Very buisy, all day at hom. Very dull day. In the morning I went up to Hazards, then around to Miss W(illiams). Mary is still sick.

FRIDAY, JULY 31, 1863

To day is the chertified (certified) day they begin to draft in the Seventh Ward. Alfred and Elijah J. are both drafted. Mary is quite worried. I hope he will not have to go. Elijah J. is over the age. Mrs. Steward was buried yesterday. Elijah J. got a carriage, and we all went.

> *Although Emilie noted that her uncle was over the age, he was later drafted and served as a private in the Sixth Regiment Company A.*

August 1863

SATURDAY, AUGUST 1, 1863

I stoped up to Hazards.

SUNDAY, AUGUST 2, 1863

I think this has bin one of the warmest dayes we have had this summer. I went down to Sunday School in the morning. Nellie was not out. In the evening.

MONDAY, AUGUST 3, 1863

I was in to Marys, she had company. Nellie treated very strangly, I can't alow for it. Mary is still sick and have not heard from Alfred.

TUESDAY, AUGUST 4, 1863

Fine day, meeting at eight this evening, at Whites. I stoped at Hazards. Nellie did not go, very few out. After meeting, I, I went around to Chases.

WEDNESDAY, AUGUST 5, 1863

To day the great picnic comes off. I went with Nellie to the office. I did not get started until after 8. When we go over, we found to our disappointment they had all gone and left us, and we did not know where to go. We staid at the Wharf until after 10. We did not get any berries and was disappointed in the bargon (bargain).

THURSDAY, AUGUST 6, 1863

Very busy all day. In the evening, we went up to Augustes

FRIDAY, AUGUST 7, 1863

Yesterday was Thanks given day. Went to church in the afternoon, very few out. Dave Cares down home to day, but didn't come to class at Nellie. Poor girl, she is quite distressed. We had quite a nice meeting last night.

Sarah got off to day. After she had gone, I found out someone had bin in my trunk. I feel it was Ella Williams.

Very warm day, Nellie spent the day in our house. She is very unhappy. I went out to church all day. Mary is quite sick to day.

I was over to Chases a little while last night, quite warm. I spent part of the morning with Mary. I wrote to Sarah and Alfred yesterday.

Frederick Douglass met with President Abraham Lincoln to discuss the unequal pay and poor treatment that black soldiers were receiving.

Yesterday, I fixed the things for Father. Elijah J. sent them to day for me. Miss Harris came for me to go out with her to the country. I promised to go on Thursday.

Meeting at Madissons. Liz and I were the only females there. We had a nice little meeting. I have bin very busy getting ready to go away.

Mary had a letter from Alfred. She was over here to day. Bell Adger was married on last Tuesday night. Nellie and George went to the reception. Very pleasant to day. This afternoon, I leave for Harrisburg. I feel very doubtful to go just at this time; Nellies in trouble and Mary sick.

Bell Adger was one of the fourteen children of Robert and Mary Anne Adger.

I had a very pleasant drive out with Mr. Harris, everything looks matured. Mr. Harris goes away to day. I wrote a long letter to Nellie and sent it in town to day.

From August 14 to October 14, Emilie lived and worked as a live-in domestic with the Harris family in East Falls of Schuylkill River, near the Falls Bridge.

I have bin very busy all day, but got along very well. I have caught a bad cold in my throat. I feel quite under the weather.

It is quite pleasant to day. I did not feel well enough to go to church. I have felt quite sick all day. I spent the morning in reading and sleeping. In the evening, Harriet (C. Johnson) and (I) took walk. We had a lovely shower last night.

This was probably Harriet C. Johnson, an 1864 graduate of the institute. During the summer months, because of the intense heat, some domestic workers would accept short-term live-in situations that were located outside of the city.

MONDAY, AUGUST 17, 1863

It is very pleasant to day. I expect letter from Nellie to day, shall be disappointed if I do not get one. The day has past and I have no letter yet.

TUESDAY, AUGUST 18, 1863

I am still looking for one to day. I have had quite a nice time out here so fare. If I only felt well, would be glad. I shall miss meeting to night. It is the first time I have missed a night for a long time.

WEDNESDAY, AUGUST 19, 1863

No letter yet from hom. Lovely day, the arir (air) is so sweet and pure. Theodore come out and Richer stoped at the house. I have had a pleasnte time so far out here.

THURSDAY, AUGUST 20, 1863

No letter yet. Im thinking friends have for saken me. Very warm. I have bin quite busy all day. It just a weeke to day since I came out here. Mr. Stiner was over to see us this evening.

FRIDAY, AUGUST 21, 1863

Very warm day. At last, I have a letter from Nellie. She has bin to Cape May. She is in good spirits. Everything is all right between her and her mother. I have bin quite sick all day, not able to do my work. I sent a note in to Elijah J. on Thursday. I hope he will answer it soon.

SATURDAY, AUGUST 22, 1863

I have bin sick all day. I hope I will be able to go to church tomorrow morning.

SUNDAY, AUGUST 23, 1863

Very warm day. I went to church in the morning. I heard a very good sermon. A young white minister that (s)poke reminded me of Johns. In the afternoon, I did not spend as profitable as I might. In the evening, we went to prayer meeting, had a spirited meeting. Our party were the only colerd people. There was about four of us.

This is one of only two entries in which Emilie racially self-identified. The other place was in the Memoranda section of the 1869 pocket diary where she wrote "her" colored people.

MONDAY, AUGUST 24, 1863

To day has bin very windy. I am going to wait to see if Nellie will write befor I answer her letter.

TUESDAY, AUGUST 25, 1863

Very pleasant morning. I received three (letters) from hom to day, one from Liz and Nellie and Elijah J. We had a hevey shower this evening.

Quite cool to day. I have written three notes home to day, one to Nellie, Liz, and Elijah J. Quite lovely out here. Ephraim cam overe this morning and stay a long, long time. I was almost chilled through standing out on the plaza.

I have bin dusting all day. Mr. Harris is in to day. Harriet, Theodore, and I went down to the Falls for ice cream, but we came back. As we went, Ephraim gave us a buck to get some ice cream.

Very busy all day, I hardly had time to think of home. The weather is so cool. I expect Hazards will be home before I am ready for them to.

Has bin quite pleasant, very windy. I should like to be home tomorrow to go to church. It's bin so long since I com out here.

To(day) has bin a lovely day. Have not bin to church. I have not bin well and my arm so laime that I am unable to raise it to comb my hair. I want to go this evening.

I went to church last night. We heard a good sermon. Johnson girls cam over and spent the evening with us. To day has bin very pleasant. In the evening Harriet, Ephraim, and I went over to Ruth. We met som of the homilzes (homliest) people I believe I every saw.

September 1863

I received a letter from Elijah J. Poor Mary (Alfred) is very sick, yet I feel very ansious about her. No word from Nellie. This evening Harriet and I went over to Johnsons. We had nice fun.

A celebration was held at Camp Penn, and thousands of spectators showed up to support the troops as they paraded and were presented with a regimental flag.

I have just finished a letter to Elijah J. and one to Mary Alfred. Poor girl, she is so ill. I feel quite worried about her.

Very pleasant to day. I have bin very busy all day sewing. I have not heard a word from Nellie. I expect a letter tomorrow. Harriet and I have had grand fun this week.

FRIDAY, SEPTEMBER 4, 1863

Very plesent day. No letter from Nellie, What can the matter be? To day we had a grand rompant on the lawn. Rochel Johnston (Johnson) came over the in the afternoon, and Ephraim, and the rest in the evening.

Here Emilie wrote that they had a grand "rompant," cf. French je rompant, *meaning "to break." Rochel Johnson was a washerwoman who lived on 807 Locust within walking distance of Emilie's home.*

SATURDAY, SEPTEMBER 5, 1863

James went off and locked us all in the kitchen. Harriet leaves in the morning, very sorry. I made cake and I went to the stores with her, then went to West Phila to see Anna Fulmer. We had a pleasant drive.

SUNDAY, SEPTEMBER 6, 1863

Lovely day. I have bin unable to go to church this morning. How I would like to be in church, it is Communion Sunday. I went to church in the evening, had very interesting sermon. The widower was with me.

MONDAY, SEPTEMBER 7, 1863

Quite plesant to day. Lizzie came out to day to coock. I am so glad. She brought me a letter from Nellie. Poor girl, she has had her own troubles since I left.

TUESDAY, SEPTEMBER 8, 1863

Agatha has gone to Washington, Jay go with her. I have bin very buisy all day. I had a letter from Elijah J., telling me he had spent all or nearly all of my money, very curoles (careless) guy.

WEDNESDAY, SEPTEMBER 9, 1863

Last night we all went over to Johnsons. We had a good bit of fun, bit I think it is the last time I will climb that hill.

THURSDAY, SEPTEMBER 10, 1863

Very fine day. Katie and I went carige riding with James. Kate got hurt. I have a letter from Harriet. Tonight I am (Emilie's pen runs off of the page)

FRIDAY, SEPTEMBER 11, 1863

I had a letter from brother to day. Theodore went home, we will miss him much. He is so full of fun. Johnson girls com over this evening. Rachel has not gone home yet. Harriet has bin gone all weeks to day.

SATURDAY, SEPTEMBER 12, 1863

I have bin as busy as a bee all day. Mr. and Mrs. Harris really had a narrow escape last night. Buggy was broken and they were thrown out, but they did not get hurt.

Very plesent after the rain. I went to church in the morning, heard a very good sermon. No church in the evening.

A letter: Elijah J. informing me that Alfred had gone to Canada. I am very sorry. Mary is still quite sick.

Very dull day, I am almost tired of the country. Burnes cam over. No letter from Nellie, I was disappointed.

I feele very ansious to be home. I received a letter heatthe [healthy] from Nellie to day. It was quite a ledger, but some bad news about Mary heatthe [health]. Answered Elijah J.s and Nellies letters.

I have bin very busy all day. It is very lonsome out her on a rainy day. I went up to Barns yesterday for my letter, met Ephraim. He invited me to go over to Mrs. Michael on Sunday. I think I will go.

To day has bin a very stormy, dreary day. The rains was very heavy. I sent some money down for Nellie to disperse.

It is quite cold to day. We had to have fire in the furnace. I only have a few more dayes oute here. I feel ansious to be home. There is no place like home, if its ever so humble.

This morning I went to church. It was quite cold in the afternoon. Ephraim taken me over to Mrs. Michael. We had quite a pleasant drive. He was quite devoded to me.

The weathe begins to be cool. It is moon light, yet it is not so dreaey.

I received a note from Paul and a letter from Mary Jones. She is quite sick, both in body and in mind. She talks as her husband has found the blessing and she is seeking fore it I trust. Nellie teles me I have a neice.

This is the only time in which Emilie mentioned having a niece. There is no indication that this was Alfred's child, since she mentioned his son Francis; nor is there any indication that this was Thomas's child, since she did not mention that he had any children; it is possible that this may have been Elizabeth's baby girl.

WEDNESDAY, SEPTEMBER 23, 1863

I have another long and interesting letter from Nellie. To day she sends me all the news. Cristy and her are on the outs. I am verry sorry, but I can not help it. I will have to take him to task when I go home.

Emilie's use of the jargon "take him to task" is quite interesting as this phrase is still used today. Most slang words do not typically retain their consistent usage. In mid-nineteenth-century jargon, as in today's language, to "take someone to task" means to lecture, berate, admonish, or hold somebody accountable for his or her actions.

THURSDAY, SEPTEMBER 24, 1863

Last night Lizzie, Ephriam, and I went over to Rutheys.

The grand review of the black troops took place at Camp William Penn in Chelten Hills near Philadelphia.

FRIDAY, SEPTEMBER 25, 1863

I have a letter from Harriet to day. I expected one from Elijah J. but I did not get it.

SATURDAY, SEPTEMBER 26, 1863

Very busy as usal, it is lovely to day. To day I have bin troubled with a sore eye, ever since Wednesday night. I will be so glad when the time comes for me to go homed.

SUNDAY, SEPTEMBER 27, 1863

Very pleasant to day. I went to church, heard a good sermon. I have not bin well. Ephraim come over in the afternoon. In the evening, we went down to the Falls to the Methodist Church.

MONDAY, SEPTEMBER 28, 1863

To day has bin blue. Monday, I did not feel like work. George Fulner was here singing for our amusement. He was great as usal.

The soldiers from the Fifty-fourth organized a public protest against President Lincoln because they were receiving unequal pay. As a result, they served without pay for eighteen months.

TUESDAY, SEPTEMBER 29, 1863

I have bin waiting patiently for a letter, but no letter came. I expect to go home this day week.

WEDNESDAY, SEPTEMBER 30, 1863

Very fine day. I walk up to Thomases to see if he had bought me a letter, but he had not. In the evening, Barns came over with one for me.

October 1863

THURSDAY, OCTOBER 1, 1863

My time is up to day. I have bin very busy washing windows. We wer to take a walk with Ephraim, but we were too tired. I answered Nellies last night.

FRIDAY, OCTOBER 2, 1863

This is my last week out here. I hope Nellies very ansious for me to com home. Alfred has come home. Cristy and Nellie are acting friendly yet.

SATURDAY, OCTOBER 3, 1863

Mrs. Harris wants me to stay another week. She has heard from Tawny, she won't be home for seven months.

The Sixth Regiment and four companies of the Eighth Regiment paraded through downtown Philadelphia on their way to a celebratory dinner at the Union Volunteer Refreshment Saloon.

SUNDAY, OCTOBER 4, 1863

Very pleasant day. I went to church in the morning, heard a excellent sermon. In the afternoon, Lizzie, Ephraim, and (I) went to see Mr. Packer. He has lovely place. He gave us some beutiful flowers.

MONDAY, OCTOBER 5, 1863

I bid my dear friends farwell last night. I hav bin busy getting ready to go home, sent my things to day.

TUESDAY, OCTOBER 6, 1863

Mrs. Harris treated me like a lady. She said she was sory she had to part with me I heard to day. Nellie was delighted to see me. I stoped at Hazards an I went down home.

WEDNESDAY, OCTOBER 7, 1863

Sarah received me very well. Poor Mary is very ill, I do not think she will be here long. I have not seen Alfred yet. Nellie and I went out shopping. I bought a clock to day.

THURSDAY, OCTOBER 8, 1863

I have bin trimming my bonnet. I am waiting and Sarah and Mary, both. I was up to Hazards this evening.

FRIDAY, OCTOBER 9, 1863

Very busy all day. Poor Mary (Alfred) is no better. I expected to go with her to see a German doct. Liz and I was out shoping. We went to meeting in the evening, very few out.

SATURDAY, OCTOBER 10, 1863

I went up to the doctors with Mary. He sayes he could do nothing for her. Her lungs is to far gone home. How sad! I feel very ansious about her.

SUNDAY, OCTOBER 11, 1863

Lovely day, did no go to church this morning. I went in the afternoon. Spent the greater part of my time with Mary. I stoped at Mrs. Cristys, poor Nellie, she is very low-spirited.

It is not clear why Emilie seems to be referring to Nellie as Mrs. Cristy; perhaps Nellie was married to Cristy at this time, or she was engaged to marry him. Unfortunately, I have been unable to find any information on either of them.

MONDAY, OCTOBER 12, 1863

I went to Hazards (in) morning. Everything is at Sue Stevens. Stoped home and at Marys. I do not think she is long for this world, if she was only prepared. I did not go to meeting tonight, it being election's night.

TUESDAY, OCTOBER 13, 1863

Very busy to day, as usal. Tonight is the party out at Clayes. I think of going.

WEDNESDAY, OCTOBER 14, 1863

I went to the party and enjoyed myself nicely. Vincent was there and came home with us.

THURSDAY, OCTOBER 15, 1863

Quite dull to day. I spent the greater part of my time with Mary. She seemed to be in a very good frame of mine. She said she would like someone to talk with here. Mrs. Jordan promised to send of her ministers, which she did.

FRIDAY, OCTOBER 16, 1863

Very rainy all day. Cristy still putting on French with Nellie. He has not bin there for foure weeks.

SATURDAY, OCTOBER 17, 1863

Beautiful day. I have bin looking for Nellie at the morning meal. Harriet was here. Mr. Cormick died yesterday. Mary Jones no better. We had singing and praying last evening.

SUNDAY, OCTOBER 18, 1863

Lovely day, like spring. I was out in the morning. Rachel's acting Frenchy. John maed me furious. This morning, Elijah J. and I called on the brid(e), Mrs. Marick. She is quite nicely.

MONDAY, OCTOBER 19, 1863

I stoped to see Mary, she is still very ill. I fear she will not get over this attack. Nellie and the girls spent the evening at Seymours. I felt so bad I did go.

TUESDAY, OCTOBER 20, 1863

Nellie stoped in as she went up to the furneal. I wrote up to father. Seminary meeting at Riders. Nellie did not go, she went over to see Mary.

WEDNESDAY, OCTOBER 21, 1863

Alfred went up to the Provost Marshall. They would not exempt him. I feel quite ansious about him. I expected Nellie here tonight, but she did not come.

The provost marshall was the officer in charge of the military police. It appears as though Alfred had tried to flee to Canada because he did not want to serve in the military. When he returned (or was returned) he then applied for an exemption based on the poor health of his wife and the age of his son.

THURSDAY, OCTOBER 22, 1863

I have bin quite sick all day. Mary is a bit (bet)ter, she think. I spent the afternoon with her. In the evening, Nellie and I went down to Gertrudes.

FRIDAY, OCTOBER 23, 1863

We spent a pleasant evening. Vincent was to come down, but did not get here, we met him. Cristy was up here this evening. We had quite a serious talk.

SATURDAY, OCTOBER 24, 1863

Nellie was up here this morning. Poor girl, she look badly. I can tell from here, but I hope they will be reconciled with each other (before) long.

SUNDAY, OCTOBER 25, 1863

Very cold and dreary. Nellie quite sick, out all day. Sue was in town. I went to church in the afternoon, heard a very good sermon. I spent part of the evening with Mary, and other part with Nellie, she seemed so low spirited.

MONDAY, OCTOBER 26, 1863

Very find day. Yesterday Sue, George, and I stoped at Aunt Janes. Poor Charlie is very ill. We did not go up to see him, Nellie is down there. I stoped to see Mary. She is very ill.

TUESDAY, OCTOBER 27, 1863

Poor Charlie died this morning at 1 o clock, he did. Beutiful meeting in Orgon, so very few out. I went down to Aunt Janes, but I had a happy time after meeting.

WEDNESDAY, OCTOBER 28, 1863

Mary is very ill to day. Alfred went on the ship to day. I feel so badly about it to think he has to go away, just at this time when Mary is so ill.

THURSDAY, OCTOBER 29, 1863

Alfred was here to day. Mr. Gibbs was to see Mary this afternoon. He said she express a hope that her sins had bin forgiven.

Nellie and I spent part of the evening with her. Then we called to see Mrs. Palmer, then went to see Aunt Jane. Charlie was buried this morning. He had a very respectable furneal. Mr. Gibbs was slighed, he was not invited to the funeral. Mr. Cattos remarks were very good.

Lizzie has bin dead three years to day. Mary is very ill tonight.

November 1863

Lovely day. I went to church in the morning, heard a very good sermon. Stoped at Mrs. Hill and at millnes (milliners). I spent the rest of my time with Mary, she is very ill.

Very fine day. I went down to see Mary, found her very ill. I'm truly helpless. Stoped over home and told Sara. In the afternoon, Nellie come up for me, Mary was dieng. I went down and staid with her.

She died last night about 7 o clock. She died very calm, she was ready. Alfred did not get to see her.

According to her death certificate, Mary died of consumption of the lungs—more commonly known as tuberculosis.

Very busy all day cleaning up the house, Mary Grew and I. Poor Mary to be buried to day. No word of Alfred. Poor little Frank is left over alone. Mr. Gibbs attented the furneal. Francis went home with Elwood, Elijah J., and fixed the things. Nellie, Mrs. Sisco, and Mary there. Mother were there.

Here Emilie called Alfred and Mary's son Francis by his nickname—Frank. Elwood was Elijah J. and Sarah's four-year-old son.

I went to Hazards to day. They all seem to simplify things with me. I have bin so very busy since I come up here. I have hardly, hardly had time to think.

Mary (and) Sue was in yesterday. I was down home a little while to day. Frank seemd to be quite contented. Tomy has come home. He come running in here yesterday. I was delighted to see him.

Nellie and (I) up to doctor this morning. He was not there.

Pleasant in the morning, I was not out. We had an excellent sermon in the afternoon. Bible class commences this evening at Mrs. Hills, very nice class. Nellie was not there, or Vincent. Tomy was up a little while.

Nellie stoped, she is still very disconsolate. I pittey her, for I have suffered the same. I finished my bonnet tonight.

Very cold and blustery. Tomy spent quite a while with me. I love to have him com up to see me. Meeting up to Whites, great many out. We had quite a nice meeting.

Very busy to day. Tomy was up to day. He comes up nearly every day. Nellie was up and spent the evening. Elijah J. worrering (worrying) me about Frank.

Very pleasant to day. Tomy came up to go out with me, but got tired of waiting. I went down to his botes (boat), spent the best part of the evening. Then went to see Mr. Lively, he was not home.

Addison Lively was a member of Shiloh Baptist Church, a musician, and Emilie's guitar teacher.

Tomy and I went to have his photograph taken. He gave me a portfolio and a set of guitar strings.

During the nineteenth century, the guitar and the harp were considered to be a genteel woman's instruments.

Very busy all day. Nellie come up to go with me to the doctor, but I could not go. I went in the afternoon. I went down home this evening.

Very rainy morning mourning I went down to church, very few out. Cristy was not there. Vincent come in just as church was out. He has forsaken me. Nellie was up this evening.

Very dull to day. Tomy went down on the receiving ship this morning. The girls went to see Mr. Lively to day to see (if he) would teach the school. He promised to let us know on Wednesday.

TUESDAY, NOVEMBER 17, 1863

Tonight the glory presentation comes off. Nellie and I went, it was very interesting, indeed, it was grand. Vincent, ever constant, come home with us. Cristy was chairman for the evening, he did not see us.

WEDNESDAY, NOVEMBER 18, 1863

Very busy to day. Hannah Brown, Celestine, and Sally Mathis, and Nellie was up here this evening. We had quite a lovely time.

THURSDAY, NOVEMBER 19, 1863

Quite pleasant, I was busy hom fixing up my things. Part of the afternoon, Nellie and I went to went down to ones, heard very cheering news. Mr. Lively has promised to teach our school. We expect to commence next Monday night.

President Abraham Lincoln dedicated the military cemetery at the Gettysburg battlefield and gave the memorable Gettysburg Address, effectively summarizing the war and the impact of the war on the nation in ten sentences. Although this has been classified as one of the greatest speeches in history, at that time one critic noted that it was "to the point" with a "pithy sense, quaintness & good feeling." Biddle and Dubin, Tasting Freedom, *302.*

FRIDAY, NOVEMBER 20, 1863

Tomy sails tomorrow. I stoped home a little while.

SATURDAY, NOVEMBER 21, 1863

Very rainy day, Nellie did not get up to day. Mrs. Powell has been quite generous to day. Have bin waching the weather all the evening. Hopes it stop raining so I could go home.

SUNDAY, NOVEMBER 22, 1863

Lizzie Brown was here last night. Very pleasant day, I went to church in the afternoon. I went to Joneses Bible class at Mrs. Boukansfea.

MONDAY, NOVEMBER 23, 1863

I have bin quite sick all day. My throat has not got well, yet I anticipat a great deal of pleasure this evening. Nellie and Mills and I went to school. We had a very nice school. Mr. Lively could not stay. We commence next Monday night.

The 1863–64 academic year at the Institute for Colored Youth started today and ended on June 6, 1864.

TUESDAY, NOVEMBER 24, 1863

Quite disagreeable day. In the evening I went to meeting, very good meeting. Nothing of interest happened to day.

WEDNESDAY, NOVEMBER 25, 1863

I have not bin out for a wander. I have bin expecting Nellie, but she did not come. Levina stoped here this evening, left a note for John Simpson.

THURSDAY, NOVEMBER 26, 1863

To day is Thanksgiven day. I went to church in the afternoon. After church, I went with Liz to call on Rachel Turner.

FRIDAY, NOVEMBER 27, 1863

I spent the day at Nellie, quite dull to what last Thanksgiven was. Many changes since then, just during one year ago. Mary (Alfred) was up here but she is gone to rest, I hope.

SATURDAY, NOVEMBER 28, 1863

Very rainy day. Nellie did not get up been, very busy all day. In the evening, I stoped home, and at Nellies. Frank is still at Elijah J.s.

SUNDAY, NOVEMBER 29, 1863

Very dull morning. I went to church, heard quite a good sermon, very few out. Bible class (at) Whites, very good turn out. Mr. Bustill come home with me. Cristy went with Mary.

Brothers Charles and James "J.C." Bustill both worked at the Institute for Colored Youth. Charles was a plasterer and worked on the Underground Railroad. James was a librarian.

MONDAY, NOVEMBER 30, 1863

Very cold, Nellie was up here in the afternoon. We went down down to school, found Mr. Lively waiting for us to. Hannah Brown was there.

December 1863

TUESDAY, DECEMBER 1, 1863

Meeting at Mrs. Turner. After meeting, we stoped at Bustills, had quite a pleasant chat.

The first three regiments (Third, Sixth, and Eighth) of the Colored Troops from Philadelphia were full. By February 1864 there were five full Philadelphia Colored Regiments serving in the armed forces.

WEDNESDAY, DECEMBER 2, 1863

Cristy still Frenchy, I do not know how to treat him. I certainly do not feel pittey some towards him. Nellie was up this evening.

THURSDAY, DECEMBER 3, 1863

Thursday very plesant. Nellie, Mrs. Jordan and I went out shopping. Nellie bought herself a coat. We went up to Harrises, then I paid several other visits.

FRIDAY, DECEMBER 4, 1863

In the evening, we went hear Fred Duglass. Yesterday, I paid a visit to the White house. I have bin so busy, I did not have time to write.

The Third Decade Anniversary Celebration of the American Anti-Slavery Society was held at the Philadelphia Concert Hall. The question that served as the theme of the event was "What Would Be the Future of Negroes in the U.S.?" William Lloyd Garrison presided and Lucretia Mott was one of the featured speakers. Frederick Douglass also delivered a speech entitled "Our Work is Not Done."

SATURDAY, DECEMBER 5, 1863

Very clear, we had not had a clear Saturday for some time. I was down home a little while.

SUNDAY, DECEMBER 6, 1863

To(day) is a very interesting to all Christians, it is our Intercommunion. St. Mary (Church) also communed with us. Bible class at Whites, good number out.

MONDAY, DECEMBER 7, 1863

Quite cold out, Nellie was up here this afternoon. We went down to school. We had quite a nice school. We organized and appointed a committee to elect officers.

TUESDAY, DECEMBER 8, 1863

Meeting at Mr. Masons. After meeting, we went to Bustills, as usal. Meeting is there next time.

WEDNESDAY, DECEMBER 9, 1863

Very busy cleaning house, everything upside down. Last night, I saw Tony Taylor and Tomy Amos was here. I hope I will get to see him. I have bin trying to collect money for the organ.

THURSDAY, DECEMBER 10, 1863

Tomy was at Elijah J.s this evening. He went down to Bustills with Nellie and I. We spent quite pleasant evening. Dave Chester was there and Vincent.

FRIDAY, DECEMBER 11, 1863

Nellie was up here, and Egerton came up in the evening. It is quite lively.

SATURDAY, DECEMBER 12, 1863

Very dull day, I have bin very busey trying to get my dress done. Tomy was up, and we went down home for a little while.

SUNDAY, DECEMBER 13, 1863

Raining. I went to church, hardey anyone out. Doct Jones preached. He gave us an excellent sermon. Nellie was up in the evening.

MONDAY, DECEMBER 14, 1863

I went down to school this evening, very few out. Nellie and I opend the school.

TUESDAY, DECEMBER 15, 1863

Meeting at Bustills, I am sorry to say I was very drowsy. After meeting, we staid a little while. Cristy and Virgil came in, and soon went. After, they came in and to our surprise Cristy came up home with us.

WEDNESDAY, DECEMBER 16, 1863

Nellie came up this evening. Tomy was not here. I was very busy trying to get my dress done, sewing all day.

THURSDAY, DECEMBER 17, 1863

I went home quite late. Sarah was busy. Mr. Gibbs was to lecture to night. Tomy went home with me.

FRIDAY, DECEMBER 18, 1863

I got my dress greased last night, but I got it out to day. Tomy was up a little while to night.

SATURDAY, DECEMBER 19, 1863

Very busy to day, I went up to the Ducts to consult him about my throat and stoped home. Nellie has made her bonnet.

SUNDAY, DECEMBER 20, 1863

Very cold, I was not out in the morning. We had a stranger preache(r) in the afternoon. In the evening, bible class at Stills. Very few out. I was sick all day.

MONDAY, DECEMBER 21, 1863

I went down to school. It was quite cold there. I cought nice cold. Very few girls down, plenty of gentlemen.

TUESDAY, DECEMBER 22, 1863

I have bin quite sick all day, not able to go meeting.

WEDNESDAY, DECEMBER 23, 1863

Sue was here this morning. I could hardly talk to her. Nellie has not bin up here since Monday.

THURSDAY, DECEMBER 24, 1863

Very cold to day, Sue was here and bought our ribbons. I went home. Very dull Christmas, and I felt so sick I had to go home soon.

FRIDAY, DECEMBER 25, 1863

Very fine day, but I could not enjoy myself, I had such a cold. Nellie and I went to Bustill and had some eggnaugh. We met Cristy. He went around to Aunt Janes with us. I had to go hom. I spent a little time.

SATURDAY, DECEMBER 26, 1863

Vincent and Nellie come up and staid a little while with me.

SUNDAY, DECEMBER 27, 1863

Raining all day, I did not get to church all day. Lizzie was sick. Nellie and Liz come up after church. We spent the evening rather dull. Vincent did not come up.

MONDAY, DECEMBER 28, 1863

Raining all day. Lizzie sick to day. I have not bin homm since Friday. I did not go to school on account of weather. Nellie was down.

TUESDAY, DECEMBER 29, 1863

Cloudy to day. Sue was here this morning. Elijah J. stoped in the afternoon and I did not get to meeting. I am sorry to say I was thankful.

WEDNESDAY, DECEMBER 30, 1863

Nice, clear morning after the rain. Very busy all day. Nellie was up here, spent the eveing. Vincent was up and staid a little while.

THURSDAY, DECEMBER 31, 1863

While clear and cold, I have bin quite sick all the week. Nellie and Tomy was up here. Nellie and went out a little while, stoped into Bustills. Then went up to visit his family and helped to trim the childrens tree; stopped at Mrs Hills. Sue went with us to Aunt Janes. I was sick.

Memoranda

I sent two letters up to Harrisburg by Harret Chester.

I do have one dollar of Sues.

I have written two letters to my Sister since and received no answer.

Addel Gordon called to see me on Friday last. I owe her a visit.

The first Sunday in every month I must cut the ends of my hair.

The Banneker Guards started for Harrisburg on the 17th(of June), returned on the 18th with out a scare.

Wednesday the 17th, 1863 will be remembered by a great many of our people. Nearly all of our best young men left for the War, but happily returned the next day un harmed.

Sarah Thomas was married on last Saturday the (27th) of June.

Monday twenty-eighth, most exciting day ever witness by many. Refugees line the streets from all the towns this side of Harrisburg and down from Harrisburg.

Emilie wrote the 28th but it happened on June 29.

The riot in New York commenced on Monday the 13th(of July), continued several days. The colerd people suffered most from the mob.

Wednesday the 5th(of August), I will always remember. Someone, while I was over in Jersey, opend my trunk, stold (stole) a ring and $6.00 and 74 cents in silver.

This was equivalent to $124.69.

I sent Alfred his notice on the 10th of August.

I had two letters from Nellie on the two weeks, only one from Elijah J.

Gorgana has bin married about five weeks. Here husband beat her and left the other day. She had to go back to because the honeymoon is not over.

Em Jones has bin married nearly a week. I hope she will make out better than poor Gorgana. Rawly has disgraced her shamfuly.

I spent a very dull Christmas this year. I was sick Christmas Eve and had to go home—New Years Eve I was out a little while. It rained so hard, I did get any where. I stopped at Bustills. Cristy was there as usaly. Nellie went to Mrs. Sicos party. Sue was up here in the evening. John com after her.

> Oh, if I had a kind friend
> A friend that I could trust
> It would be a source of joy to me
> To know that I was blest
>
> With one in whom I could confide
> My secrets hopes and fears
> And who would not in coldness turn
> From me in furture years
>
> But, oh I fear I never shall
> Have that consoling thought
> To help me on through lifes cold stream
> Though very close I've sought
>
> To find this jewel of a friend
> That poets so applaud
> And as I have not found one yet
> I fear it is all a fraud.

A World Imagined

During the nineteenth century, the church, the schools, and the clubs were places of refuge and stability for the free black community. The pastors and the teachers were often actively involved in the political arena and were considered to be part of the leadership, providing guidance and direction. These places were anchors that connected families and communities. Within the enslaved communities, the church was the place where families could gather and fellowship on Saturday evenings or Sunday mornings. Although plantation owners determined when or if the enslaved families could have a church meeting, some families would steal away for short periods of time to meet and worship in private. It was a place where they could imagine the chariot swinging low and coming forth to carry them home.

For Emilie, the church was an important part of her life, and she spent a significant portion of her week either in service or at Bible study. Since it was so close, it was located at 915 Bainbridge within a five minute walk of her home, it is easy to see how she could have built her life around it. First African, which was also known as either Seventh Street Presbyterian Church or the First (Colored) Presbyterian Church, was that type of place and fostered that type of involvement and engagement. John Gloucester Sr. founded the church in 1807 with the encouragement and support of the white presbytery of Philadelphia for the purpose of training black Presbyterian missionaries. When it opened in 1811, it was the first black Presbyterian church organized in America, the fifth black church founded in the city, and it was a pillar in the Seventh Ward community. It was an uninteresting-looking building, built of plain brick, sixty feet long and thirty feet wide without any ornamentation either within the building or outside it. On the main floor, there were four rows of pews with a gallery on each side and one on the end, a high ceiling, and enough space to comfortably seat 370 people. On any given Sunday, every seat was filled, and there were people standing in the gallery area in the back. At once a legend and a mythical hero, Gloucester was known for being able to draw a large crowd. During the early days before the church was built, Gloucester used to hold services on the street corners and people would line up to hear and support him. Prior to coming to Philadelphia, Gloucester lived in Tennessee and was the body servant of Reverend Gideon Blackburn, who encouraged him to become a minister. Blackburn took Gloucester to Philadelphia to meet with the Evangelical

Society of Third Presbyterian Church and later freed him so that he could work unencumbered as a "missionary among colored people."[1] Although Gloucester was freed, his family was not, and he spent the next twelve years traveling through the North and throughout England to raise $1,200 to purchase his wife and his children.[2] The church members were primarily middle class, living in and around the Seventh Ward, and had an annual income of $1,538.[3] Prior to 1844, First African Presbyterian Church had over five hundred members and received an annual church income of $3,338 from the members. To put it in perspective, during the latter half of the nineteenth century, white working-class incomes fell below $900 per year, middle-class incomes fell between $900 and $3,500, and upper-class incomes were above $3,500 per year. In the free black communities of Philadelphia, where a majority of the families lived at or below the poverty line (which was approximately $650 per year), the annual income level of First African Presbyterian reflected both the social status and the color classification of the members (since mulattoes were typically educated, skilled, and had more disposable income).[4] Even though he founded the church, Gloucester actually never served as their official pastor, working as their resident minister until he died of tuberculosis in 1822. Prior to his death, Gloucester had laid out a detailed succession plan, which included his oldest son, Jeremiah, stepping in to lead the church. It is not known whether Jeremiah grew up in the church or joined his father there after he graduated from Presbyterian Synod School of New York and New Jersey but what is known is that several members of the church rejected Gloucester's plea.

They submitted a petition asking the presbytery to select Samuel Cornish to lead the flock.[5] Jeremiah decided to leave the church, taking approximately 80 percent of the members (some of the oldest and most respected black families in the city) with him. They built and founded the Second African Presbyterian Church on St. Mary's Street between Sixth and Seventh Streets. Less than twenty years later (after the building was destroyed during the 1842 riots and Jeremiah traveled to England to try to raise funds to build a $12,000 church), his brother Stephen, along with most of the members of Second African, petitioned and founded the Lombard Street Central Church.[6] Gloucester's youngest sons were John Jr., a student at Ashmun Institute (now Lincoln University), a Presbyterian minister, and a close friend of Emilie; and James, who founded and served as the minister of Siloam Presbyterian Church in Brooklyn, New York.

In 1842, when Emilie was just a toddler, First African, under the leadership of Charles Gardner, began, to rebuild its membership and its reputation. When Gardner resigned six years later and the church began to lose members (again), Jacob C. White Sr. stepped in and worked to have the building remodeled. By the time William T. Catto arrived in 1854 to assume the leadership of the church, it was valued at $8,000 and had an active membership roster of 180 people.[7] Catto was an established member of the free black Philadelphia elite. He had relocated to Philadelphia in 1848 after establishing himself as an activist and a minister. During Catto's tenure, White served as the Sunday School superintendent and the first president of the church's newly established board of trustees In addition to serving as a stop on the Underground Railroad, First African also had established educational ties outside of the city—with both Ashmun Institute (now Lincoln University) and Princeton Theological Seminary—to allow their seminary students and teachers to conduct their practicums at the church.[8] It was a place of intense activity and activism, holding service every Sunday at 10 and 3 and hosting weekly lectures at the Benezet Institute on Friday nights.

In addition to attending church with the White family, Emilie wrote of visiting them to attend either Bible study or a meeting and of being at the same social events with them. On July 24, 1863, after spending the day shopping with her friend Nellie, Emilie wrote, "Nellie and I went up to Whites and staid until meeting time. I spent quite a pleasant visit. I had the pleasure of meeting some rebels (people who were opposed to the Civil War) that were opisite." Here she attended Dave's wedding: "Dave was married tonight, I had to march in. Jon (John Simpson), Gorge (George Bustill White), and Jake (Jacob C. White Jr.) were at the wedding." Although she did not write of visiting the home of the Cattos, she does mention listening to Catto preach, "I went down to church. Mr. Catto preached, very few out."[9]

Emilie lived about five minutes from her school, the Institute for Colored Youth (now Cheney University). The school opened in 1837 after Richard Humphreys, a Quaker and a silversmith, bequeathed $10,000 (one-tenth of his estate) to design and establish a school for "the benevolent design of instructing the descendants of the African race in school learning, in the various branches of the mechanic arts and trades, and in agriculture, in order to prepare, fit and qualify them to act as teachers."[10] The institute was known for its rigid entrance examinations, its tuition fee of ten dollars per semester plus the costs of books and stationary, the pyramidal structure of its classes (since passage from one grade level to the next was highly competitive and extremely rigorous, the upper-level classes were much smaller than the lower-level classes) and its strong liberal arts curriculum. The school's mission was to train black teachers using other black teachers. Additionally the curriculum included composition, Greek grammar, algebra, plane and spherical trigonometry, geometry, poetry, classics, sciences, and classical Latin. Students had to complete an intensive, difficult examination in geometry, Latin, Greek, and plane and spherical trigonometry. Their passing scores were usually published and determined their ranking. Although it is the oldest black institution of high learning, it did not actually grant degrees until 1914 when it adopted a curriculum of a normal school (teacher training). Even still, those who completed the rigorous program were considered to be the "surviving elite within an elite."[11]

From 1863 to 1865, Emilie took evening classes on Monday night in the institute's seminary program, which included instruction in Bible and spelling. It also appears as if Emilie took language courses in French and German. Courses began in October, and the school had both a winter and spring session. It is not clear whether these courses were strictly for credit or if they were informal classes that were organized to serve the community. Here she mentioned taking language and spelling classes: "I expecte to go home to day. No girls come but I taken French leacn [lessons]"; and "Examination in the afternoon, it was very much crowed. Cristy had a special spelling class in the afternoon for our benefit." She also used some French and German words in her entries. In one example that suggests her knowledge of French, Emilie wrote, "It was a perfect jure" (cf. French *jour*, meaning "day"). Similarly, in another example, Emilie used a spelling that suggests knowledge of German: "They went down to see the Fralerne" (cf. German *fräulein*, meaning "young woman").[12]

At the Institute for Colored Youth, female teachers typically taught female students, but in Emilie's case, in 1863, her evening classes did not have a regular teacher, and the institute seems to have had some difficulties in hiring one. Several men and women substitutes taught her class until they hired a permanent teacher. On January 19, 1863, after classes had been in session for three weeks, Emilie noted, "I went down to school. We had no teacer but will have one next Mondy night." The following week she complained, "Very poor school. No teacher, Dave De-Clones teaching us again."[13] Throughout the semester Emilie wrote about not having a permanent teacher, of having to open the school herself, and of finally deciding not to attend class until the institute hired a permanent teacher. It would not be until November that the issue was finally resolved, and Emilie happily wrote, "Heard very cheering news, Mr. Lively has promised to teach our school. We expect to commence next Monday night."[14]

Addison Lively, Emilie's guitar teacher and the director of the Shiloh Baptist Church choir, was born in Virginia around 1820. Since he is listed as colored in the 1860 U.S. Census, he was probably born enslaved. Slavery had been legally recognized in Virginia since the mid-1600s, and the state had quickly grown over time to have the largest population of enslaved black Americans of any other state in the Confederacy. Lively was born around the time that David Walker, a black abolitionist and writer, had written and issued his *Appeal to the Coloured Citizens of the World*, a public call for black people to unite in the fight against injustice. Somehow Lively had found his way to Philadelphia and had established himself as a musician, choir director, and music teacher.[15]

As are revealed through both the content of Emilie's diary entries about her educational pursuits as well as her actual diary entries themselves, which are written in a relatively standardized English, Emilie was actively involved in expanding her literacy. For nineteenth-century black women, the active process of becoming literate meant that they were taking the power and authority to know themselves, they were gaining the skills they needed to read and write, and they were learning how to act with authority and confidence based on that knowledge.[16] Literacy and fluency undergirded a nineteenth-century black woman's ability to actively construct and maintain her agency. Indeed Emilie was part of a very small percentage of black women who were literate and who consciously pursued education beyond elementary and middle school. Additionally she lived in a ward that had the highest rates of literacy for black people in the city.

Though she probably lived in a community of homeowners—mulattoes were three times more likely to own property than blacks—Emilie did not own her own home; instead she lived in either a boardinghouse or a private home that took in boarders. At the same time, given that the boardinghouse culture was built on and maintained by gambling, prostitution, and anonymity, it seems highly unlikely that Emilie lived there. Respectable boardinghouses rarely accepted single female lodgers because women's wages were so low, and any unattached woman was usually viewed as a "woman of the town" (that is, a woman who was involved in illicit activities). Boardinghouses were considered to be the antithesis of private homes: whereas "if boardinghouses were crowded, homes were spacious; if boardinghouses were public, homes were private; if boardinghouses offered unappealing victuals, homes served delectable meals."[17]

Because of Emilie's lifestyle, specifically her constant contact with the free black Philadelphia elite and her membership at First African, it is more probable that Emilie lived in a private home that took in boarders rather than in an established boardinghouse. Also, since Emilie often wrote of going "down home" to visit her family and friends, she probably would not have chosen to stay at a place of questionable repute, such as an established boardinghouse, when she could have remained at home. Before her father moved to Harrisburg, Emile visited him on a regular basis. Moreover Emilie had frequent female and male visitors, including church members, college students, and members of some of the most established and well-known black families in Philadelphia. Because she often worked as a short-term live-in domestic in the Fifth Ward, she probably lived in a private home near that area.

Based on her diary entries, regardless of whether Emilie lived in an established boardinghouse or in a private home that took boarders, we do know that she kept her belongings in a trunk that was accessible to other people. In the Memoranda section of her 1863 diary, she wrote, "I will always remember someone while I was over in New Jersey opend my trunk and stole a ring and $6.00 and 74 cents in silver." For a live-in domestic and *modiste*, this was a lot of money, particularly because she supported her ailing father and other family members. She frequently worked with families outside of Philadelphia and would regularly send money back home. Here she wrote at the end of a difficult week, "To day has bin a very stormy, dreary day. The rains was very heavy. I sent some money down for Nellie to disperse."[18]

The few things that are known about Emilie paint a picture of an everyday working-class woman who struggled with her finances and who did not live an elite lifestyle. In addition to making dresses and trimming bonnets, her primary income came from her work as a short-term live-in domestic. From 1863 to 1865, she worked with three families on a regular basis: the Harris family in Harrisburg and the Hazards and Powells in Philadelphia. During the summer of 1864, she lived and worked with the Wister family in Germantown.

According to Du Bois, domestic work was classified as a devalued occupation even though over 90 percent of legitimately employed black women worked as servants, waitresses, launderers, and cooks.[19] As a domestic Emilie earned about three to six dollars (equivalent to $55.50–111.00) per week and probably contributed about two dollars (equivalent to $37.00) a month to pay for her room.[20] In 1860 this was a typical wage for a domestic, with an average amount of four dollars and fifty cents (equivalent to $83.25).

At the same time, although she did not make much money, Emilie had a powerful social network, which granted her access to some elite privileges, such as education, club memberships, and invitations to private events, meetings, or parties. She also occasionally visited the homes of elite families and attended parties hosted by them. It seems that when Emilie was invited to public and private events in and around the city that were hosted by elites, it was mainly because of her connections with others who had higher social status within the black community and her friendships with elite families. She was accepted into this closed community, and she socialized with and had close connections to members of the community.

At the same time, a contradiction arises when Emilie's notions of service and activism are considered. In her three years' worth of entries, Emilie never specifically wrote about or mentioned *noblesse oblige*—that notion (popular among elites of the era) that privileged individuals had a responsibility to work on behalf of the less fortunate. Emilie also did not act as a public agent of change in her community, nor was she a leader in the abolitionist movement. Nevertheless she did participate on a grassroots level. She sold tickets to abolitionist concerts, was a member of the Ladies' Union Association, and attended speeches given by antislavery activists. It is very likely that she was involved in these types of discussions, though she chose not to write about them in her personal diaries. Because *noblesse oblige*, both as a theory and an ideal, was important to the free black community, Emilie probably believed in it even if she did not write about it or find more involved ways to practice it in her life. Although her diary does not reflect this, she had to be aware of the points of tension that led up to the moment (the start of the U.S. Civil War) that informed and shaped the environment and the world in which she lived.

Philadelphia and the Year of Jubilee

In February of 1861, even though Emilie's life may not have changed very much, the fabric of the nation dramatically changed as the states in the South that were fiercely committed to "forever enslavement" chose to secede rather than concede.

By the end of the year, the Confederate States of America (CSA), led by Jefferson Davis, consisted of eleven states and roughly nine million people—3.5 million of whom were enslaved.[21] It also had very few railroads, naval powers, and shipyards. The Union, led by newly elected President Abraham Lincoln, consisted of twenty-four states, roughly twenty-two million people and 85 percent of the nation's factories.[22] Lincoln was a moderate antislavery Republican who struggled both privately and publicly with the issue of slavery. In 1858, when Lincoln first accepted the Republican nomination to challenge Illinois senator Stephen A. Douglas, he stated, "I believe this government cannot endure, permanently half slave and half free. I do not expect the Union to be dissolved. I do not expect the house to fall but I do expect it will cease to be divided. It will become all one thing or all the other."[23] Before that, he was an advocate for "Slaveocracy," or the so-called political power of the southern slave owners and he appeared to be deeply divided over the issue.

In April 1861, two days after the Confederacy opened fire on Fort Sumter in Charleston, South Carolina, Lincoln put forth a call for able-bodied volunteers. Black men across the North rushed to sign up, only to be informed that "able-bodied" applied to white men, and consequently they were not allowed to enlist. By August the country was in the midst of a full-blown war that was philosophically, economically, and socially separating the country, families, and communities. In the first two years it was seen by Lincoln and white male power brokers saw the Civil War as nothing more than a "simple misunderstanding between gentlemen, a white man's War," a misunderstanding that had nothing to do with slavery, freedom, or black people.[24] It was clearly stated in the Crittenden-Johnson Resolution, passed by Congress on July 25, 1861, that the purpose of the war was reunification and that the government was not going to take any actions against slavery. And although most free and enslaved blacks would have disagreed, this prevalent ideology guided Lincoln during the early stages of the war as he struggled both to win and to keep the nation together without the assistance and input of its black residents. Lincoln was committed to not allowing slavery to spread beyond its assumed boundaries, but not to ending it. By his own admission, he was less interested in addressing the moral implications of slavery and more interested in finding viable and plausible ways to reunite the nation. In an 1862 open exchange of letters with editor Horace Greeley, Lincoln argued that his primary goal, as the elected president of the nation, was to save the Union, and if that included freeing some slaves and leaving others alone, then that was what he was prepared to do.[25]

This was clearly the path that Lincoln planned to take with the Emancipation Proclamation, although it was not that clear or obvious less than a year before this exchange. As the war continued and the death toll increased, black and white abolitionists and antislavery activists increasingly pressured Lincoln to publicly refocus the goal of the war. They wanted Lincoln to make this a war to end slavery, and they wanted a revolution, one where change came "from the bottom up that required power and authority from the top down to give it public gravity and make it secure."[26] At the same time, there was also mounting pressure from the other side not to take that type of stand. In the midst of all of this clamor, one man stood out among the rest, a runaway slave from Maryland who was considered to be the "giant of abolitionist giants," Frederick Douglass (neé Frederick Augustus Washington Bailey), a man who on many accounts was remarkably similar to Lincoln: in background—Douglass was enslaved, and Lincoln grew up in an impoverished home; in education—Douglass never formally attended school, and Lincoln had less than one year of formal schooling; and in cause—both of them were actively involved in moving the nation beyond slavery, whether reluctantly as in Lincoln's case or because they no choice but to work to change the world, as in Douglass's case.

Born enslaved in Tuckahoe, Talbot County, Maryland, Douglass was working as a caulker in Baltimore when he met Anna Murray, a freeborn woman whose parents were manumitted before she was born. After Douglass escaped to the North, Murray later followed him to New York, and after getting married, they adopted the surname Douglass and settled in New Bedford, Massachusetts. In short order Douglass began to speak out and tell his story about his life on slave row. He was an enormously popular speaker, at once humorous, engaging, serious, and most important, authentic. He was an anomaly, a runaway who could speak intelligently about his personal experiences with American slavery. Standing on the stage with his hair slung back, a full nappy beard, and a deep booming voice, Douglass captivated the audience, particularly the women. When suffragist Elizabeth Cady Stanton saw Douglass on the stage for the first time, she noted that he "stood there like an African prince, conscious of his dignity and power, grand in his physical proportions, majestic in his wrath, as with keen wit, satire and indignation he portrayed the bitterness of slavery, the humiliation of subjection to those who in all human virtues and capacities were inferior to himself."[27] He had initially been hired to speak about his experiences by William Lloyd Garrison, the editor of the radical abolitionist newspaper the *Liberator* and one of the founders of the American Anti-Slavery Society. As the "prize exhibit," Douglass was instructed to give only the facts and then let the white abolitionists give the philosophy.[28] It was not long before Douglass, as he began to mature as a speaker and writer, began to move from simply describing slavery to proscribing it: "When they tell the world that the Negro is ignorant and naturally and intellectually incapacitated to appreciate and enjoy freedom, they also naturally publish their own condemnation, by bringing to light those infamous Laws by which the Slave is compelled to live in the grossest ignorance."[29] He became the moral voice and the face of the antislavery movement both in the States and abroad.

In 1847, when Lincoln was first elected to the House of Representatives and Jefferson Davis entered the Senate, Douglass—after publishing his autobiographies; embarking on a hundred-city antislavery tour with Charles Lenox Remond, a freeborn abolitionist and the first person of color to take the antislavery message abroad; and eventually purchasing his freedom—began to copublish the *North Star* newspaper with Martin R. Delany, an abolitionist and physician. The newspaper rivaled Garrison's *Liberator* as a major voice for the abolitionist cause.[30] The paths of these three men would intersect some fifteen years later, in the fall of 1862, when Lincoln made the decision to listen to the words of Douglass and other abolitionists and to draft and present a proclamation that would force the nation to move from being a slave society toward becoming a free one. Additionally a number of national and international events had occurred that might have convinced Lincoln that his decision to move forward with the release of the document was correct. In April slavery was abolished in Washington, D.C., and a treaty was signed between the U.S. and Britain that suppressed the African slave trade; and in July Congress passed the Second Confiscation Act, which explicitly freed slaves who were living on plantations owned by persons who were against the Union.

In August 1862, one month before Lincoln issued his preliminary Proclamation, an 8-page "Appeal from the Colored Men of Philadelphia to the President of the United States" was released as a response to Lincoln's push for colonization. In it, the writers spoke out against colonization and called for the immediate emancipation and citizenship of all American slaves. "We believe that the world would be benefited by giving the four millions of slaves their freedom, and the lands now possessed by their masters. They have been amply compensated in our labor and the blood of our kinsmen. These masters 'toil not, neither do they spin.' They destroy, they consume, and give to the world in return but small equivalent. They deprive us of 'life, liberty, and the pursuit of happiness.' They degrade us to the level of the brute. They amalgamate with our race, and buy and sell their own children."[31]

One month later Lincoln gave a speech in Antietam, Maryland, where he issued a preliminary Emancipation Proclamation, designed to provide the Confederate states with a final opportunity to join the Union or risk the immediate emancipation of their slaves. Even though this was both a political and a social statement, Lincoln did not intend for it be viewed as a pro-black, benevolent document. It was a war tactic. He even waited until after a Union victory to announce it. This did not matter to the black community because they defined it and viewed it as much more than just that. As Jacqueline Jones Royster explains, emancipation "was not a gift bestowed upon passive slaves by Union soldiers or presidential proclamation; rather it was a process by which black people ceased to labor for their masters and sought instead to provide directly for one another."[32]

Some black Americans, both enslaved and free, were not certain until the last moment whether Lincoln would follow through on his promise. One of the reasons for the initial skepticism—over whether or not he was going to release it—was that Lincoln was a vocal proponent for American colonization as a way to end the race problem. He had recently signed a contract to relocate five thousand American blacks to Haiti at a cost of $250,000, had secured control of over $600,000 for additional black colonization, and had approved an outlandish deal between the United States and the Chiriquí Improvement Company in hopes of relocating black Americans to the republic of Columbia.[33] Lincoln believed that black and white Americans were better off separated, and he tried to convince black Americans to adopt his solution as a way to end this "problem." In a speech at the White House, where he asked black leaders to persuade their people to emigrate to Chiriquí to become coal miners, Lincoln stated: "You and we are different races. We have between us a broader difference than exists between almost any other two races. Whether it is right or wrong I need not discuss, but this physical difference is a great disadvantage to us both, as I think your race suffers very greatly, many of them by living among us, while ours suffers from your presence. There is an unwillingness on the part of our people, harsh as it may be for you free colored people to remain with us."[34]

With all of the tension and the uncertainty of the moment, on December 31, 1862, black and white America counted down the moments until the Proclamation would either take effect or be withdrawn. Many spent the night in prayer and turmoil, while others celebrated, confident that freedom was at hand. One fugitive slave attending an all-night meeting at a "contraband" (enslaved men and women who fled plantations) camp in Washington, D.C., stood up moments before the day ended to proclaim: "We'se free now, bless the Lord! They can't sell my wif an' child no more, bless the Lord! No more that! No more that! No more that, now!"[35] Matilda Dunbar, the mother of poet Paul Laurence Dunbar, described it in similar terms when she noted that on the day she heard she was free, "I ran 'round and 'round the kitchen, hitting my head against the wall, clapping my hands and crying, 'Freedom! Freedom! Freedom! Rejoice, freedom has come!'"[36] At the historic Tremont Temple in Boston—the place that Dwight L. Moody once called "America's pulpit" and where the first public reading of the Emancipation Proclamation in Boston took place—orator and women's suffragist Anna Dickinson, slave narrative author and historian William Wells Brown, and Frederick Douglass spoke about what this moment meant to America. Douglass, as expected, was the last one to address the audience, and his words seem to capture the emotion and sentiment that had been moving throughout the country: "We were waiting and listening as for a bolt from the sky, which should rend the fetters of four millions of slaves; we were watching as it were, by the dim light of stars, from the dawn of a new day, we were longing for the answer to the agonizing prayers of centuries. Remembering those in bounds as bound with them, we wanted to join in the shout for freedom, and in the anthem of the redeemed."[37]

When the news of emancipation swept across the nation, the night of celebration that followed was electric. When a formerly enslaved man and two women began to sing out the words to "My Country 'Tis of Thee," Colonel Thomas Wentworth Higginson, a Harvard-trained Brahmin and abolitionist, who led the First South Carolina Volunteer Regiment stood waving an American flag.[38] He later noted that the "wonderfully unconscious" tribute to the news of Jubilee sounded like "the choked voice of a race at last unloosed."[39] One enslaved woman remarked that when she heard that "Lincum done signed de mancipation," she packed her bags and "started out wid blankets an' clothes an' pots an' pans an chickens" on her way to the Union lines.[40] Although weeping had endured throughout the long nights of slavery, the joy that came in the morning of freedom was a "worthy celebration of the first step on the part of the nation in its departure from the thralldom of the ages."[41]

As Fredrick Douglass and other abolitionists quickly realized, the document was designed only to "abolish slavery where it did not exist and leave it intact where it did."[42] Instead of freeing enslaved people in the states in which he exercised presidential authority, Lincoln's proclamation applied only to rebel states and counties, in which he had no executive authority, voice, or control. It was designed to free all of the enslaved men, women, and children who were living in ten states that were acting in opposition to the Union. It did not apply to the 450,000 enslaved people living in Delaware, Kentucky, Maryland, and Missouri; nor to the 275,000 living in Tennessee; nor to the tens of thousands of enslaved men, women, and children living in the Union-controlled areas of Louisiana and Virginia. Furthermore, the document did not outlaw slavery and did not provide provisions, resources, or citizenship for the newly freed populations. At the same time, the spirit of this document provided many enslaved people with the impetus they needed to "free themselves" by running away from their plantation owners and joining the Union Army. As Union soldiers moved further into Confederate territory, they were met by hundreds of enslaved people "coming garbed in rags or in silks, with feet shod or bleeding, individually or in families," seeking protection, employment, and assistance, many echoing the words of one former slave who said, "you give us free, and we helps you all we can."[43] In less than two years, by the beginning of 1865, close to seven hundred thousand out of nearly four million enslaved black Americans had achieved some form of emancipation—either by running away or by being freed by the Union armies. Free black men and women also engaged in this new mobilization effort, with some enlisting in the armed services, others working to raise monies for the troops, and still others seeking opportunities to advance the cause of freedom in cities at home and abroad.[44]

The implementation of the Emancipation Proclamation, on January 1, 1863, along with Frederick Douglass's efforts to call black men across the country to arms and the thousands of contrabands (those who fled or were "freed") who worked with the Union soldiers, drastically changed both the direction and the purpose of the war. What began as a fight to save the Union without the assistance of black men and women now became a fight to end enslavement with the much-needed aid of free and enslaved black men and women. One black soldier, when asked if black men were ready to fight for the Union, responded: "General, we come of a fighting race. Our fathers were brought here because they were captured in War, and in hand-to-hand fights, too. We are willing to fight. Pardon me, General, but the only cowardly blood we have got in our veins is the white blood."[45]

Even though they were needed in this war, black soldiers typically received substandard equipment, were relegated to fatigue duty, and, up until 1864, were scheduled to receive only $10 a month, with $3 going towards the cost of their uniform (White soldiers received $13 plus uniform allowances). Even though section 2 of the Militia Act of July 1862 enabled the President to pay black soldiers the full $10, most did not receive this pay adjustment for up to eighteen months after it was approved. Many black regiments, led by the famed Fifty-fourth Massachusetts Volunteers, chose to fight without pay rather than accept lower wages.[46] Two of the better-known men of the Fifty-fourth Volunteers were brothers Charles Remond and Lewis Henry Douglass, whose father, Frederick Douglass, had been instrumental in helping to release and publicize the historic "Call to Arms," which was a recruitment effort designed to encourage black men to enlist in the armed services.[47] Some of the other lesser-known (but equally important) black soldiers include Emilie Davis's uncle, Elijah J.; her brother, Alfred; and her beau, Vincent; and a number of other male friends from school and from the Banneker Institute, all of whom were drafted or volunteered in Philadelphia and went off to war in the fall of 1864. These men were a large part of Emilie's life, offering guidance, direction, and in some instances instruction, and it seems to have been important to her to maintain these close bonds, no matter the cost.

Establishing Community

Although she had a large community of friends, she was in close and constant contact with her family. She wrote of going "down home" to visit them and of exchanging weekly correspondence with her father, once he moved to Harrisburg, and with her sister, Elizabeth. Here she wrote on June 28, 1863, "I sent a letter to Father last night," and two days later—when the city received news that Harrisburg might be invaded—"I am all most sick worsen (worrisome) about Father. The city is considered in dangue." Here she mentions her aunt, most likely her father's sister: "After church, we went to see Barker (Henry Barker Black) and Aunt Jane (Davis), she is quite sick." On July 16, 1864, after her brother had been mustered into the armed services: "I had a letter from Liz this week. I have bin sick to day. Last night I wrote a letter to Lenox. I was out a few sarcanes [seconds] this afternoon. I received a letter from Sister and a photograph from my dear brother (Alfred) in Montreal." She does not mention Elizabeth coming to visit until 1865: "Very busy. Did not get to the Fair this morning. I went down home. Sarah was better. Sister come down this morning. I went out with her. She staid all night withe me."[48]

Emilie's diary provides very little detail about her other family members. Other than a listing for her mother and two of her brothers, Elwood and William, in the 1850 U.S. Census, further information has not been found about them, and they are not mentioned in Emilie's pocket diaries. An omission on Emilie's part would have been unusual, since she not only wrote about attending weekly funerals or being present at someone's death bed, but she also noted the passing anniversary of a person's death. For example, on October 30, 1863, she wrote, "Charlie [Aunt Jane's husband] was buried this morning. He had a very respectable furneal," and on the following day she wrote, "Lizzie [a family friend] has bin dead three years today." Additionally, on January 29, 1864, she wrote, "Elwood [Emilie's nephew, Elijah J.'s son] is still suffering but I think death will soon end his suffering," and the next day she sadly wrote, "Elwood is dying. I hurried home and staid until he breathed his last. He died at 11 o'clock this morning. His spirit has gone to his Father, that quick."[49]

During a typical week, Emilie spent much of her time away from home. She faithfully attended church, taught or participated in a biweekly Bible study, attended classes at the Institute for Colored Youth, and socialized with her friends almost daily. In the 1860 U.S. Census, Emilie is listed as a domestic, but she wrote in her pocket diary about her occasional work as a *modiste*. Her work pattern, as noted in her diary entries, seems to suggest that she worked as a seamstress when she could secure clients and as a servant when she could not. In this census, Elijah J. is listed as a waiter; Sarah, as a seamstress; and Elizabeth as a domestic (in 1850, she was listed as a student). At first glance, it seems as if Emilie and her family may have been part of the working poor since waiters and domestics were not always guaranteed a steady and secure income. With a closer reading, the facts emerge that since Emilie's father was literate (as evidenced by the letters) and was able to provide education for all four of his children (Emilie, Elizabeth, Tomy, and Alfred); and that Emilie possessed a valued skill, it actually suggests that her parents were part of a small number of working-class black and mulatto families who were able to secure long-term work.

Information about Emilie's life can also be gleaned from her assigned racial status as well as the racial status of the members of her family. In addition to listing a person's neighborhood, age, job, and place of birth, the 1850 U.S. Census introduced two categories to denote the racial status of people of color: *mulatto*, which included octoroons (1/8th black ancestry), hexadecaroons (1/16th black ancestry), quadroons (1/25th black ancestry), and quintroons (persons having one white and one octoroon parent), and *black* (if a person was white, the space was left blank). It was also the first time that free people were listed individually instead of by family, and that there were two questionnaires, one for free inhabitants and one for slaves. Prior to 1850, the racial categories were white, slave, and other (which was used for either free born black people or persons who were free but did not look white).

Since instructions were not provided to help the census takers determine color classifications, Theodore Hershberg and Henry Williams conclude that the census takers probably made an educated guess based upon a person's skin color and not ancestry. Furthermore in some cases the census takers would see only one member of the family and make a color designation for the entire household based on that person.[50] Additionally, because census takers changed every decade, a person's color designation sometimes changed, as well. Twenty-six percent of those reported as black in 1850 were reclassified as mulatto in 1860, while forty-seven percent of those reported as mulatto in 1850 were reclassified as black in 1860. Even though race in the nineteenth century was, as Eric Foner points out, an "amorphous category amalgamating ideas about culture, history, religion, and color," it correlated very closely with a person's socioeconomic status.[51] In 1860, thirteen percent of the blacks that were reclassified as mulatto had an upward shift in their socioeconomic status.[52] Since the U.S. Census was conducted every ten years, many economic shifts, either rising or lowering, took place during that time. Because of the rising, lowering, and reclassification that took place in the 1860 U.S. Census, Roger Lane questions the large demographic survey's validity. He notes that because the census took place after the passage of the 1850 Fugitive Slave Act—which greatly affected black Philadelphians, since slave catchers would travel north to kidnap black people—and after the passage of two resolutions by the Pennsylvania state legislature to ship black Philadelphians back to Africa, black people were not open to the idea of providing detailed information about themselves to a "group of strange white men."[53] Although racial categories were routinely added and removed from the questionnaire, it was not until 1870, with the end of the Civil War and the passage of the Thirteenth, Fourteenth, and Fifteenth Amendments, that the U.S. Census removed the mulatto category and reclassified all people of color as black (but this was not a definitive change as the term mulatto was routinely added and removed from the Census up until 1930).[54]

During the antebellum period, Philadelphia had one of the largest populations of black people of any city. With over twenty-two thousand black people, it was second only to Baltimore in this regard, and it was the largest black American city outside of the enslaved South, with 3.9 percent of the population.[55] Compared to blacks, mulattoes tended to have higher incomes and greater access to education, and tended to be endogamous, with eighty-five percent of mulatto men marrying mulatto women. Similar marriage patterns occurred within the black community, with ninety-three percent of black men marrying black women.[56] The few blacks who were allowed within mulatto communities seem to be either the direct descendants of wealthy or well-known abolitionist blacks or they possessed highly valued, lucrative skills, such as in medicine, law, education, and the arts. In Philadelphia mulattoes usually lived within the exclusive First, Fifth, or Seventh Wards. The Seventh Ward, which had the highest concentration of mulattoes and wealthy blacks, was a large epicenter of concentrated black wealth, and most of its residents were educated, wealthy, and liberally trained. They were the clerks, teachers, merchants, and professionals of the black community.[57] Additionally the ward boasted the most respected black schools, churches, and clubs, and the major points of distribution of the black press.[58]

Within this and other free black communities, lighter-skinned blacks also created socioeconomic groups that excluded most darker-skinned blacks. For example the Philadelphia-based Pythians Base Ball club, which was founded in 1867, was one of the first black teams in the U.S. and was an elite men's club with more than seventy percent of the members classified as mulatto. The team was made up of teachers and students from the Banneker Institute and the Institute for Colored Youth. Both Octavius Catto and Jake were officers—captain and secretary respectively—and players. The club had an annual fee of five dollars, and most of the members belonged to the Pennsylvania Equal Rights League. The Philadelphia Committee to Recruit Colored Troops had a majority of mulatto members who were property owners, literate, and seen as the voices of the black community. Additionally some of the members of the committee wielded economic power outside of the city, owning property in other areas of Pennsylvania, New Jersey, and Washington, D.C. The Ladies' Literary Society of Philadelphia's membership included only women who were considered to be the elite of the black community.[59] In the South, a person's skin color was closely associated with his or her social status: darker skin typically denoted enslaved status, while lighter skin typically denoted free status. In the North, however, lighter skin color guaranteed access to certain elite social circles, particularly among women.[60]

Emilie was classified as a mulatto in 1850 and 1860, which probably meant that she had fairer skin and finely textured hair. In her pocket diary, in one of only two entries where she racially self-identified, Emilie referred to herself as colored. While visiting a church in Harrisburg with friends, she wrote: "In the evening, we went to prayer meeting, had a spirited meeting. Our party were the only colerd people. There was about four of us."[61] Furthermore Emilie did not mention anyone else's color unless they were white. For example, in that same diary entry, she continued, noting that she "heard a very good sermon, a young white minister that (s)poke reminded me of Johns."[62] Although the terms *mulatto*, *black*, and *colored* can all be used to describe Emilie, she chose, within her private space, to call herself colored. Since skin color was so closely connected to a person's socioeconomic class, one wonders why an educated and literate woman would choose to classify herself this way.

In addition to her skin color, Emilie was also privileged because she was literate, which placed here in within a small category of nineteenth-century literate black people and within an even smaller category of nineteenth-century literate

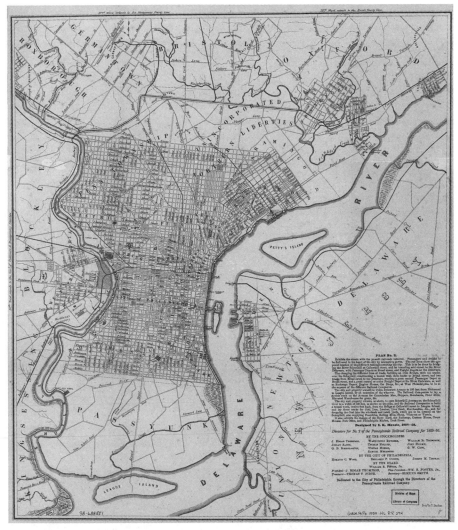

1857–58 map of Philadelphia. Pennsylvania Railroad Company.
Courtesy of Library of Congress.

black women. During the mid-1800s literacy rates among free black people in Philadelphia were low with only one out of every four free black households sending its children to school.[63] Beginning in 1853 the board of education of the Pennsylvania Society for Promoting the Abolition of Slavery, in an effort to ascertain the yearly educational conditions of black people over the age of twenty-one, visited households in the twenty-three Wards, interviewed the residents, and categorized their responses into four different educational areas. The four categories noted whether

"Distinguished Colored Men" (c. 1883). Library of Congress.

individuals had the ability to read, write, and cipher (or "work out sums on a slate through long division") in what was categorized as "simple rules;" had the ability to read and write legibly; had the ability to read only; or were unable to read. In 1859 the Seventh Ward, where Emilie Davis lived, had the highest percentage of black people that could read, write, and cipher in the simple rules. The number of men greatly outnumbered the number of women; but the report also states that the men were generally not home during the surveys and that the women answered on their behalf. [64]

In 1779 the first school for free black people opened in Philadelphia, and, by the time Emilie came of school age in the 1850s, there was an active, thriving free black school system with public, charity, benevolent or reformatory, and private schools. The average attendance in Philadelphia ranged from fifteen students at the Banneker School to 193 at the grammar schools. Although elite families tended to educate both their sons and their daughters, male students typically outnumbered female students at a rate of 1.5 to 1.[65] Since Emilie attended school, she was also part of a small number of black women who had access to and took advantage of the school system. It is obvious not only that she was literate but also that she constantly immersed herself in educational environments, either at her church or by taking classes, in which she was intellectually challenged, thus placing her within an even smaller category of black American intellectuals.

Lerone Bennett Jr. wrote that after the Revolutionary War, black intellectuals began to emerge and succeed in a number of cultural, economic, religious, and social arenas. He outlined four categories that can be used to classify and analyze black intellectuals. First is the "Jupiter Hammon" category, referring to blacks that, like Jupiter Hammon, voluntarily created intellectual work that allowed whites to buttress their worldview. Hammon was an enslaved man from New York who is known as the first black published author with his poem "An Evening Thought: Salvation by Christ, with Penitential Cries" (1760). The second is the "Phyllis Wheatley" category, referring to blacks that, like Phyllis Wheatley, subtly challenged the system by focusing their work on the slave system but offered no direct challenge to the existing political and social hegemony. Wheatley was an enslaved girl from Africa whose book, *Poems on Various Subjects, Religious and Moral* (1774), was the first book of published poetry by a black woman and the second book published by an American woman.[66]

Third is the "Othello" category, referring to blacks that, like the anonymous Othello who wrote and published harsh antislavery essays in 1788, militantly challenged both the intellectual and cultural mores of white dispensation. Finally, there is the intellectual category, referring to blacks that worked to create and develop organizations of change. This fourth category is loosely based on men like Richard Allen and Absalom Jones, two men who had purchased their own freedom and cofounded the Free African Society, the first independent black organization, considered to be the predecessor to the black church; and Prince Hall, who established the first black Masonic lodge.[67]

In placing her life within the larger stratum of black intellectuals, Emilie Davis falls within both the "Phyllis Wheatley" and the "Othello" categories. On the one hand, like Phyllis Wheatley and other black intellectuals who fall within this category, Emilie Davis offered no direct challenge to the existing political or social system. Outside of her pocket diaries, Emilie's name and experiences are not recorded in the published annals of black women's archival history. She was not a lecturer, a published author, or a known abolitionist. Yet, at the same time, Emilie Davis can also be viewed as falling into the "Othello" category in that through the simple act of recording her everyday experiences, Emilie unknowingly asserts authorial agency and identity. Her diary—her life in her own words—can thus be viewed as directly challenging the intellectual and cultural mores of everyday freeborn black women and how their experiences have been constructed by the male historical dispensation. Furthermore an analysis of Emilie's diary can be viewed as being a direct challenge to the historical and contemporary void of information about the lives and experiences of everyday freeborn black women.

Politics and Abolitionist Activity

In addition to her leisure activities, church, and work, Emilie was actively involved in abolitionist fundraising activities. In 1863, the Hutchinson Family Singers, the first American close-harmony quartet who traveled throughout the Northeast and England singing and raising money for the abolitionist, temperance, and women's rights movements was scheduled to host a concert to raise money for the abolitionist cause. Emilie was one of the many church members who sold tickets for this event. On the day the concert was announced, she wrote, "The Hutchinsons give a concert next Thusday night for the benefit of our church." She spent the week trying to sell her tickets: "I have bin very buisy trying to sell ticets for the concert. Alfred brought one." On the day of the concert, she happily noted, "I sold all my tickets. Nellie and Rochel [close friend] over, went to the concert. It was good, every one seemed pleased."[68]

These types of celebrations were common in the free black community, so at the same time that the formerly enslaved were celebrating their freedom, some freeborn Philadelphia black women, like Emilie, who were actively involved in abolitionist fundraising activities, also celebrated their contributions to the freedom struggle. Although these women had not been born enslaved, they had probably heard discussions about legalized slavery around the dinner table or in their classrooms, and they were probably familiar with the lectures of Frederick Douglass and Maria Stewart, the first black woman to speak to a diverse audience of men and women. They likely would have heard the great escape stories of Henry "Box" Brown, who escaped slavery by having himself mailed from Virginia to Philadelphia, traveled around with his crate, and spoke about his experiences.

Women like Emilie would have also understood the implications of the 1850 Fugitive Slave Act, which required all free states to return fugitive slaves to their plantation owners, putting the onus on the captured black person (enslaved or free) to prove that he or she was not the legal property of the plantation owner, and which was seen as a threat to all black Americans, freeborn, freed, or fugitive. They likely would have been familiar with the details of the U.S. Supreme Court's 1857 *Dred Scott v. Sanford* decision, which ruled that black Americans were not U.S. citizens and therefore had "no rights that the white man was bound to respect."[69] And they were probably aware of the ongoing organized struggle against enslavement that had been taking place in the free communities since 1777, when Prince Hall and eight other free blacks successfully petitioned the Massachusetts legislature to abolish slavery.[70] These were the types of issues—the ones that directly affected their lives and economic and social status—that were being written about in the newspapers and discussed in the meeting halls by the free black community.

With her background knowledge of enslavement and resistance, Emilie's activities on January 1, 1863, provide an insight into how free black women celebrated the occasion: "Today has bin a memorable day. I thank God I have bin here to see it. The day was religiously observed. All the churches were open. We had quite a Jubilee in the evening. I went to Joness to a party, had a very blessest time."[71] Within this entry are two telling indications about Emilie's life: first, she wrote that the day was religiously observed; second, she celebrated at the home of the Jones family. Emilie was an active churchgoer who missed very few Sunday services in 1863 and as a member of First African Presbyterian, she was probably there that night.

Her pastor, Reverend Jonathan Gibbs, focused his sermon on the message of freedom:

> O God, we appeal to Thee. Let this strife be so decided that justice, truth, honor, may not be put to shame. You, my country, entered into a solemn covenant with God in 1776a and declared before highest Heaven that your first and only purpose was to foster and cherish the equality and fraternity of man. How have you kept this covenant? Let Dred Scott decisions, fugitive-slave laws, the judicial murders of Denmark Vesey, Nat Turner, John Brown Gabriel and numerous others testify... Your destiny as white men and ours as black men are one in the same; we are all marching on to the same goal. If you rise, we will rise in the scale of being. If you fail, we will fail; but you will have the worst of it.

After Emilie attended church, the party she mentioned at the Joneses may have referred to the relatives of Absalom Jones, the founder of the African Church of St. Thomas, which was one of the first black churches in the North. Throughout the year, Emilie frequently wrote of attending parties either at the home of or with the Jones family. One year later, on January 1, 1864, Emilie celebrated with the Joneses again: "I feel thankful that I am spard to see another year. Home all day. In the evening, I went to Jones. I enjoyed myself very much. Great many changes have taken place since last New Years."[72]

Some of the changes that Emilie is referring to are probably connected with her work with the Ladies' Union Association of Philadelphia. Formed on July 20, 1863, for "the Purpose of Administering Exclusively to the Wants of the Sick and Wounded Colored Soldiers," the members were actively involved in raising money and collecting clothes and articles of mental improvement to aid black soldiers. Emilie was not only at that historic meeting, it was held at her house; but in her typically terse style, she simply noted, "Meeting was at our house. Very good meeting. Pop Steward is seriously impressed."[73] Although she never held an office (from 1863 to 1866), she was actively involved in the group. On December 12, 1864, she attended a subcommittee meeting at the Masonic Hall to collect donations to send to Charleston, South Carolina. Having raised over $950 in less than fifteen months, the committee noted the following donations to be sent to Charleston: twenty-one Dresses; twenty-four Shirts; twelve pairs of Drawers; fifteen pairs of Pants; twenty-seven Coats; thirty pairs of Shoes; fourteen pounds of Sugar; fifty-two sets of Under garments; one-hundred pieces of Children's clothing; nine vests; and $7.50. Additionally they recorded that they had $500.00 in their personal treasury, with Emilie's aunt, Mrs. Elijah J. Davis (Sarah), acting as the association's treasury. As before, Emilie in writing about the meeting, simply noted, "Ellen come up and spent the day. Liz stoped before meeting. We all went together. Had a very good meeting. Quite a number out."[74]

Like noted in the earlier entry, there are telling indications in this one of the access that Emilie had to the elite community through her friendships and activities: she mentioned that Ellen and Liz stopped to visit, and they attended a meeting together. Ellen Black and Emilie were close friends and church members who often shopped with and visited one another. Ellen's father was Ebenezer Black, the corresponding secretary at First African Presbyterian, who worked with Elijah J. on the 1863 "Call to Arms" and who owned several real estate properties. Within First African, Ellen had gained a reputation for openly challenging the elders about the conservative devotional music. On April 16, 1859, some of the younger members of the church, including Ellen Black, Elijah J., George Bustill White, Elizabeth White, Jake White, and Emilie, formed the church's Singing School Association and submitted a formal petition designed to change the "manner in which the singing is performed in the devotional exercises of the Sabbath Day." This was, of course, quite controversial.[75]

Elizabeth (Lizzie) Harriet Stevens Gray Bowser was the second wife of David Bustill Bowser, a local activist and painter and the grandson of Cyrus Bustill. David was fourteen years older than Lizzie and was the grandmaster of Carthagenian Lodge No. 901 of the Grand Union of Odd Fellows benevolent society for mutual assistance where Elijah J. was a member. Founded in 1848, Lodge No. 901 was one of the three Philadelphia chapters of the well-known, nationally recognized black male secret fraternal voluntary organization. Focusing primarily on recruiting and retaining young members, many of the founders were members of other fraternal organizations, including the Banneker Institute. The lodge sat at the corner of Lombard and Seventh Streets, and the members met weekly and held themselves to a "code of proper moral conduct," including paying established fines if they were involved in adultery and gambling or if they had refused to pay their monthly dues. The members professed a moral stature, an attentiveness to family and community responsibilities, and a commitment to improving personal prospects and collective standing of the members.[76] Lizzie was also a member of the House of Ruth, the female counterpart to the Odd Fellows. Although she was the wife of an activist and the mother of a five-year-old, since she and Emilie were both members of the Ladies' Union Association and attended the same Bible study class, they socialized about twice a month. Here Emilie wrote on July 17, 1863, "I am all most tired of doing nothing everyday. I went up to Lizzes with some things. Lizzie gave me som lunch, witch was very nice"; and on July 23, she wrote, "Nellie and I went out shoping. Stoped to see Lizzie at 16th and Walnut."[77] In May 1865, at the Ladies Annual Fair, Lizzie single-handedly organized and sold over $1,200 (equivalent to $22,200) worth of goods at her table for the Ladies' Union Association. In her pocket diary entry on May 12, 1865, Emilie wrote only, "In the evening, I went to the meeting. Very interesting."[78]

Additionally Caroline Rebecca Le Count, an 1863 graduate of the Institute for Colored Youth, a descendent of the Le Count family—one of the black elite families in Philadelphia (her father, James, was a cabinetmaker-turned-undertaker who sent all three of his children to the institute)—and the companion to Octavius Catto, was the corresponding secretary of the Ladies' Union Association and a part of the subcommittee with Emilie. She was very well known throughout the school, having received almost perfect test scores on her May 1863 institute exams. Le Count taught at the Ohio Street School in 1865, and by 1868 she was promoted to principal. She later became actively involved in the Philadelphia political scene, helping Catto to integrate the streetcars, after she was forcibly removed from one on March 25, 1867.[79]

The Ladies' Union was a very active association. Throughout the War, they were constantly raising money and collecting goods for sick and wounded soldiers and when the War ended, they turned their attention to working on behalf of the freedman. In their 1867 Report, they noted that they made this change not only because the War had ended; but, because the freedman, "by the Providence of God through the late war, [had] bursted the fetters which bound them for so many years," needed their assistance. They worked very closely with Rev. Gibbs (He was traveling between Philadelphia and South Carolina laying the groundwork for his transition from First African to working with the Freedman of Charleston.) who received and distributed goods on their behalf and kept them aware of what was happening within the free community. On January 29, 1865, after receiving a shipment of books, Gibbs sent a letter of receipt from Charleston:

> Dear Friend:
> I obtained to-day your two boxes of clothing sent by Express, valued at $250, for gratuitous distribution among the Freedman. Present my sincere thanks to the Ladies of this noble association for their valuable gift to the destitute and suffering among the Freedman. There is a vast among of suffering here, which is the direct result of the villainous doings of the "rebs." Hundreds of Freedmen have come into this city, driven from the plantations where they have worked last year, by the rebels, without a penny for their entire year's work. I will state one case out of a score, just such:—I brought to the office of the Leader, three Freedmen I met among a company of 150, who were an open lot, just as they left the cars, for several day. These men said they belonged to a gang that had 14 *full hands* [emphasis in original]. They engaged last April to work for one-fourth the crops and be fed up to Jan'y 1, 1866. They raised 300 bushels of Shelled Corn, 100 bushels Shell Peas, half bale of cotton and some other things of value. Two months ago the man refused to find food they were compelled to shift as they could. They received for their entire work *one bushel of corn* [emphasis in original] to a hand, and the reb refused to let them stay on his place because they would not agree to work for the same this year. Negroes wont work![80]

As a member of the Association, Emilie received firsthand information of what was happening in the newly freed black communities. Though she did not record what was discussed, it is not unreasonable to conclude that they did discuss it and the fact that she participated in these types of private meetings and abolitionist endeavors speaks again to the fact that she held social status as a mulatto woman within Philadelphia's free black community. Though Emilie did not occupy the ranks of the elite, it is nevertheless clear that she possessed a fair amount of cultural and social capital, exemplified through her education, her connections to other powerful members of the black community, and her regular association with them at social and political events.

In general black women with higher amounts of cultural capital, which included lighter skin color, material wealth, familial ties, education, and linguistic fluency, had decidedly more access to positions of power and to lives of prestige.[81] The process of acculturation into the white society for these women was easier, and it was expected.[82] At the same time, many of these women committed their lives to helping others, which led to the creation of temperance societies, moral improvement societies, and literacy societies. For elite freeborn women, there was a clear economic line of class demarcation between them and the majority of free black women who lived at or below the poverty line. Yet Emilie occupied a space between elites and those at the poverty line. Emilie, as an "everyday" mulatto woman, adds another class distinction within the too-broad parameters of free and enslaved women. A close examination of Emilie's life thus provides another avenue for historians to reconceptualize how freeborn black American women of various class standings negotiated their status during this time period.

~3~

A World Created

Within the black community, freedom—as a concept, an idea, and a dream—had probably been talked about since slavery was first legalized. Within the enslaved communities, the further the generations were removed from Africa, the harder it probably was to imagine a life without being owned. Within the free black communities, particularly in the life of someone like Emilie, freedom was probably a term of immense contradictions. Even though the free black communities had access to money, privilege, and opportunities, they understood that they had a tenuous and slippery hold on freedom. Their lives were defined and limited in so many ways by the color of their skin, even the terms *elite* and *privileged* meant something different to white people than they did to black people. Within the white communities, a family could be defined as either elite, which applied to "those individuals who were the most successful" and stood "at the top of the functional class hierarchy, "or as upper class, which applied to "a group of families whose members are descendants of successful individuals of one, two, three, or more generations ago."[1]

In the free black community, the lines were much more blurred in that the elite were the upper class. It was a close-knit community that was difficult to penetrate, and for formerly enslaved black Americans—who lacked money, were illiterate, and had darker skin—it was almost impossible to gain entrance into these private networks. In her article on the black Philadelphia elite, Emma Lapsansky makes it clear that the black elite was not on the same level as the white elite. The black elite had power but not political power, they often had working-class incomes, and their status in the black community was based on personal qualities rather than on possessions or background. They were encouraged to live comfortably but to do so within their means so that they could give back to help "cultivate feelings of piety and gratitude" within the unfortunate masses.[2] Emilie did not write about this tension or about the challenges she faced as an "everyday" free black woman. For reasons unknown she chose not to use the page to discuss the enormity of the events that she experienced on a daily basis nor to discuss the tensions she felt as a mulatto and working-class free woman who lived during America's war to end slavery. The social, economic, and political policies and laws that guided America during Emilie's time had been constructed and implemented as early as the seventeenth century, and they affected how she lived her life. The examination of these social points of tensions is not simply to have us participating in Jacqueline Jones Royster's public discussion of the "discourse of differences" but to bring an understanding to Emilie's very complicated social, political, and economic situation.[3]

Historians have long recognized that the free black community in Philadelphia produced and trained generations of black male and female leaders who had national reputations before, during, and after the Civil War.[4] In Emilie's world these were the men and women that she came into contact with at social and political events throughout the city. These leaders were born and bred in some of the most elite—mostly mulatto—families within the free black communities. Many of the families had been in Philadelphia for more than three generations and had amassed personal family wealth and property that placed them within the top eleven percent of the black population economically. By the 1840s, black-owned wealth in Philadelphia was distributed on three levels: the top one percent possessed thirty percent of the wealth, the middle ten percent possessed seventy percent of the wealth, and the bottom fifty percent possessed five percent of the wealth. However, these figures only accounted for sixty-one percent of the black population; the assumption must be that the final thirty-nine percent of the black community did not possess any material wealth. By 1860, more than twenty thousand black Philadelphians were a part of this elite cohort that had assumed dominant leadership positions in most of the city's numerous black organizations.[5]

Their children were taught at a young age—either in school, at church, or at home—that they had a responsibility to contribute to the advancement of black people, both enslaved and free. In 1832, shortly after Pennsylvania introduced a bill that required all blacks to carry identification passes, Sarah Mapps Douglass, the daughter of well-known abolitionists Robert and Grace Bustill, wrote:

> One short year ago, how different were my feelings on the subject of slavery! It is true, the wail of the captive sometimes came to my ear in the midst of happiness, and caused my heart to bleed for his wrongs; but, alas! the impression was as evanescent as the early cold and morning dew. I had formed a little world of my own, and cared not to move beyond its precincts. But how was the scene changed when I beheld the oppressor lurking on the border of my own peaceful home! I saw his iron hand stretched forth to seize me as his prey, *and the cause of the slave became my own*" (emphasis added).[6]

This work, as abolitionists and antislavery activists, was discussed and carried out both in private, in the work of the conductors of the Underground Railroad or in conversations around the dinner table, and in public, at churches, and at male and female antislavery, fraternal, and benevolent societies.

The "Call to Arms"

It is within this environment of activism and action that Octavius Valentine Catto, a well-known and outspoken antislavery activist, played an integral part in shaping and directing the political and social agendas.[7] Catto was born in Charleston, South Carolina, in 1839 to William, a former slave, and Sarah Isabella Cain, a descendant of a respected South Carolina mulatto family. Catto grew up in Philadelphia (his family moved north shortly after his father was freed) and arrived at the Institute for Colored Youth in 1854, eventually becoming the valedictorian of the 1858 graduating class. After he completed his graduate work in Washington, D.C., he returned to the Institute for Colored Youth to work as the assistant to the Yale- and Dartmouth-educated principal, Professor Ebenezer Don Carlos Bassett. He soon became a member of the Banneker Institute and was elected as their recording secretary. Later he was hired as the principal teacher of the institute's male department.[8] He was young, outspoken, and charismatic. Though Emilie never mentioned Catto by name, he was best friends with Jake White, and Jake's brother was George Bustill (one of Emilie's suitors, who would later become her husband), and he was a teacher at the Institute; it is reasonable to conclude that she knew him.[9] Catto also visited Emilie's church on a regular basis, as his father was both an elder and a Sunday School teacher. Additionally Catto was one of the primary organizers, along with Emilie's uncle Elijah J., of Philadelphia's first all-black volunteer troop organized in response to Abraham Lincoln's 1863 call for emergency troops.

At this time, the city was charged with the news of the Civil War. People were dying, battles were being won and lost, and although these conversations were happening around Emilie, for the first two months of her 1863 pocket diary entries, she did not reference the war. Perhaps she viewed it as a male activity, or maybe she felt that she was disconnected from it. In either case everything changed on March 17, 1863, after she attended an event held at the Mother Bethel African Methodist Episcopal Church. Founded by Bishop Richard Allen, Bethel was one of the first black churches in America and had been a pillar in the First Ward since 1794. It was located at the corner of Sixth and Lombard Streets and was a central meeting place for the free black community.[10] On this evening Frederick Douglass was in town and was scheduled to deliver a lecture, "Men of Color, To Arms." It was a highly anticipated event because it was common knowledge that he was on a speaking tour to recruit black men into the armed services. That evening, as expected, Douglass put forth a "Call to Enlist" for black men to leave Philadelphia and join the Massachusetts Regiment. This was important as earlier that year, Massachusetts Governor John A. Andrew had received the authorization to form the Fifty-fourth Massachusetts Colored Regiment, the first black regiment organized in the North.

In response Andrew sent forth a number of black recruiters including Douglass, Charles Lenox Remond, Thomas Morris Chester, and Martin Delany. The *Philadelphia Public Ledger* covered the event and noted how passionately Douglass spoke as he worked to call black men to action: "As a measure of sound expediency, you and I should rush to the service of the U.S. I should like to be Colonel, but to say I would not, for that reason, serve in the ranks, would be like asserting that I would not go near the water until I learned to swim. My advice to colored men is to get an eagle on your button and a musket on your shoulder as soon as you can, and when that is done, all the devils in Jeff. Davis' dominions cannot keep you out of citizenship."[11]

On this night the church was filled with local black leaders as well as church and community members. The event was publicized in advance, and, unlike other lectures and events, it was free. It was an emotional time in the life of the war. The Emancipation Proclamation had finally been enacted, and free blacks were anxious to involve themselves in securing victory for the North, thereby securing freedom for all.[12] Pennsylvania was one of the few northern states that had not yet allowed black men to enlist. Prior to the event, the fifty-four members of the Committee to Recruit Colored Troops (the Philadelphia Committee) issued a four-by-eight-foot "Call to Arms" broadside in the Seventh Ward. The Philadelphia Committee consisted of Catto and his father, John W. Simpson, Robert M. Adger, David Bustill Bowser, Jonathan Gibbs, Jacob C. and Jake White, and Elijah J. Davis, among many other black and mulatto men who were considered to be the spokesmen for the black community. These men actively espoused the "ideals of patriotism and public service" as they consciously pushed their social, political, and economic agenda. In addition to the broadside, flyers were being circulated throughout the city, challenging the black community to act, "now or never[,] . . . to prove to the South that they were men and not craven cowards without soul, without manhood, without the spirit of soldiers."[13] This was one of the many war-related events that were happening in and around Philadelphia, and the flyers were designed to get everyone excited: "For generations we have suffered under the horrors of slavery outrage and wrong! Our manhood has been denied, our citizenship blotted out, our souls seared and burned, our spirits cowed and crushed, and the hopes of the future of our race involved in doubt and darkness. But now the whole aspect of our relations with the white race is changed. If we love our country, if we love our families, our children, our homes, we must strike now while the country calls."[14]

Emilie, as a part of this community, was probably aware of the event long before it was publicized. It is reasonable to believe that she was beginning to realize that the war was going to personally affect both her and her family. Emilie's friend Vincent escorted her to the lecture. In her diary she noted, "Last evening Vincent looked perfectly staid. Went we went in Fred Duglass lectures. To night meeting at Stills. Mr. Gibbs was down in the room but did not take part, any part in the meeting."[15] Vincent, she wrote, "looked perfectly staid," which most likely described both his dress and his mood. This was an introspective time for young black men throughout the city, who knew that at some point, they would probably have to go to war or become actively involved in the war recruitment efforts. After the event Emilie wrote that there was a "meeting at Stills," which was the home of well-known abolitionist William Still, who lived at 410 Sixth Street, within walking distance of the church.[16] For fourteen years, while working on the Underground Railroad, Still—who has been called the Father of the Underground Railroad—interviewed hundreds of enslaved people en route to freedom and documented their experiences. He later hid the material in a cemetery during the Civil War, and in 1872 he organized and published his collection.[17]

She also mentioned that Jonathan Gibbs, her minister and a highly respected abolitionist and activist, was there but did not take part in the discussion. Gibbs had grown up in Philadelphia and had attended a local Free School. He completed his secondary education at Kimball Union Academy (one of the oldest private boarding schools in the country) in Meriden, New Hampshire. He was a Dartmouth graduate and was the third black person to graduate from the school and the second black person in the nation to deliver a college commencement address. He was a long time member of First African, having joined with his brother Mifflin right after their father died. It is not clear why he joined the Presbyterian church (since his father was a Methodist and his mother was a Baptist) but it worked to his advantage as First African paid for his tuition at Kimball and Dartmouth. After graduating from Dartmouth, Gibbs studied theology at the Princeton Theological Seminary and attended the 1855 New York Colored Men's State Convention. Although he did not graduate from the seminary, he was ordained and became the pastor of Liberty Street Presbyterian Church in Troy, New York. In 1860, when he finally returned to Philadelphia to become the pastor of First African, he had already made a name for himself as an outspoken antislavery activist. So it was unusual for him to attend a meeting with Stills and Douglass and not actively participate.[18] For the past year, Gibbs had been involved in a number of events that may explain his reticence: first, he had recently been involved in a very public and messy separation from his wife, Anna Amelia Harris, an elite free black woman (her father was a merchant) from New York. Jonathan and Anna had three children. The girls, Julia Pennington and Josephine Haywood, went with her and their son, Thomas Van Renssalaer (who later cofounded and was the vice president of Florida A&M College) stayed with his father.

There was some talk that Gibbs was either thinking about or had started seeing another woman. Emilie, upon hearing this, noted, "There is a gaddys wonder out about DJJG and his lady, allso about Mr. Gibbs because he thought he would take a wife to himself. There is great deal of dissatisfactoon in the church about it."

DJJG was Dr. James J. Gould Bias, a former slave, Methodist preacher, and Mason. Bias was also a founding member of the Grand United Order of Odd Fellows along with Emilie's uncle. Perhaps the gaddys wonder about him and his wife is that they were working with Charles Tourney, a white minister, to help runaway slaves escape north to Baltimore. They were part of a vast network of conductors including Frederick Douglass, Stephen Smith, Robert Purvis, and Still. Although she wrote about Gibbs, Emilie decided not to talk about the situation with her friends: "Hannah Brown stoped here to night," Emilie wrote, "to see what I had to say about Mr. Gibbs. I had nothing to say."[19]

Second, Gibbs had upset the church membership by announcing that he was thinking of leaving the ministry to work with the formerly enslaved populations in South Carolina. Throughout the year, it appears as if the Trustees of the church had a public disagreement with Gibbs about his lifestyle and his future at the church. Three months after the meeting at William Still's house, Emile attended a private trustees' meeting and wrote with much frustration, "Last night they had quite a disloyal meeting about Mr. Gibbs. The Trustees were about to turn Mr. Gibbs right out of the church." This was a racially and politically charged time in both the black and white communities, and Gibbs as an activist and pastor was right in the middle of it. By 1864 Gibbs had participated in the Colored People's Convention, which produced the National Equal Rights League to protest against racial discrimination, and was firming up his plans to leave First African to work with the newly freed community in Charleston, South Carolina.

Finally, Gibbs seems to have been battling an illness. On March 8, 1863, Emilie wrote: "I went to church in the morning. Mr. Gibbs was sick, consiquneely Mr. White (Jacob C. White Sr.) held lecture. Very few out"; on March 15, two days before the meeting: "This afternoon, Doct Joneses preach, Mr. Gibbs is still sick"; and later on March 29: "Mr. Gibbs still sick, he didn't preached this afternoon."[20] Although Gibbs did not participate, he was present, and given the gravity of Douglass's speech and the fact that the meeting was held at the home of William Still, it is quite reasonable to conclude that it was a place where the stage was set for what would eventually happen in June.

Countdown to Camp William Penn

Throughout the year, the local newspapers provided daily reports about the Civil War, and when the Confederate troops invaded Cumberland, Pennsylvania, in June 1863, and later advanced into Gettysburg, Pennsylvania, the free black community knew that this was happening. Word was received in Philadelphia that General Robert E. Lee and the Army of Northern Virginia were moving towards southern Pennsylvania. As a response Governor Andrew Gregg Curtin issued "A Call to Arms" for men who were "capable of bearing arms" to volunteer to defend the state.[21] Octavius Catto, along with a number of black leaders including Elijah J., responded by helping to mobilize a full company of ninety black soldiers (including a number of teenage boys) under Captain William Babe.

On Tuesday, June 16, on the evening before the black volunteers were scheduled to depart, Emilie attended a meeting where Jacob C. White Sr. made a frightening announcement: "Mr. White frighten us by saying that a great many of his dear frien(d)s expeced to go to Ware (War) at 12 o'clock. After meeting, I asked who, he said all the boyes." All the "boys" included Institute for Colored Youth teachers Octavius Catto and Jake White, students Raymond Burn, Henry Boyer Jr., and Joseph G. Anderson Jr., and Emilie's uncle. The next day, the volunteers marched from City Arsenal on Broad Street to the Harrisburg Station. Emilie traveled to the Independence Square train station for the festivities that were organized to send them off to war. She was almost giddy with excitement: "To day has bin the most exciting I ever witness. We went to see the boyes start for Harrisburg. I left home about 9 o'clock. It was almost 12 when I came home."[22] It was a day of excitement for everyone except Major General Darius Nash Couch. Although they had been received and fitted without question at the City Arsenal when they arrived in Harrisburg, Couch—who was in charge of mustering the provisional forces and home guard levies for Pennsylvania—refused to receive them.[23] His excuse was that Congress had provided for the enlistment of black men only for a minimum of three years. Sadly they were sent back to Philadelphia. "This morning, the first thing I heard was that the boyes had bin sent back. I feel glad and sorry." Even though this happened, the boys were not deterred and were still "talking about going to ware (war)."[24]

This invasion changed everything for Pennsylvania. Previously the state had had a difficult time getting white men to enlist. There had been a general feeling of disdain about the Civil War, which had now been supplanted by feelings of fear and concern. This event probably substantiated President Lincoln's and Frederick Douglass's concerns that every state needed to actively recruit, draft, and enlist black soldiers. Two weeks later Pennsylvania issued a mandatory draft and a letter was sent to Thomas Webster, Esq., from the U.S. Army granting permission for Philadelphia to raise three all-black regiments of infantry.[25] The volunteers were set to rendezvous at Camp William Penn in the Cheltenham Township, Montgomery Country, near Philadelphia. Camp Penn was the first and largest camp organized for black troops, and it sat on land belonging to Quaker abolitionist Lucretia Mott. "To day has bin the exciting day," Emilie wrote, "I have witness refuges are comin from all the towns this side of Harrisburg. The greetes excitements prevails." In addition to watching black men march on Sixth Street in Philadelphia en route to Camp William Penn, Emilie also saw black and white refugees coming into the city in advance of General Lee's invasion of south central Pennsylvania.

The city began to draft black men ward-by-ward, and by the end of July, the draft had finally reached the Seventh Ward. Emilie, who was both glad and sorry to see "the boyes" return from Harrisburg, anxiously wrote, "Today is the chertified (certified) day they begin to draft in the Seventh Ward. Alfred and Elijah J. are both drafted. Mary is quite worried, I hope he will not have to go. Elijah J. is over the age."[26] Emilie was right to be anxious about Alfred because he was a reluctant soldier. His wife, Mary, was very ill and was suffering from constant chest pains and coughing spasms, and since they had a young son, Alfred probably did not want to leave her. Less than two months after he was drafted and while Emilie was working with a family in Harrisburg, she received a disturbing letter from Elijah J. that informed her that "Alfred had gone to Canada" and "Mary is still quite sick."[27] It is not clear why Alfred had gone to Canada, either the military had sent him, or he was attempting to flee the country before he had to report for training. If he were fleeing, it is quite possible that he used the Underground Railroad because in addition to helping enslaved people move toward freedom, it did help black men who were fleeing the draft. (There was also a large community of free blacks in Ontario near the American border, which may have offered him refuge.) When he returned (or was returned), he applied to the Provost Marshall, the officer in charge of the military police, for an exemption—perhaps because of Mary's poor health or the age of his son. In either case, his request was denied.

In contrast Elijah J. wanted to go to war. Not only had he both volunteered and signed Frederick Douglass's March 1863 "Call to Arms," but he was also actively involved in the local recruitment efforts. Although Emilie wrote that Elijah J. was "over the age," he was later drafted on November 23, 1864, and served as a private in the Sixth Regiment Company A of the U.S. Colored Troops. He was mustered out of service on September 20, 1865. In total eleven black regiments were mustered, though they were credited as part of the regular force and not Pennsylvania's or Philadelphia's.[28] In writing about these everyday experiences in her life, Emilie captured the mixed feelings of black men who were excited about having an opportunity to fight as well as those who were reticent about joining the service and leaving their families.

In 1863 a call had been issued, and the free black men and women of Philadelphia had boldly stepped forward to answer it, which was not a new position for them. In 1858, less than five years earlier, Frederick Douglass had stated that the city (and the black people) of Philadelphia holds "the destiny of our people."[29] This did not just start in 1858; Philadelphia had long been a place where black people were shaping their own destiny and, by extension, the "destiny" of all black people.

Philadelphia and the Social Construction of Race, Class, and Gender

The mulatto families in Philadelphia had long been considered by many to be the "elite" of the free black population. These families had the far-reaching ability to influence and shape community activism. They were a unified force, "rigidly class-conscious, inbred, intensely conservative and impractical in the extreme." They were also regarded by many as "traitors" to the cause of other northern blacks, both because of their ongoing struggle to assume leadership of the black community and because of their decision to focus attention on perceived irrelevant issues while diverting attention away from the bigger questions of slavery, freedom, and economic security.[30] These struggles—which took place from 1787 to 1848, during the time when freeborn Philadelphia blacks began to greatly outnumber formerly enslaved blacks—situated the elite black community to become the leadership base from 1850 to the end of the Civil War.

To the free black communities in Baltimore, New York, and Boston, as well as to the enslaved southern blacks, Philadelphia stood as a gateway between the enslaved southern plantation communities and the free northern communities. From its earliest development, Philadelphia struggled to define, organize, and regulate the spaces where black people lived, worked, and interacted. Next to Baltimore, which had the largest population of free blacks at 25,600, Philadelphia had one of the largest concentrations of free black wealth and talent with a free black population of 22,098.[31] Within that number further distinctions are made when the black and mulatto populations are evaluated separately. Since color classifications were arbitrarily selected by census takers, they adversely affected the rights of black people while positively affecting the rights of mulattoes.

An analysis of the issues of race, class, and gender and how they shaped Emilie's world must begin with outlining and understanding the four moments when these issues were socially and politically constructed in America prior to the ending of the Civil War. By delineating these moments it helps to further the understanding of the unique "nexus between Africans and Americans which, though token and perverted as it may be" should not be "neglected by the careful student."[32]

The first wave, which took place in the seventeenth century, began with the charter generation and marked the beginnings of black life in America. In 1619, one year before the Mayflower arrived at Plymouth, Massachusetts, and 246 years before the ratification of the Thirteenth Amendment, the first twenty Africans set foot in British North America at Jamestown, Virginia. Although the European slave trade began in 1444, this first connection with the permanent American settlements marked the beginning of the triangular trade system in which approximately forty million Africans were forcibly taken from their homes in Africa and scattered throughout the Americas. This story would never be fully documented, but over time it defined the categories of race and gender throughout the Americas. It would take almost forty-five years, before slavery was legalized and America became a slave society.[33] The difference was that in a society with slaves, slavery is one of the many forms of labor. In a slave society, not only does slavery stand at the center of the nation's economic production, but the master-slave relationship provides the model for social interaction between whites and blacks.[34]

In 1662, one year after legalizing slavery, Virginia's House of Burgesses went one step further by approving legislation that uniquely conjoined a black woman's womb with capital accumulation by giving the white plantation owners an "incontestable right of access to black women's bodies."[35] This essentially allowed white plantation owners to either impregnate their slaves or have them impregnated without impunity, thereby actively reproducing their own labor force. It was during this plantation generation that the social conditions between blacks and whites were further solidified, with whites rising in social status and blacks losing their social status. As a result skin color became closely connected with social status and social conditions, as America rapidly became two nations—one white and free and the other black and enslaved.[36] It was at this time that the idea of race became associated with skin color, intellectual and linguistic deficiencies, and internal capabilities.[37] Also during this time, enslaved people began to construct their African-American identity as a result of the social conditions on the plantation, which included the close living quarters, the intermingling of Africans from different ethnic groups, and the forced English-only communication with the owners and with each other. This resulted in their African identity's being supplanted with a constructed survivalist identity. This identity, which was created in an effort to ensure their survival, combined their African history with their European exposure and their American environment.[38]

Second was the plantation generation, which took place during the eighteenth century as colonial America became wholly dependent on enslaved labor. With the legalization of slavery, the second wave of New World Africans were subjected to more increased levels of violence, isolation, exhaustion, and alienation, which resulted in a substantially higher number of fatalities than the previous generation. This happened because the enslaved populations contested the legalization of slavery at every opportunity, either through conspiracies, or open rebellion, or by running away; and they were unable to handle the harsher working conditions and the diseased low country environments. Between 1619 and 1807, millions of captured African people were transported by ship from the coasts of Africa to the ports of America. This six-to-ten-week journey, the "Middle Passage," was absolutely brutal, and one captain described it as having "a sense of misery and suffocation" so overwhelming that "the slaves not infrequently would go mad before dying and suffocating." Bennett likens the selection process to the rolling of a roulette wheel: wherever the wheel stopped (or the slave ship docked), the future of the African people in that area was forever to be linked with enslavement.[39]

Third was the revolutionary generation, when some enslaved people sought and found ways to actively engage in the struggle to end slavery, and many southern and northern slaveholders chose to either manumit their slaves or allow them to purchase their freedom. This revolutionary spirit took place during the early part of the nineteenth century and moved across the North as the society with slaves began to slowly transform itself into a free nation. This also marked the beginning of the "Black Pioneer Period," in which urban populations and cities began to grow as newly freed blacks established households, founded sociopolitical institutions, and took leadership positions in the free black community.[40] Additionally the term "African" was unofficially adopted as the largest population of African people, outside of Africa, became one tribe and no longer classified themselves as anything other than the free Africans.[41] It is interesting that this discussion did not end with this universal acceptance of the term "African." By 1831 black Americans were openly debating in the letters section of the *Liberator* newspaper about what to call themselves.

Fourth was the migration generation, which dramatically reshaped the African American communities as both the institution of slavery and enslaved people began to migrate across the West. It was during this period, the mid-nineteenth century, that the slaveholders bought, sold, and relocated enslaved people from the exterior states to the interior ones, permanently altering the remaining enslaved populations. Families were separated as younger men and women were transported west and older ones were left behind.[42] Fugitive slaves became the most active voices against the institution of slavery, and plantation rebellions occurred in response to the depressing conditions.[43] Also more enslaved people were choosing to run away to the North rather than continue to negotiate the conditions of enslavement. The ideas of eventual freedom slowly replaced the notions of forever enslaved, as both the black and white populations closely followed the 1860 presidential election. The final wave was the freedom generation, which began in 1865, with the ending of the Civil War and the ratification of the Thirteenth Amendment, which ended legalized slavery. Once removed, the yoke of slavery was replaced with the burden of living and defining freedom in a world that had never experienced such a radical and sudden internal change. The next steps forward found both the free and newly freed communities subjugated to a different yet vastly similar situation that defined their existence, limited their freedoms, and continued to use race as the cogent and deciding factor that defined social status and condition.

From the charter to the migration generations, race, class, and gender were shaped and defined as socially constructed categories that determined social, political, and economic behavior and relationships within a young America. In Philadelphia the realities of slavery, resistance, and freedom began to intersect during the early part of the seventeenth century and continued up until the nineteenth century. During this time a small number of free black Philadelphians established communities and started competing for jobs and housing with both the Irish immigrants and the newly emancipated blacks migrating from the South. Their community began to slowly grow and experience economic progress. At the same time, enslavement as an institution continued to grow, and the enslaved population continued to increase in numbers with many of them coming from other colonies in the beginning of eighteenth century (particularly South Carolina and the Islands) and from Africa by the middle of the century.[44] Northern slavery was much milder than southern slavery because the enslaved in the North were not subjected to the harsh living conditions found in the South, and they typically received better food, more expensive clothing, and better housing.[45] In Philadelphia the enslaved men were trained as either house servants or farmhands, or they were taught a trade, while women were primarily trained as housekeepers and cooks. At the same time, milder did not necessarily mean better since enslaved women faced additional difficulties as a result of language barriers and exposure to new diseases.[46]

From Slavery to Freedom

During the 1700s there was increased tension between the Quakers (Society of Friends), who argued for the regulation of slavery, and the councils of the state churches, who sought to impose harsher and more restrictive slave laws. With the increased number of mulattoes, Pennsylvania ruled that the child of a free woman and an enslaved man would be enslaved for ten years, while the child of an enslaved woman and a free man would be enslaved for life. Thus mulattoes formed two classes: either they were classified as servants for a termed number of years, or they were enslaved for life.[47] Additionally the rights of free black women were so entangled with the restrictions and restraints that their freedoms were severely limited.[48] As the Revolutionary War continued, the Quakers called for an end to slavery, ordered manumission, and worked to end it by statute.

It would not be until 1750 that slavery in Philadelphia would finally begin to decline and voluntary emancipation began to take place across the city. Less than twenty years later, Anthony Benezet, an early abolitionist and Quaker, opened the Negro School, the first school for free children, and five years after that, he opened a school for girls. Benezet later founded the first antislavery society, the Society for the Relief of Free Negroes Unlawfully Held in Bondage.[49] At this time it was the Quakers that continued to take the lead in establishing schools for the free black communities. In 1792 they founded the Cherry School for black women, which focused primarily on teaching academic rather than household skills. The curriculum included reading, writing, and arithmetic and was taught by Helena Harris, a black woman who had previously taught white children. In less than five years, the Quakers had opened seven schools around the city.

Three years after the end of the Revolutionary War, Pennsylvania enacted the Act for the Gradual Abolition of Slavery, which stated that any child born after 1780 was born free and any child born to an enslaved person would remain in servitude until the age of eighteen. This act led to an increased number of free and fugitive blacks migrating into the city as the black population experienced a 210 percent increase over a ten-year period, 1790–1800, approximately three times more than New York and almost four times more than Boston.[50] This freedom and protection was extended in 1788 when the act was expanded to prevent the internal and foreign slave trade and correct kidnapping and other abuses.[51] The passage of the act along with the work of the Quakers and abolitionists and the surfeit of trained and talented free men and women, transformed the city into a battleground where the free mulatto communities interacted and competed with the white, free black, and fugitive communities.

During this time black leaders also began to emerge and establish organizations of change. In 1787 Richard Allen, a former slave who belonged to the Chew family, and Absalom Jones, from Delaware, met with six other prominent black men—Samuel Boston, Joseph Johnson, Cato Freeman, Caesar Cranchell, James Potter, and William White—to cofound the Free African Society (FAS) and take the first "wavering step" toward "organized social life" by founding a black mutual-aid society.[52] In their opening statement, the Free African Society outlined their ideology:

> Whereas, Absalom Jones and Richard Allen, two men of the African race, who, for their religious life and conversation have obtained a good report among men, these persons, from a love to the people of their complexion whom they beheld with sorrow, because of their irreligious and uncivilized state, often communed together upon this painful and important subject in order to form some kind of religious society, but there being too few to be found under the like concern, and those who were, differed in their religious sentiments; with these circumstances they labored for some time, till it was proposed, after a serious communication of sentiments, that a society should be formed, without regard to religious tenets, provided, the persons lived an orderly and sober life, in order to support one another in sickness, and for the benefit of their widows and fatherless children.[53]

By consciously selecting the term "African," Ira Berlin suggests that it marked the moment when black people transcended their tribal and ethnic backgrounds to become a unified nation of people.[54] These eight are considered to be the founders of black America, and they were well educated and extremely religious. Their meeting took place one month before the first session of the Constitutional Convention, and though the purpose of the two groups was different, the *esprit de corps* was not. One was organizing to establish a nation for white male property owners, while the other was organizing identity and personhood for both the free and enslaved black communities. The one common thread is that each group worked to create a social compact without having women present and accounted for at the table.

These slow steps toward organizing the black experience helped create a sense of community and recreate a social identity. Bennett argues that the creation of this religious and political organization established the nascent black America and propelled Jones and Allen onto the local political scene.[55] When the yellow fever epidemic spread across the city in 1793, Jones and Allen were the only two volunteers who answered Mayor Matthew Clarkson's call for help.[56] As a result, the Free

African Society became the major agency of relief work during the epidemic. This level of commitment to the community, the city, and black people was the first step toward establishing a black American existence. The second was the establishment of the independent black churches across the North and South. Although Jones and Allen later parted ways and established separate churches, they both continued to work within the free black communities to openly challenge and resist discrimination and segregation in an attempt to define what it meant to be black in America.

Even with all the progress, the road from enslavement to freedom was gradual, and Edward Raymond Turner compellingly presents the idea that a race movement was taking place stage by stage across the city, as the black community moved swiftly from slavery to limited servitude to apprenticeship and finally to continuous freedom.[57] Between 1820 and 1840, Philadelphia was one of the most critical cities in the nation for free blacks and fugitive slaves because it connected the road of slavery in the South with the road to freedom in the North. Because of its close proximity to the South, it was a major point of destination for fugitive blacks.[58] This is really where Emilie's story begins. On the 1850 and 1860 U.S. Census, it states that both her father and her uncle were born in Maryland but there is no information about how or why they relocated to Philadelphia. Her mother was born in Pennsylvania but outside of the 1850 U.S. Census there is no information about who she was, how she lived her life, or what happened to her after 1850. As a result of this lack of information, Emilie's story—like that of so many other black people at this time—can only start with her. Her diaries provide a record of her life but the history of Philadelphia provides the much needed context for how she lived out her life.

Growing Up in Philadelphia

W. E. B. Du Bois suggests that five social developments took place during the early 1800s that shaped and defined the experience of the Philadelphia "Negro." It started with the industrial revolution and its impact on the nation's economy and was followed by the nation's recovery effort that took place after the War of 1812 and continued into the 1820s. Shortly after that, there was a high influx of Irish Catholics and German immigrants into the city who were competing with the free black communities for jobs and homes. This was followed (and perhaps influenced) by the growth of the free and fugitive black communities. The final social development happened when the Quaker and abolitionist communities became actively involved in furthering the antislavery agenda.

Additionally, by 1829 the free black community began to experience an increase in racially charged events and white repression that would spark a massive retrogression in their economic and social gains. These racially charged events—which included race riots, fires, periods of lawlessness, increased violence, and increased poverty—continued until after the Civil War. Some of the events, such as the 1838 burning of both Pennsylvania Hall, a newly dedicated center of antislavery agitation, and the Shelter for Colored Orphans, happened primarily because Mayor Clarkson failed to provide adequate police protection.[59]

Although blacks and whites lived and worked in close contact with one another, there was an ongoing undercurrent of racial tension. This racial divide manifested itself at every point within the community as Frederick Douglass noted when he said, "there is not perhaps anywhere to be found a city in which prejudice against color is more rampant that in Philadelphia . . . It has its white schools and its colored schools, its white churches and its colored churches, its white Christianity and its colored Christianity, its white concerts and its colored concerts, its white literary institutions and its colored literary institutions . . . and the line is everywhere tightly drawn between them."[60]

Despite these significant social problems, the elite free black community never stopped struggling to create a more improved situation for their children. They continued to purchase property and increased their attendance in schools, benevolent societies, and churches—all choices that were largely influenced by a person's economic status. They also continued to meet, organize, and invest, and they found ways to agitate the policy makers. In 1832, in response to a piece of legislation that was designed to curtail their activities, the black community responded by producing tax receipts that showed that they held approximately $350,000 in taxable property. The numbers had significantly increased by 1837, when a piece of legislation was put forth in an effort to disenfranchise the free black community. The Pennsylvania Abolition Society undertook a census to prove that black people paid their taxes, cared for their underprivileged, and actively participated in building Philadelphia's economic infrastructure. They found that the free black community, who made up only 8 percent of the Philadelphia population, owned sixteen churches, had close to $310,000 in unencumbered property, had organized one hundred active benevolent societies, and had enrolled roughly 1,700 of their children in public or private schools. Even with these figures, black men in Philadelphia still lost the right to vote, which they had enjoyed since 1790, and did not receive suffrage until the Fifteenth Amendment was ratified in 1870.[61]

In 1847, less than ten years after the legislation passed, the elite free black communities of Philadelphia would see more than 1,800 black students attending school, a $200,000 increase in real estate holdings, including acquisition of three more churches, and the establishment of six more benevolent societies. They also operated their own insurance companies, libraries, building and loan associations, labor unions, and branches of fraternal organizations. This experience of black economic, political, and social growth was unique to Philadelphia. There were other northern cities, like New York, Baltimore, or Boston, that had free black communities, but they did not have the social, political, and economic influence that black Philadelphians wielded.

By 1857 the numbers had almost doubled as the free black communities, on the eve of the Civil War, experienced a season of rapid financial growth, community respect, and neighborhood stability.[62] At the same time, elite free blacks were discriminated against by white Philadelphians who wanted the color lines to be clearly drawn and maintained and wanted to be clearly separated from a majority of black families, who owned $60 or less of real estate.[63] Free blacks fell within four different social and economic levels: Grade I were the talented and successful, the aristocrats of the black community who had access to education, travel, property, and money; Grade II were the laborers who possessed highly valued skills working as waiters, teachers, ministers, seamstresses, barbers, and tailors; Grade III was made up of the working class; they possessed devalued skills and worked as live-in domestics, day workers, and street cleaners; and finally, Grade IV, the uneducated and unemployed, which Du Bois dubbed as the "submerged tenth." These were the fugitive blacks that did not possess any marketable skills and therefore lived on the fringes of black Philadelphia society.[64]

Further delineation is made when mulattoes and blacks are studied separately. Within Philadelphia, mulattoes and blacks tended to live in separate wards with the largest concentration of wealthy mulattoes situated in the Seventh Ward. In the Seventh and Eighth Wards, which extended from Chestnut to South Streets and from Seventh to the Schuylkill River, over eleven percent of residents were either black or mulatto. In the Fourth Ward, which stretched from Old Southwark to South and from the Delaware to Broad Street, ten percent of residents were black. The largest concentration of black Philadelphians—at twenty-one percent—was in the Fifth Ward, which sat at the center of the city between Washington Square and the Delaware, and Chestnut and South. The First, Second, and Third Wards were primarily all-white neighborhoods, and their residents would occasionally move in and out of the Seventh Ward to attend meetings, church, social events, and to hire day workers. The largely mulatto Seventh Ward had a lower rate of crime than the Fifth and Eighth Wards, which had more black residents and higher rates of crime.[65]

By 1860 the mulatto population had increased by 93 percent in Philadelphia, while the black population had declined by 4.3 percent. A disproportionate number of mulattoes migrated into the city within a ten-year period. At the same time, the mulatto populations of Maryland, Delaware, and Virginia all decreased. Hershberg writes that both the passage of the 1850 Fugitive Slave Laws, which made it easier to recapture runaway slaves and kidnap free blacks and ship them to the South, and the 1857 *Dred Scott* decision probably provided the impetus for mulattoes, who had a greater sense of mobility, to migrate and relocate.[66] In 1860 the Philadelphia and Delaware River Railroad Company's horse-drawn cars carried an estimated forty-six thousand people into and out of the city per day. Two years earlier the city council had begun laying iron rails in the most densely populated neighborhoods, following the arc of the Delaware River, in an attempt to ease traffic and provide additional speed and comfort over the omnibus. As a result horse-drawn cars were situated in the Fifth Ward and were near the Seventh Ward; many blacks and mulattoes populated these two neighborhoods. Out of the nineteen cars, eleven did not allow people of color to ride, and the remaining eight allowed them to ride only on the outside platform with the driver.[67]

Three out of four black and mulatto families were nuclear, characterized by two-parent households. Mulatto households generally consisted of just the parents and their children, while black households tended to have a higher proportion of older relatives living in their homes. The pattern seems to indicate that mulattoes tended to get married and move out to start their households, usually with very large church weddings and familial support, while black families tended to marry and either move into parents' homes or have their parents move in with them. Such moves pooled economic resources and explained why individual blacks were less likely to own property than mulattoes. The 1860 Census shows that mulattoes owned property at a rate of 3-to-1 in comparison to blacks.[68]

Marriages in 1860 tended to be endogamous: blacks tended to marry other blacks while mulattoes tended to marry other mulattoes. The U.S. Census shows that 93 percent of black men married black women and 85 percent of mulatto men married mulatto women. Black women had the lowest rate of marrying outside their color group, while mulatto women had the highest rates of exogamy at 31 percent. Black men who were at the top of the occupational ladder, such as businessmen and skilled laborers, were more likely to marry mulatto women than black men who were unskilled laborers. Mulatto women disproportionately married black men who had access to money, which extended to access to better educational opportunities, social and cultural outlets, and communities.[69] Since social status was directly linked to racial identity, many mulatto women chose to marry up in color classification or economic status.

Noblesse Oblige and the Black Elite

During the nineteenth-century, the elite of the free black communities, within their genteel and closed circles, possessed a sense of *noblesse oblige*, in that they believed that they had a moral and social obligation to work on behalf of the less fortunate. In 1855, Maltilda A. Jones, a mulatto student at the School for Colored Girls, wrote a letter to author Mary Elizabeth Dewey, the daughter of well-known American Unitarian minister Reverend Orville Dewey, in which she attempted to answer the question of why education was so important to the lives and the future development of free black people:

> Two years ago your mother asked our school, "if we would be more
> happy, with these educational advantages?" & I was among the number,
> who replied to the question. Two years have passed since then, giving

us a great experience, & some can truly say, I am much happier with the knowledge obtained during that time. My feelings are entirely different from what they were when I first came to Miss Miner's school. I not only need intellectual cultivation, but partially a moral development of character, as did many others. We need [education] more than your people do, & ought to strive harder, because the greater part of our people, are yet in bondage. *We that are free, are expected to be the means of bringing them out of Slavery, & how can we do it, unless we have proper educational advantages. We must get the knowledge, & use it well.* (emphasis added)[70]

In addition to relentlessly pursuing education, amassing wealth and property, and practicing gentility—which were the social, political, and financial dictates of the community—the elite also had active antislavery agendas. Although middle-class status was sometimes hard to achieve and maintain, the black and mulatto families that were able to reach (and in some cases, surpass) these social levels, like the Fortens of Philadelphia, the DuSables of Chicago, and the Halls and Cuffees of Massachusetts, helped create environments in which their children were exposed to activities that seemed best suited to fit their class and endowment.[71]

At the same time, these families were aware that they were living as free people during a time when bondage was the assumed norm for people of color. They also understood that to be free and black in America with an agenda of social freedom

The effects of the proclamation—freed Negroes coming into the lines at Newbern, North Carolina. 1863. Courtesy of Library of Congress.

and equality meant that they had to teach their children at a young age how to "bear up under the daily insults" whenever they were "shamefully abused" and "the arrows of death are flying about [their] heads."[72] These communities maintained political and social networks and family ties across the North as elite families intermarried and supported one another, financially, politically, and socially. This was the landscape where Emilie had come of age. These were the social, political, and economic issues that indelibly marked her childhood and shaped who she was—a literate freeborn woman. Perhaps one of the reasons Emilie chose to record her life was that she understood how quickly the fabric of a country could shift and how easily communities can change.

With the tensions associated with the Civil War, the release of the Emancipation Proclamation, and the constant threats associated with the Fugitive Slave Laws, elite families were also aware of the precariousness of both their freedom and their bourgeois culture.[73] Similar to the work of black men who vigorously worked to expand the American ideology of social freedom, black women, in response to these social realities, continued to find ways to be both politically involved and intimately connected with family and friends. They did so through, among other avenues, the creation of female-centered spaces in which public conversations could take place within private environments. These were the arenas where they shared their friendship albums, their private diaries, and their thoughts and feelings. It was an environment that was created by women and situated as a place where women were able to bond with one another. Moreover it was an environment that Emilie fully participated in and where she constructed and maintained her vast network of female friends.

Emilie Davis, 1864

"To day has bin a great day. 6,000 slaves have bin declared free in the state of Maryland. It has bin generally ahseehed (assisted) here by our people."

Diaries, Memoranda, 1864

In 1863 Emilie had many changes in her life: her father, Charles, after battling a short illness, moved (back?) to Harrisburg; her sister-in-law, Mary (Alfred's wife), passed away from consumption of the lungs (tuberculosis); and her brother, Alfred, was reluctantly drafted into the United States Colored Troops (USCT). She did not hear from her sister, Elizabeth, and she saw her younger brother, Tomy, only a few times. Even though she had a number of visitors per week, she still complained of having no friends. She ended the year with a poem in which she yearns for friendships. In 1864 the country is in the third year of a vicious "civil" war. Neither the Union nor the Confederacy seemed to be open to any type of compromise: on the surface the Union needed to win to save the country, while the Confederacy needed to win to save their way of life. (It was, of course, much more complicated than that.) The number of lives lost continued to increase, as both black and white soldiers died in the midst of battle or from complications sustained by injuries. Additionally an untold number of enslaved men, women, and children of color were making the bold decision to "free themselves." Even though the Civil War continued to rage around her, Emilie seems to have carved out a simple life for herself. She spent her days visiting, shopping, making dresses, and occasionally working with her families. Her activism seems to have been limited to her work with the Ladies' Union, which consisted of selling tickets for lectures and concerts, and attending meetings held at the homes of abolitionist and antislavery workers. Both the larger world and her personal world seemed to be changing around her, and yet, in so many ways, she remained the same. With all of the sickness and the deaths, she opens the New Year thankful and hopeful.

January 1864

FRIDAY, JANUARY 1, 1864

I feel thankful that I am spard to see another year. Home all day. In the evening, I went to Jones I enjoyed myself very much. Great many changes have taken place since last New Year.

I staid home last night. Bitter cold day I stoped in to see Nellie, poor girl. She is very unhappy. Sue was here to day and two strang ladies. I ran out and bought my diary to day.

Very cold this morning. I was not at church in the morning. I feel thankful that I have bin spared to see the first Sabbath in the New Year. Very good attendance in the afternoon. Dave was down, no Bible class. It was quite a disappointment. Nellie and I went to church.

Very cold. It commenced snowing this morning. Before night, we had quite a snowstorm. Sue was up and staid while until school time. I went down to school had a very nice school but we had no fire. I had to hurry home soon.

Quite cold to day. I was out a little wayes, went to town Sunday. I went to see Em Warwich then out to see Lizzie. Meeting tonight at Rachel, after meeting we went to visit Bustill then to the Fair. Staid at Nellies all night. Vincent come home with me. I do not know how I could get along with him.

> *January 5–7, the Ladies' Union Association hosted a fair at Sansom Street Hall to raise money to support sick and wounded black soldiers.*

Nellie and Sue were both here to day. They are going to spend the evening with the girls.

Quite cold to day. Sue was up to day. I went out to Harries then to see Lizzie then over to Sarah Whites. It was six o'clock before I got home. In the evening, we went to the Fair. Had quite a nice time. Vincent came home with us. Cristy was there and acted quite strangely.

> *Emilie wrote that she was visiting Sarah White; if she had been talking about the sister of George Bustill and Jake, then Sarah would have been only around eleven years old. Perhaps Emilie visited Sarah in an effort to see George, one of her suitors, whom she later married.*

Nellie was up to day I feel so sorry for her. Tomy made me a present last night. I was up to see Hannah Brown. Sue has not bin here to day.

Bitter cold to day. Very busy all day. Mrs. Briscoe come up in the afternoon. I went with her to get a clock in the evening. I went down home. I bought my guitior up.

SUNDAY, JANUARY 10, 1864

Very cold. I went down to church, one of Mr. Gibbses friends preached for us. We had a very good sermon. I expected Sue up here but she did not get here. I spent quite a lonsom evening all by myself.

MONDAY, JANUARY 11, 1864

Quite cold but clear. Nellie was up in the afternoon. Sue spent the evening with me. I went down to school and stoped at Mrs. Hills and Mrs. Hawkins paid up my areas (arrears). We had a very nice school. We elected three officers George, John an Nellie.

TUESDAY, JANUARY 12, 1864

Meeting (at) Mr. Washington, very spirited meeing. Lizzie was up and staid up until the meeting time. Nellie did not go.

WEDNESDAY, JANUARY 13, 1864

Very busy to day. I have bin waiting patiently for Nellie to come up this evening but she did not come. She went to millery to a memding presentation.

THURSDAY, JANUARY 14, 1864

Very disagreeable to day. The walking is very hard. I went down to the commisation office and to Bustill and Hills. Spent part of the evening in home and the rest of the evening in Nellies.

FRIDAY, JANUARY 15, 1864

Sue come up and spent part of the day and evening. Nellie was sick. I sent a letter to Will yesterday.

SATURDAY, JANUARY 16, 1864

Elwood was quite sick Thursday. Nellie stoped an took my skirt to mend. I was down home. Stoped in Nellies.

SUNDAY, JANUARY 17, 1864

Very disagreeable evening. I was not at our church all day, it being Intercommunion at St. Marys. Ms. Cares sick, Liz and me out. Great suffering at (Mother) Bethels. Bible class at Mary Jones. Very nice class.

MONDAY, JANUARY 18, 1864

Running around all day. Nellie stoped for me to go to school but I did not go on account of the rain.

Reverend Gibbs met with the congregation of First African and informed them of his decision to leave the church to become a missionary in the South. His resignation received unanimous approval.

TUESDAY, JANUARY 19, 1864

Still raining. I gave a letter for Sister on Sunday. Meeting at Defees very few out. Mr. Gibbs was not there since hes still quite sick. Nellie did not go to meeting. Sue stoped here a minute.

WEDNESDAY, JANUARY 20, 1864

Beautiful day after the rain. Nellie come up to spend the evening. She has received her little budget of [affectation or affection?]. Sue and John stoped in a little while.

THURSDAY, JANUARY 21, 1864

Nellie is up here ironing. I went out to Mary DeClones. She was not home. Called on Em McCrell she was out. Spent the rest of the day home. In the evening we went to the lecture. Mr. Stanford lectured—his subject was the fire of Malachi.

FRIDAY, JANUARY 22, 1864

Lovely day. I was down home and stoped for Nellie to come up and make a finish. I was down to Bustill a few minutes.

SATURDAY, JANUARY 23, 1864

Very busy all day. Tomy was up in the morning and bought Nellies guitar. I went down home Bub (Elwood) was very sick. Sarah is quite worried about him.

Here Emilie uses her nickname for Elwood—which was Bub.

SUNDAY, JANUARY 24, 1864

Very dull day. Nellie was not at church this morning. She was sick. Elwood was very ill this morning. Elijah and Sarah are very ansious about him. Sue and John, Nellie and Vincent come up to see me. In the evening we spent quite a pleasant evening frimeayr.

Here Emilie wrote "frimeayr," cf. French je frimer, *meaning "to show off."*

MONDAY, JANUARY 25, 1864

Elwood is still very sick. I went down to school, had a very full school. Miss Little was down. I staid home all night with Elwood. He is very low. The fever has gone to his head. Poor little fellow. He suffers very much. Meeting at Bustills I could not go.

TUESDAY, JANUARY 26, 1864

Elwood has not spoken since this morning. I staid with him all night last night. Lizzie come home to day. Rachel goes to.

WEDNESDAY, JANUARY 27, 1864

This evening I spent most of the evening home. Elwood is not better. Mary B(lack) and Mother attend to him faithfully. I went to see Mrs. Marshall and to send some things out to Frank.

Mary Black was a member of the Ladies' Union Association.

THURSDAY, JANUARY 28, 1864

Elijah J. has call in Doct Morris but I think it is to late for any earthly power to help him.

FRIDAY, JANUARY 29, 1864

I stayed home last night. Elwood is sinking fast to day. I was to go down to see Frank but I can't go. Elwood is still suffering but I think death will soon end his suffering.

SATURDAY, JANUARY 30, 1864

Tomy come for me this morning. Elwood is dying. I hurried home and staid until he breathed his last. He died at 11 o'clock this morning. His spirit has gone to his Father, that quick.

According to his death certificate, Elwood died of congestion (swelling) of the brain.

SUNDAY, JANUARY 31, 1864

Very cloudy day. I went down home and staid until after ten. The girls all stoped to see me. There was a great many people in to see Sarah and Elijah J. I wrote to Alfred this evening.

February 1864

MONDAY, FEBRUARY 1, 1864

Very rainy all day. Nellie was up. We went for our guitars. I did not go down to school. Sue was down. They had quite a nice time.

TUESDAY, FEBRUARY 2, 1864

Quite dull this morning. This is the day we have to part with our little Elwood. I went down home in the morning. Mrs. Williams laid him out. Very nice but he did not look like himself. Mr. Gibbs spoke beautifully over him.

WEDNESDAY, FEBRUARY 3, 1864

I staid home all the afternoon. I did not go up to the Hazard until 10. I went down to Bustills with Hannah. Sue come in to have her head dressed.

THURSDAY, FEBRUARY 4, 1864

Very fine day. Nellie come up this evening and Hannah Brown. I got my guitar yesterday. I went up to Augustines with Sue then down to Bustills. I spent the evening at Bustills. I received a letter from Tomy and one from his friend. Vincent come home with me.

FRIDAY, FEBRUARY 5, 1864

Mr. Gibbs has a daughter. Egerton is sick. He looks badly. I have bin waiting for Nellie to come up all day but she has not made her apperance yet. This evening she stoped on her way to meeting.

Jonathan Gibbs was first married to Anna Harris, and they had three children. After they divorced, he married Elizabeth, and they had one daughter, Anna, who died in infancy.

SATURDAY, FEBRUARY 6, 1864

Very dull and dreary. I have not bin well all day. I went down home a little while and stoped in to Nellies.

SUNDAY, FEBRUARY 7, 1864

Very dull all day. A great many out in the afternoon Mr. Gibbs preached a service concerning the several deaths which has ocured in our church during the past month.

MONDAY, FEBRUARY 8, 1864

Beautiful day. I went down Chestnut St this afternoon, meet Meal Williams. We went down to school in the evening we had a very hard lesson. We picked several pieces for Wednesday evening.

TUESDAY, FEBRUARY 9, 1864

Sue stoped here this morning. Quite busy all day. I sent a letter to Tomy yesterday. Meeting at Offerts. Liz and I went. Nellie did not go. We had a very good meeting, few out.

WEDNESDAY, FEBRUARY 10, 1864

Quite (quiet) to day. Mrs. Rock is to be buried this morning. Jemi and I went up Chestnut St to see the colored soldiers. They went away to day. In the evening we went to Madame Raf in Reading. She has quiet (quite) a good house. Dave was down.

The Twenty-second Infantry Regiment of the U.S. Colored Troops marched from Camp William Penn through the streets of Philadelphia on their way south to fight at Yorktown and Petersburg.

THURSDAY, FEBRUARY 11, 1864

I went up to Daves. This afternoon stoped home, went on erand for Elijah J. We went down to Bustills spent part of the evening there and the other part at Nellies.

FRIDAY, FEBRUARY 12, 1864

Sue come up and spent the day. John come up in the evening. Nellie was up a little while. I have not bin out to day. John and Sue had French on.

SATURDAY, FEBRUARY 13, 1864

Quite pleasant. I inted (intended) up staying in the house this evening but Nellie come up here and bought here (her) guitar and for me to take down. I did not go home.

SUNDAY, FEBRUARY 14, 1864

Quite a blustery day. I did not go out in the morning. We had a very good service an bible class at Nellies. Great many there I had to marsh (march) home.

MONDAY, FEBRUARY 15, 1864

Quite cold but clear. I went down to school. We had a very full school. Mr Lively divided the classes. I stoped at Docts. Tomy is quite sick.

TUESDAY, FEBRUARY 16, 1864

Quite windy. To day meeting at Mrs Whismons. Very few out, only Nellie, Mary, and Liz and I there. Mr. White writes that the meetings are very poorly attended.

WEDNESDAY, FEBRUARY 17, 1864

Bitter cold day. The coldest this winter. I had to go out very much against my will. Sue has not bin up this weeke.

THURSDAY, FEBRUARY 18, 1864

Still quite cold. To day is my birthday. I went home then to Mr. Lively. He was not home. I feel thankful that I have bin spared to see another birthday. Vincent came up her to meet me. It was almost eleven o'clock.

FRIDAY, FEBRUARY 19, 1864

Tomy is still sick. Nellie and I spent last evening in. Mary plaed (played) several pieces for us.

Charlotte Forten's father, Robert Bridges Forten, published a poem in the Liberator *newspaper urging black men to enlist in the armed services.*

SATURDAY, FEBRUARY 20, 1864

Very pleasant to day. Busy all day as usal. In evening I went down home. Nellie was up in the afternoon. Sue was here in the evening. She has gone to the docter to spend a couple of dayes.

SUNDAY, FEBRUARY 21, 1864

Lovely morning. I went down to church. Nellie was not out there. But Liz and I after church, we went to see Aunty. Hollis stoped in Bustills a minute. Vincent was up to see me this afternoon.

MONDAY, FEBRUARY 22, 1864

To(day) is very fine. There is to be a grand parade pass our house. To day in the afternoon Scott and Lizzie Agustes stoped to see me. In the evening I went down to school, we had a nice time.

TUESDAY, FEBRUARY 23, 1864

To day I have bin sick. All day I did not go to meeting. I have not seen Nellie since last night. Meeting was at Mary Black, she is quite sick.

WEDNESDAY, FEBRUARY 24, 1864

Busy as usal to day. Sue come up from Chesters this morning. She is quite sick with a bad cold. She was here most all the morning. Nellie did not come up. I was quite disappointed.

THURSDAY, FEBRUARY 25, 1864

Quite pleasant to day. I went down to Mr. Livelys but did not take a lesson. I was out collecting this afternoon but did not rass (raise) a cent. In the evening, Nellie and I went to Bustills.

FRIDAY, FEBRUARY 26, 1864

Quite dull to day. Nellie was up.

SATURDAY, FEBRUARY 27, 1864

Busy as usal. Nellie stoped up this morning in the evening. Pline (Pliny Ishmael Locke) and I stoped at Nellies. We went up Eleventh St and seen a sight.

This was probably Pliny Ishmael Locke, a student at the Instiute and the son of Ishmael Locke, the first principal of the Institute.

SUNDAY, FEBRUARY 28, 1864

Pleasant. I went to church in the afternoon. Heard an excellent sermon. After church Liz and I went to Bustills and spent quite a pleasant time. In the evening we went to bible class at Ayers.

MONDAY, FEBRUARY 29, 1864

Lizzie went down to Mr. Livelys and stoped at Mrs. Potters. We had a very nice school. Great many out. We have two classes then Vincent went home with me.

March 1864

TUESDAY, MARCH 1, 1864

Very stormy all day. Snowing fast all day. Meeting at Mrs. Childs very few out but we had a good time.

WEDNESDAY, MARCH 2, 1864

Nellie did not come up as usal. Sally went to her place this morning. I hope she will like it.

THURSDAY, MARCH 3, 1864

Very pleasant. I went up to Chesnut St looking for new hat. Did not find one. I stoped in Augustines to see Cristy.

FRIDAY, MARCH 4, 1864

Pleasant to day. Lizzie Holms stoped in to see me.

SATURDAY, MARCH 5, 1864

Raining to day. Very busy all day I did not go home. Nellie stoped this morning.

SUNDAY, MARCH 6, 1864

Beautiful morning. I went to church in the morning. Communion in the afternoon I am sorry to say I was not out in the afternoon.

In the morning, Sall and Nellie came up. John and George and I spent the evening. I went down to school. This evening went to Mr. Livelys. First we had a very nice school.

Quite pleasant to day. Meeting this evening at Mrs. Browns. We had quite a sharing. Mr. Benedict died suddenly this afternoon. He was at church on last Sunday morning.

Mrs. Brown is quite sick. Sue and little girl was here to day. It seems an age since Nellie has bin up here on Wednesday evening.

Quite a disagreeable day. I went out shoping and got a pair of tickets for the ministers. I stoped home a while then Nellie and I went down. Nellie didn't go in. I went in and spent quite an agreeable time then I went to Aunt Janes and took tea. Barker cam up home with us.

[No Data]

I went down home a little while. Nellie was not very well. I came home and commenced practicing.

Very pleasant to day. I did not go out. I wrote three letters in the morning. In the afternoon I went to church and heard a very good sermon. In the evening to bible class at Mrs. Riders. Nellie did not go.

Lizzie stoped this evening to go to school. I had to leave her and go to Mr. Livelys. We had quite a number out. Mr Lively was not there. I came out before school was out.

Meeting at Mr. Stewards, great many. We had a real old time prayer meeting. Mrs. Thomas was there.

Very busy all day. I expected Nellie in the evening but as usal she did not come. I received a letter from Martin yesterday.

THURSDAY, MARCH 17, 1864

Lovely day I went up to Harrises. Lizzie was quite sick. I stoped to see Sue a little while. Nellie and (I) went to Mr. Melles then to Mrs. O'Neils and Brown. We spent the evening with Sue. Mrs. Hill gave me the children's pothographs (photographs).

FRIDAY, MARCH 18, 1864

Quite busy to(day). Sue stoped in a few minutes yesterday. I stoped at Mrs. Potters put my name for a situation.

SATURDAY, MARCH 19, 1864

Nellie was out to come up a little while this evening. I went down home and cut out a dress for Mrs. Burton.

SUNDAY, MARCH 20, 1864

Quite raw and cold to day. I went down to church in the morning. Very good sermon. After church we went to see some sick members. Liz and I staid at Mr. Gibbs. In the evening the girls came up. Vincent, John, and Barker—we spent an agreeable time.

MONDAY, MARCH 21, 1864

Quite cold. I went to Mr. Lively as usal then to school. We had quite a nice school. Barker was down. Peterson and Barker came home withe me.

TUESDAY, MARCH 22, 1864

Very chilly and cold. Sue stoped here to day, her and John speaking again. Meeting at our house. We had a very happy meeting. Elijah J. was out. Sarah did not come up.

WEDNESDAY, MARCH 23, 1864

Quite a snowstorm. It snowed all night. Very disagreeable out. Sue ran in a minute. There was a funeral down at the church this afternoon, (a) stranger. I did not go down.

THURSDAY, MARCH 24, 1864

Very fine day. I did not go out until late not being well. I went down to see Mrs. W(illiams) stoped to see Mrs. Brown. Stoped at church. Spent the evening with Nellie.

FRIDAY, MARCH 25, 1864

Sue stoped a little. Nellie was up. I expected Barker but it comenced raining and he did not come. I was quite disappointed but I was so busy sewing I did forget it.

SATURDAY, MARCH 26, 1864

Raining and very disagreeable all day. I finished my dress and taken it home. They scolded me at home for coming out in the storm.

Lovely day, after the rain. This is Easter Sunday, it ought to be solemnly observed. I went to church in the afternoon heard a very good sermon. In the evening I went to Bible class. We had an interesting class. It was at Mr. Livelys.

Quite pleasant to day. I went to Mr. Lively had a very nice lesson then went down to school. Sue and Vincent went to the Fair.

The fair lasted for about a week and was held at the Concert Hall.

I went down home and fitted Sarah's dress then went to meeting. Very nice meeting. After meeting Mary and I went to the Fair. It was very nice.

Quite disagreeable all day. Raining. Barker came up and spent the evening with me. We had quite a nice little chat. Nellie and Beck, Cristy stoped on their way to the Fair.

Very dull to day. I went down to Mr. Livelys had my lesson in the afternoon. I went home and sewed. Nellie came for me to go out. She bout her dress and we paid tree (three) visits in the evening. We went to the Fair. I enjoyed myself very much. I had several dress cuts given to me.

April 1864

Nellie was out there tonight. I did not go.

Another rainy Saturday. I have not seen the girls since Thursday. Meale and Nellie stoped for me to go to the Fair. There was two presentations, a chains (chance) to receive waghes (wages).

Rather cloudy and damp. I went to church. Heard a very good exortation from one of the gentlemen at the college. We went to (Mother) Bethel after church. Nellie was not out in the evening. Sue and Nellie John and Vincent and Barker come up. We spent an agreeable evening. Barker goes away to day.

Cloudy to day. I went to Mr. Livelys and taken my lesson then went down to school. He was not there. Vincent was not there. We had quite a full school.

TUESDAY, APRIL 5, 1864

Very stormy to day. It has bin raining, cloudy and storming. Mrs. Beck led for us this morning (?). Quite a sorrowful time. The rain prevented me from going to meeting.

WEDNESDAY, APRIL 6, 1864

Lovely day. I have bin quite busy all day as usal. In the afternoon I went out on an errand stoped home a minute. Found a letter there from Mary Williams with her potograph (photograph) enclosed. It was quite a joyful surprise.

THURSDAY, APRIL 7, 1864

Beautiful morning. I went down to Mr. Livelys but did not take my lesson. My finger was too sore. Mr. Lively advised me not to. I went around to see Mrs. Bridyal and stoped at Aunt Janes. Sue and (I) went out shoping. Mary H and I went to see the Fair. Mr. Farbeaux, he was hurt by the explosion on Wenesday. He looks very badly.

The boiler exploded at the offices of Merrick & Sons, located on Foundry between Fourth and Fifth Streets. In addition to being an elder at First African, Jacob Farbeaux worked at Merrick as a messenger.

FRIDAY, APRIL 8, 1864

It has bin a very fine day to day. I have not bin out. Sarah sent me word yesterday that Charles Seymour was dead. It does seem that death is in the land both among young and old.

SATURDAY, APRIL 9, 1864

Very dull this morning. It commenced raining before dark. I did not get home tonight.

SUNDAY, APRIL 10, 1864

Quite a rainy morning. I did not go to church in the morning. I went out in the evening. Nellie was not out. Her finger is still quite bad. Bible class at Mrs. Williams. Very few out.

MONDAY, APRIL 11, 1864

Beautiful day I went to see Cristy. He was hurried to day. I went down to Mr. Livelys then to school. We had collected $30 towards paying the debt on the organ.

Thirty dollars is equivalent to $555 in today's market.

TUESDAY, APRIL 12, 1864

Meeting at Mrs. Chases. Sunrise was there and spoke beautiful. We had a very good meeting. Mrs. Brown is still very ill.

WEDNESDAY, APRIL 13, 1864

An otherwise rainy day, I have bin busy as usal. Nellie did not get up. The (Camp William Penn) soldiers were to parade to day but was posphoned on account of the rain.

THURSDAY, APRIL 14, 1864

Quite an Aprile day. I went down to Mr. Livelys as usal. The soldier parade to day, I saw them. Nellie, Lizzie, and I went down to Eighth and Lombard and saw them in their glory. It seemed to be a free day.

FRIDAY, APRIL 15, 1864

Beautiful morning I went out on errand. Stoped at Lizs and Bustills. I had quite a prominade.

SATURDAY, APRIL 16, 1864

Clear for the first time in three weeks but commenced to rain before night. I went and left my bonnets. Stoped home and Ellen Kate and Sue were here.

SUNDAY APRIL 17, 1864

Lovely morning I went to church. Mr. Sunrise preached for us. He gave us the plain doctrine in the evening. Sue came up. Nellie did not come. Vincent and John came up late.

MONDAY APRIL 18, 1864

Beautiful day, quite like spring. Tomorrow the wedding is expected. I went down to Mr. Livelys had a very good lesson then went down to school. I had to open school and light up (the fires).

TUESDAY, APRIL 19, 1864

Another beautiful day. Sue was here, she was not down to school. Last night meeting at Mr. Wells very good meeting. Poor Nellie had to go home. Her finger pained her so I went up to the (Hestonville) Depot but was to late. The folks had commenced. I was so disappointed. They are stoping at Hardings.

WEDNESDAY, APRIL 20, 1864

Nellie was up this evening, She has not bin up for some time but her finger is better.

THURSDAY, APRIL 21, 1864

Lovely day. I went down to Mr. Livelys had a nice lesson. In the afternoon I went up and sit for some potographs (photographs) then went down to call on the girls. They were gone out. Went back home and found them there. I went with them to pay off some bills. I taken tea with them and spent the evening withe them. We had a grand time. Nellie and Sue did not like it.

FRIDAY, APRIL 22, 1864

I went up to the Depot yesterday but they did not go until half past 10 at night. Nellie received some hansome presents. They all looked lovely.

SATURDAY, APRIL 23, 1864

Nellie was up this evening. I got a pair of garters.

A garter was an elasticized band either worn around the leg to hold up a stocking or sock or on the arm to keep the sleeve rolled up.

This a lovely Sabboth morning. I would like to go to church this morning. I went in the afternoon, Sunrise spoke for us. Bible class at Mrs. Hills. I heard some very bad news to day.

Yesterday I wrote to Mary Williams. I went for my potographs (photographs). They were not very good. I sent one to Mary Williams. Gave one to Mrs. Hill. I went to Mr. Livelys as usal then to school. We had a very nice school meeting at Mr. Whites.

Very few out. Lizzie gave me one of his pictures to day. My album is almost full.

Since Emilie uses the word "his," she may have been talking about Lizzie giving her a picture of her son or she may have been referring to one of David's pictures. (He was a well-known painter.)

Rainy day. Busy as usal, Sue was here but I did not see her. Nellie come up and spent the evening with me. She is trying to sew withe her hand. I am so busy I cou(ld) not help her.

Fine day I went up to Harrises. Stoped at hotels I heard of a situation to go to Germantown for the summer. Nellie and I were out shoping. I spent the evening with Mary and Nellie. Meal was there. Sue was not down. I have not seen her since Monday.

Home all day. Meal promised to come over tonight but did not.

Lovely day I went out to Germantown to Mrs. Wister and engaged to go to her the first of June. I did not get home to, is the last of Aprile.

May 1864

Rather cloudy this morning. I went to church we had a stranger to speak for us. After church, we went to Bethel. Sue and Nellie and John and George were up in the evening.

Beautiful day. Busy as usual on Mondays. In the evening I went to Mr. Livelys. I did not know my lesson very well. I went down to school, had a very nice lesson. Vincent was not there, it being the first Monday in the month.

TUESDAY, MAY 3, 1864

Quite warm to day. I went down home and received my circular for the exsamination. Meeting at Mrs. Millers, few out.

WEDNESDAY, MAY 4, 1864

Another bright day. Mrs. Wister called to see Mrs. Powell to day. I have promised to go out on the 7th of June. I did not get to the exsamination to at all. Nellie went. It was very interesting. Sue was here last night and Vincent.

THURSDAY, MAY 5, 1864

To day is quite like summer. I went down to Mr. Livelys but my mind was at the Sansom St. Hall, I wanted to greet the alumni. Sue and I went out shoping. We bought our bonnets in the evening. We all went to the school exercise at Concert Hall. It was grand. Vincent came home with us. Nellie was up a little while. She is still thinking about Egerton.

> *The Alumni Association of the Institute for Colored Youth held a celebration at the Sansom Street Hall at 716–718 Lombard Street for the class of 1864.*

FRIDAY, MAY 6, 1864

Nellie and Sue were both here this morning. In the evening I went down home found Mary Williams there.

SATURDAY, MAY 7, 1864

I went for my bonnet, it is beautiful.

SUNDAY, MAY 8, 1864

It is a lovely morning. I Iow would I like to go to church morning service, is the last part of the day. I spent part of the morning in reading and writing. Bible class closed this evening at Mrs. Hawkinses. Very few out.

MONDAY, MAY 9, 1864

Very fine day but very warm. I went down to Mr. Livelys. Had a nice lesson then went down to the school. Very few out. I hear the girls are losing their interest in the school. We had one name to report, Mr. Sayers.

TUESDAY, MAY 10, 1864

Another warm day. Very busy. Sue was here a little while in the evening. I went down home. Stoped at Nellies. She was not home. I did not get to the meeting at Aunt Marys. Nellie was not there. Very good meeting.

> *The Twelfth Annual Commencement Activities of the Institute for Colored Youth were held at the Concert Hall. Octavius V. Catto, valedictorian of the class of 1858, gave the commencement address.*

Pleasant to day. Miss Williams and Mr. and Miss (Hiram) Fry called on me this morning. Nellie did not come as I expected this evening. Miss (Elizabeth Taylor) Greenfield concert comes off tonight.

Although Elizabeth Taylor Greenfield, the "Black Swan," had been born enslaved, she was later freed and had gone on to become an internationally renowned opera singer. She had an astonishing range and had an active singing career in England and America.

Quite cloudy. I went down to Mr. Livelys. He was not home. Consequently I lost another lesson. I have not bin well all day. I went home and put away some of my things. In the evening, I went down to Bustills.

I spent the evening with Nellie. Sue was there. We all went to the ice cream soloon. Quite a dull day. It commenced raining about evening. I have not bin out to day. I received a very interesting letter from Alfred Thursday. I sent one to Sister on Wednesday.

Very showery to day. I was out in the afternoon. In the evening, I went down home found a letter there from Mary Williams.

Quite an April day. It has bin showering every little while. I went to church in the morning. We had a very good sermon but I did not enjoy it much as I had the toothach. The girls came up. There was quite a growing riot last night. The boyes was in it, John and Vincent.

The riot took place on Seventh and Little Pine Streets and involved both men and women.

I have not bin here all day. I went down to Mr. Livelys but did not go to school. My tooth would not let me.

I suffered very much last night with my face. I have not bin able to (do) anything. Nellie come before meeting. I was so sorry I could not go.

My face is better to day. Lovely morning but rainy afternoon. Nellie came up and spent a little while withe me.

THURSDAY, MAY 19, 1864

Pleasant, I went down (to) Mr. Lively but did not take a lesson. I went down home in the afternoon and staid there until I went to the concert. The concert was spelendid (splendid). The children all sang well. After the concert, we all, about 8 in number, went to the ice cream soloon through Mr. Harrises kindness. Mr. Harris called here for me to go to the concert but I was afraid of taken cold.

The concert that Emilie may have been referring to actually happened on May 17 at the National Hall. The pupils of Lombard Street Public School (Colored) performed, and the proceeds were set to benefit the Sanitary Fair.

FRIDAY, MAY 20, 1864

Butiful morning. My tormentors have come. The worms, I think, three on me this morning.

Emilie was probably suffering from hookworm disease, a skin condition characterized by skin lesions that look like worms under the skin.

SATURDAY, MAY 21, 1864

Nellie was up this evening I did not go out.

SUNDAY, MAY 22, 1864

Lovely morning. I did not go to church as I would liked to this morning. I went to church in the afternoon, Dr. (John Sella) Martin preached. He spoke beautiful but most to lenthy in the evening. Nellie and I went to the Central (Lombard Street Central Presbyterian Church), heard a very good sermon.

Reverend Dr. John Sella Martin was a black Presbyterian minister. Stephen Gloucester founded the Lombard Street Central Presbyterian Church in 1842.

MONDAY, MAY 23, 1864

Fine day. Nellie and Sue were bothe here. I went down to Mr. Livelys had quite a nice lesson then went down to school. We settled the business concerning the organ.

TUESDAY, MAY 24, 1864

Clear, very busy all day. Sue was (up) a little while in the evening. I went home before meeting I heard some very distressing news. Poor Sony Taylor died on Thursday, last 19th. Lizzie is quite (quiet) from shock.

WEDNESDAY, MAY 25, 1864

I went to meeting had a very good time met Mary out. Thomas went up home this morning. Nellie was here this afternoon. Johns was here yesterday. Mary and Meal, Maggie, Elijah J., Ellen E., Susy J., George S. were all here, last evening. We spent quite a pleasant time.

THURSDAY, MAY 26, 1864

Very stormy. I have bin keep in by the rain all the afternoon. Evening, I was sadly disappointed I did not stop mourning all the evening.

FRIDAY, MAY 27, 1864

Raining this morning again but it cleare up in the afternoon. I went down home in the evening. Sue and Nellie were up here. They had bin out shopping.

SATURDAY, MAY 28, 1864

Butiful day. I have bin very busy indeed. It my last weke up at Hazards for some time. I went down home found a letter from Porter A, he is in Norfolk, VA.

SUNDAY, MAY 29, 1864

It is a lovely morning. I went to church. We had a stranger to speake for us. He spoke butiful. I realy enjoyed his sermon in the afternoon. Nellie and I went to Johny (John E.) Browns furneal.

According to his death certificate, John E. Brown died of consumption—more commonly known as tuberculosis.

MONDAY, MAY 30, 1864

Lovely day. I have bin quite busy to day getting ready to go away. Mary went home to day. I went up the dock in the evening. I went down to Mr. Livelys as usual then to school.

TUESDAY, MAY 31, 1864

Quite pleasant. Very busy all day. In the evening, we all went to St. Thomas to see Mary Rilly married, then to Mr. Farbeaux to meeting. We had quite a nice meeting.

St. Thomas Protestant Episcopal Church was located at the corner of Adelphia and Fifth.

June 1864

WEDNESDAY, JUNE 1, 1864

To day has bin quite a dull day. We had quite a large fire in our neighborhood. This afternoon. Several houses had their roofes burned off. The fire was below us.

THURSDAY, JUNE 2, 1864

Quite wet. I went down to Mr. Livelys an received my last lesson for the summer. In the evening, I regret to say I went with Vincent to the Odd Fellows anniversary. I shall ever regret it. They turned it into a regular Hall. I have felt very uneasy all morning. Nellie was very very much prepared to my going.

The Grand United Order of Odd Fellows was a nationally recognized black male secret fraternal organization that was founded to provide mutual assistance. Members included Elijah J., David Bustill Bowser (who served as the grandmaster), Dr. James J. Gould Bias, and Vincent.

FRIDAY, JUNE 3, 1864

She (Nellie) is very angry at with me. I went to the lecture last evening. It seemed as if Mr. Gibbs was talking to me in his discours, as usual.

SATURDAY, JUNE 4, 1864

Nellie and I went up to Bayards in the evening.

SUNDAY, JUNE 5, 1864

This is a very solemn day. It is Communion, we have had a very rainy day. Mr. Gibbs baby was Crisenne (Christened) this morning. Lizzie Dolly was down at church.

MONDAY, JUNE 6, 1864

Beautiful morning. I have bin busy getting ready to go to Germantown but it come up with a shower and I did not go out. I went down to school. We had a very nice school.

TUESDAY, JUNE 7, 1864

This morning, Pliny and I started for Germantown. Vincent was at the Cares. I not time barely to speak to him. I arrived safe. It is very pleasant out in Germantown.

Dr. Owen J. Wister was a medical doctor who worked in Germantown and Philadelphia, with his wife, Sarah Butler.

WEDNESDAY, JUNE 8, 1864

Beautiful day. I have keep very busy since I have bin out here. I sent a not(e) to Nellie to day. It is quite lonsome out here. I have plenty time for thought and meditation.

THURSDAY, JUNE 9, 1864

Raining this morning. We have had rain for several Thursdays but it cleard up in the afternoon. I do not have much idle time. Mrs. Wister is shur (sure) to find something for me as soon as I have finished one piece, she has another.

FRIDAY, JUNE 10, 1864

It is a lonely morning. I received a letter from Martin I do not quite like the tenor of it. I also received Mary Jones' photograph. It is like her but I did not recognize it at first.

SATURDAY, JUNE 11, 1864

It has bin very pleasent to day but it did not seem like Saturday. I have only bin out once since I have bin here. I miss going down home.

SUNDAY, JUNE 12, 1864

It is a lovely morning. I did not get to church. I had to stay with the boy. I spent part of the morning in reading Christ's Sermon on the Mountain. In the afternoon, quite unexpectly, Rachel Turner and Pliny come. I was delighted. We went out had a plesant walk in the evening.

Owen Wister Jr. was four-years old.

MONDAY, JUNE 13, 1864

I went to church with Miss Grant, heard a good sermon. I have just answered Alfred's letter.

TUESDAY, JUNE 14, 1864

Very pleasant. Not letter from home yet. My throat has bin sore ever since I have bin out here. I know I would like to go to meeting but I would have to hold meeting to myself.

WEDNESDAY, JUNE 15, 1864

Very warm to day. I have very few idle moments to day. I received a very pleasant letter from Nellie. She telles me Meli Agusters was married on Sunday morning and I believe Mary is to be married tonight.

THURSDAY, JUNE 16, 1864

I received a letter from Mary Williams to day. I sent one to Sarah. I don't have time to be lonsome out here.

FRIDAY, JUNE 17, 1864

Very warm to day. I received a note from Sarah saying Dave was drafted in the country. I answered Nellies note this evening.

SATURDAY, JUNE 18, 1864

I have bin very busy all day and not very well. I went out a little while in the evening. It is very unpleasant to go out. The soldiers are [Emilie stopped writing in the middle of the sentence]

SUNDAY, JUNE 19, 1864

Beautiful morning. I did not get through in time to go to church. Rachel cam up and spent the morning with me. In the afternoon, I went up to see Pliny. She has gone home. I went to church. Heard a good exortation after church, I went to see Miss Ushner.

MONDAY, JUNE 20, 1864

Lovely morning. Rachel bought my guitar out this morning. I hope I will find time to practice. This afternoon I spent over in Wisters with Martin. In the evening, I went down to May Winestrong and had some strawberrys.

TUESDAY, JUNE 21, 1864

I stole a few minutes this morning to practice but had not patience to tune it but in the evening, I went up to Miss Winell.

WEDNESDAY, JUNE 22, 1864

Very warm. I am all most out of patience with my situation. Already it is so confining here. Wednesday and Nellie is not come yet.

THURSDAY, JUNE 23, 1864

Very warm. I have (been) quite busy as usal. I do not think Nellie is coming out. This evening I told Mrs Wister about her table.

FRIDAY, JUNE 24, 1864

This morning, this morning I had a note from Sarah this morning. Estelena was here this afternoon. I went down to the station with her. I had quite a pleasant walk.

SATURDAY, JUNE 25, 1864

Here is I think it warmest day we have had. I went to town with Mrs. Wister to see the Fair. I did not get home. I was delighted with the Fair. It was beautiful.

Although Emilie calls it a "warm" day, the papers note that there was a severe heat wave in effect with temperatures ranging from the mid-90s to the 100s. The Great Central Fair, which opened on June 7 in Logan Square, was the second highest grossing fair in the U.S. after New York—they collected just over $1 million for the Sanitary Commission.

SUNDAY, JUNE 26, 1864

Rather pleasant to day. I did not go to church during the day. I spent the morning in reading and writing. In the afternoon, I went to see Rachel. In the evening, went to church.

MONDAY, JUNE 27, 1864

The evening it was very warm. I enjoyed myself very much. Yesterday I received a letter from Nellie at last saying she could not come out. She expect to go away this week. Consequently, I don't expect to see her.

TUESDAY, JUNE 28, 1864

Very plesant to day. How I wish I could go to meeting this evening. I amuse myself by practicing and reading. If I had not my guitar I think I would be very lonsome.

Congress repealed both the 1793 and the 1850 Fugitive Slave Acts (or Fugitive Slave Laws), which required all free states to return fugitive slaves to their plantation owners. It had placed the onus on the captured black person (enslaved or free) to prove that they were not the legal property of the plantation owner.

WEDNESDAY, JUNE 29, 1864

I am busy through the day and in the evening when it is not too warm. I practice this afternoon for the first. I was out walking in town.

THURSDAY, JUNE 30, 1864

This is the last of June. It has bin quite cloudy all day with a little rain in the afternoon. It commenced pouring. This is my evening but I not make much as of it.

July 1864

FRIDAY, JULY 1, 1864

This is the first very pleasant this morning but we had a certified stom in the afternoon. I enjoy myself in the evenings, reading the Word.

SATURDAY, JULY 2, 1864

Quite cloudy all the morning. I expect to go to town this afternoon. I started for town at 2'o. It comenced rainy just as I got out of the car.

Emilie wrote "car" but she is referring to the streetcar. Since she was inside of the streetcar, she was riding on a designated "colored" car.

SUNDAY, JULY 3, 1864

Lovely day. I went to church in the morning. Hear a good sermon. We stopped at Aunt Janes and to see Rachel. She is quite sick. Vincent even kin (can) come up for 15 m. Stopped in to see Egerton, was there looking like a lost sheep. I started for Germantown about half past 5 in the afternoon.

MONDAY, JULY 4, 1864

I went out with Owen. I felt very lonsome in the evening.

TUESDAY, JULY 5, 1864

Fine day but very warm. Mrs. Wister went to town with Owen. She could not do a better thing. I have bin quite busy all day. How I would like to go meeting very much.

WEDNESDAY, JULY 6, 1864

Quite pleasant this morning but in the afternoon very warm. I did not have much time to practice to day. Very busy. I sent a note to Sarah on Tuesday.

THURSDAY, JULY 7, 1864

Exceedingly warm to day in the afternoon. It commenced raining. Martin was at Tomys on Sunday. He stoped at the house but I did not see him.

FRIDAY, JULY 8, 1864

Very warm. Bin marketing. I had a talk with Mrs. (Wister) about the all absording topic. I wrot to Nellie and Liz to day. I see I will not be able to spend the summer in Germantown.

SATURDAY, JULY 9, 1864

Rather cloudy and warm. We were all called up this morning to receive our ration of sugar. I told Mrs. Wister that I would have a tittle for it. I went down to Maryes to tell Herneil.

SUNDAY, JULY 10, 1864

It is a beautiful morning. I could not go to church in the afternoon. I spent the afternoon in reading. In the evening, I went to church. They had no preaching. After church I went home with Becky Smith. Mr. Johnson was with me.

MONDAY, JULY 11, 1864

Exceedingly warm to day. I was out this afternoon. Stoped to see Miss Whimon. Rachel come and spent the evening with me.

TUESDAY, JULY 12, 1864

Very warm. I have had my first lesson on the sewing machine. Succeeded admirablely. I worked all the afternoon. No word from home this week of yet.

Singer sewing machines were first introduced in 1855 and cost about $50 (which is equivalent to $925). They could be purchased through a hire purchase or installment plan.

WEDNESDAY, JULY 13, 1864

Very pleasant to day. I have bin practicing a little on the machine. No word from Nellie yet. In the evening, Mary M. and I went to see Rachel, spent quite a pleasant time.

THURSDAY, JULY 14, 1864

Quite pleasant. I thought I certainly would get a letter to day but no letter as yet. I am porly looking for Vincent this evening but he did not come.

FRIDAY, JULY 15, 1864

Cool this morning but pleasant. Quite busy all day. I practice a little to day. Rachel was here this afternoon. This evening Becky Smith and Anna come up and spent quite a nice little time.

SATURDAY, JULY 16, 1864

I had a letter from Liz this week. I have bin sick to day. Last night I wrote a letter to Lenox. I was out a few sarcanes (seconds) this afternoon. I received a letter from Sister and a potograph (photograph) from my dear brother (Alfred) in Montreal.

SUNDAY JULY 17, 1864

Beautiful morning. Home as usal but I shall indeavor to improve my time at reading. I have bin quite sick to day. I am sorry I have not bin to church to day.

MONDAY, JULY 18, 1864

To day pleasant this morning. I feel very much as if I would like to head home. Mary went home to day. I received a letter from Nellie to day. At long last, I am not very well pleased with it.

TUESDAY, JULY 19, 1864

I have bin running the (sewing) machine nearly all day. To day is the afternoon, Dan and I went to take a walk. I was very glad after sitting all day.

WEDNESDAY, JULY 20, 1864

Exceedingly warm to day. Busy as usal. I have bin to day with the machine. In the evening, Mary M. and I went to see Becky and we had a lovely time.

THURSDAY, JULY 21, 1864

Plesent to day I wrote to Liz to day. I had plenty of visiters this afternoon. Rachel, Miss Whisom and Miss Wood. I feel very low spirited to night owing to disappointment.

FRIDAY, JULY 22, 1864

Very much like rain to day, wich is very much needed. I went down to Marys this evening. Rachel lives so far that I can not go to see her often.

SATURDAY, JULY 23, 1864

I wrote to Nellie yesterday. I may expect an answer about next week. Not of my many friends have bin out to see me yet. I have bin sick all day.

SUNDAY, JULY 24, 1864

Very pleasant. I went to church this morning. The first Sunday I have really enjoyed since I have bin out here. I heard a beautiful sermon. After church, I went to see Rachel. I wrote to Sister yesterday. Mary come up and spent the evening last evening.

MONDAY, JULY 25, 1864

I received a letter from Nellie to day. It was rather different from the last one. I had nice time practicing in the evening.

TUESDAY, JULY 26, 1864

Quite pleasant to day. I have bin busy as usal. I answered Nellie's letter. This evening Rachel was up. Went to Marys and spent a pleasant time.

WEDNESDAY, JULY 27, 1864

It has began to get warm again. Lizzie's cousin in trouble. I would like to see her. I was out early this evening. Went over to Miss Whismons then to Saumaker's Lane.

THURSDAY, JULY 28, 1864

Exceedingly warm this morning. Sarah Jones was out here but not to see me. Vincent come out this evening. I was pleased to see him. We went over to see Miss Whisom. Liz has gone to see Uncle William.

FRIDAY, JULY 29, 1864

Very warm to day. Quite like August. Anna and her friend were to see me this evening.

Very warm to day. I have bin busy as usal, doing a little of everything and not much of anything. Mary was up this evening.

Lovely morning. I did not go church. Very warm in the evening. I went down to Rachels. We went to the Lutherian Church. After church, we stoped in Marys.

August 1864

Quite sulty. I have had no letter from home since I come out this last time. Mary was up this evening. If (it) was not for her, it would be quite dull.

Very warm with rain, wich is much needed. I received a letter to day from Sue, quite unexpectedly. I spent the evening with Mary.

Pleasant to day. In the afternoon, I went up to see Estelena but she had gone. I went down to Maryes. It commenced raining. I spent the evening with her. She gave me an a excellent tea wich is very rare out here. I answered Mary's letter this evening. I have had not time to write to day.

Very warm to day. The excitement still continues about the rebels. The girls here, down at Shoremakers Lane. We went down to Maryes.

Not quite as warm as yesterday.

I went home in the [evening] Nellie was glad to see me. I went to Bustills.

I feel so happy to be permitted to worship in my own church. Mr. Cristipher spoke in the morning. Mr. Gibbs delivered a powerful sermon in the afternoon. I spent the Sunday very pleasant.

We went out this morning. In the afternoon, Mary and Vincent were their. Martin came out here this afternoon. He met a cold presentation.

I had a letter from Tomy and answered it. I expected Nellie and Barker out last night.

WEDNESDAY, AUGUST 10, 1864

Very rainy all day. I have bin very busy sewing my dress. I thought I could not stand the heat. I did go out until evening. I went over to Mrs. Whimone. I had a pelesent time. I went to Maryes, we went down the Lane.

THURSDAY, AUGUST 11, 1864

Very warm. I did not go out this evening. In the afternoon, I went to take a little walk. I spent part of the evening in practicing. I sent a note to Nellie.

FRIDAY, AUGUST 12, 1864

Not quite as warm to day as it has bin. Busy as usal. In the evening, the girls come up. Mary and I went to walk with them. They are very wild.

SATURDAY, AUGUST 13, 1864

Very salty to day. This almost intolerabel but we must bear it. I have not heard from home. I have not seen Rachel. We had a very heavy shower this evening.

SUNDAY, AUGUST 14, 1864

Lovely morning, after the rains. I did not go to church in the morning. Vincent and Dave did come out this morning, paid me quite a pleasant visit. In the evening, I went to church with Ms Lemmens.

MONDAY, AUGUST 15, 1864

Things glum as usal. Mary was up, she is my only comfort mon out here.

Here Emilie wrote "confort mon," cf. French confort mon, *meaning "my comfort."*

TUESDAY, AUGUST 16, 1864

Quite pleasant to day. To day, I have bin sewing on the machine. It gives me a great deal of trouble. I have bin very busy sewing this evening. I finished my dress body at last.

WEDNESDAY, AUGUST 17, 1864

Quite warm again. I had a letter from Nellie yesterday. Quite a heavy shower, this afternoon. In the evening, we went to see Rachel but she had not got home yet. I left a letter for her.

THURSDAY AUGUST 18, 1864

The girls were over this evening. Mary was up.

FRIDAY, AUGUST 19, 1864

I received a huge letter to day from Alfred. It is almost like a newspaper. He gives me a detail observation of what he is doing while he is away.

SATURDAY, AUGUST 20, 1864

It has bin exceedingly cool to day almost like fall. I have bin sitting this day with my charge [though] I am ready to go home before my time is up.

SUNDAY, AUGUST 21, 1864

Very pleasant this morning. I have bin quite sick all day. I have not bin well enough to go to church. Rachel was here in the morning and Becky and Mary in the evening.

MONDAY, AUGUST 22, 1864

Pleasant. I received a letter from Tomy to day. Elijah J. has not written to me for some time. I attemped to write to Nellie but did not finish.

TUESDAY, AUGUST 23, 1864

Rachel was here this morning bought me a letter from Sue. I do not feel like answering it at present. I surely need he(lp) in finishing Nellie's letter.

WEDNESDAY, AUGUST 24, 1864

This morning Miss Whimon bought me a letter that I auht (ought) to have had weekes ago.

THURSDAY, AUGUST 25, 1864

Quite pleasant. I went down in the Lane this afternoon to see Rochel. In the evening, Mary and (I) went to a Festival. I had a great deal of fun. The country gents were very gallant. The ladies, most of them, were dressed as if for a party. I expected Vincent this evening but he did not come out.

FRIDAY, AUGUST 26, 1864

Pleasant to day, everything goes on pretty much as usal. I feel discontent with myself. I know I do not read my bible or meditate as much as I ought but I am resolved to try to do better.

SATURDAY, AUGUST 27, 1864

I have not heard from Nellie. I expect she thinks she will not write because I am coming in soon, mean thing.

SUNDAY, AUGUST 28, 1864

Very pleesent. This morning I did not go to church. I expected Rachel but she did not come up. I am reading a book called *In More Holy*. Very interesting. I wrote a long letter to Alfred.

MONDAY, AUGUST 29, 1864

This moning commenced to be quite pleasant. To day I received a letter from Elijah J. He heard from Father. I went to church last evening and up to Meals. I made Mary go up with me.

TUESDAY, AUGUST 30, 1864

I have tacked down little pieces in our sewing book for the future.

WEDNESDAY, AUGUST 31, 1864

Lovely day. Rachel and I decided to go out together to the shore. Vincent up to take me walking in the evening.

September 1864

THURSDAY, SEPTEMBER 1, 1864

Very pleasant. Vincent came out to see me quite unexpected. I expected Elijah J. but he not get here.

FRIDAY, SEPTEMBER 2, 1864

Quite cool this morning. I had a very sad letter from Sister to day. It made me feel very badly. Father is quite feeble. I finished writing to Nellie this evening.

SATURDAY, SEPTEMBER 3, 1864

Cloudy to day. I went to the city this afternoon. I stoped at Estelena. Stoped at the shoes makers and at Rachels. It commenced raining.

SUNDAY, SEPTEMBER 4, 1864

Very rainy morning. I was quite disappointed. I did not get to church in the morning. I(t) rained in the afternoon but I went to church. We only had two tables. Very good exortation. I spent the evening, very pleasant.

MONDAY, SEPTEMBER 5, 1864

I come out in the strom all day and all the evening. I received a letter from Elijah J. saying he would be out.

TUESDAY, SEPTEMBER 6, 1864

Raining still. Mary did not come up this evening. I expect Nellie, Foster and Vincent out on Thursday.

WEDNESDAY, SEPTEMBER 7, 1864

Quite pleasant. I went up to the Depot, met Estelena then went to see Caroline. She is sinking very fast, I think. I spent the evening with Mary. Rachel goes away on Saturday.

THURSDAY, SEPTEMBER 8, 1864

Rather cloudy. Nellie came out but my Sister did not. Vincent came. We spent quite a pleasant evening.

FRIDAY, SEPTEMBER 9, 1864

Quite like fall to day. I feel very low spirited and worried. I went up town this evening. Very sad with all the time out here. I had very little recreation out here.

SATURDAY, SEPTEMBER 10, 1864

Quite warm again. I had a letter from Tomy on Thursday. This afternoon, Owen and I taken a very long walk.

SUNDAY, SEPTEMBER 11, 1864

Rainy day but not quite as hard as last Sunday. I went to church in the morning, herd a good sermon.

MONDAY, SEPTEMBER 12, 1864

Clear morning. School commences this evening. I would like to be in town. I was down to Maryes this afternoon.

The 1864–65 academic year for the institute opened with 114 students, between the high school and the preparatory school

TUESDAY, SEPTEMBER 13, 1864

Owen an I were out for a walk. I wrote to Sister and to Father on Sunday and to Tomy. I very ansious about Father. I have not had an answer from either of my letters.

WEDNESDAY, SEPTEMBER 14, 1864

I very much disappointed to day. Nellie sent me a note saying Mary was out with Foster. I expected to go in the evening to a party, got all ready and was disappointed.

THURSDAY, SEPTEMBER 15, 1864

Lovey day to day. Vincent come in the evening. He was not well.

FRIDAY, SEPTEMBER 16, 1864

Foster paid me quite a pleasant visit on Wednesday evening. I have bin quite industrious to day and evening. Mary did not come up.

SATURDAY, SEPTEMBER 17, 1864

Very pleasant morning. I have felt very happy all morning. I hope I am not going to hear any bad news.

SUNDAY, SEPTEMBER 18, 1864

Very pleasant. I was home all day. In the evening, I went to see Caroline then went to church. I heard a very good sermon.

MONDAY, SEPTEMBER 19, 1864

Lovely morning. I am waiting patiently for my parcel come from Germantown. In the evening, Mary and I went to Bobbyes. Spent quite a pleasant time. I feel gay and happy.

TUESDAY, SEPTEMBER 20, 1864

I expecte to go home to day. No girls come but I taken French leacn [lessons]. I went to meeting, enjoyed the meeting very much.

WEDNESDAY, SEPTEMBER 21, 1864

I have bin very busy puting away my clothes. In the afternoon, I went to help make mourning for the poor litte orphan. In the evening, Mr. Foster taken Nellie and I to the festival.

THURSDAY, SEPTEMBER 22, 1864

Mr. (Samuel) Steward was buried to day. He was taken to the church. Mr. Gibbs spoke very well.

Samuel Steward died on September 18 of hemorrhaging lungs.

FRIDAY, SEPTEMBER 23, 1864

Have bin very busy all day getting ready to go to see Father. In the evening, I went to meeting. Very few out. Some missionary from Africa spoke. Foster was there, he is quite a beau.

SATURDAY, SEPTEMBER 24, 1864

Busy as usal. I will not get off to day. Quite excitement this afternoon. Mr. (Alfred B.) Green was molested and defended himself by shooting one of his asalasints. He was arreseted. Nellie and I had a talk with Sue.

Alfred B. Green was a quartermaster at Camp William Penn and member of the Banneker Institute. He was attacked by three men and fired his gun twice, hitting one of them in the leg.

SUNDAY, SEPTEMBER 25, 1864

Quite cool this morning but pleasant. I went to church, hearid very good sermon. Stoped at Aunt Janes, Vincent was with us. Church in the afternoon. In the evening, we were disappointed. Vincent did not come and Foster went to church. Vincent come late.

MONDAY, SEPTEMBER 26, 1864

Busy washing so I went out in the afternoon. Stoped at Mr. Livelys and Mrs (Mary) Proyers. Vincent was down to tell me Caroline (Miller) was dead. He was down in the evening, brought me som cream. He was very affectionate.

Caroline Miller died of tuberculosis.

TUESDAY, SEPTEMBER 27, 1864

Lovely day. I started for Harrisburg at half past. I had a very tiresom journey. I rived about 8'o, found all well. Father was delighted to see me.

WEDNESDAY, SEPTEMBER 28, 1864

Rainy day. I am in for the day. I expect Father has gone to the Depot. I went around to Mary Williams and to Chesters this evening.

THURSDAY, SEPTEMBER 29, 1864

It is very dull up here. Raining again this morning but clear in the afternoon. I was out a little whil. Alex was to come around but he did not come.

FRIDAY, SEPTEMBER 30, 1864

It rained very hard last night. Very cloudy this morning. I sent a letter home yesterday I went down to see Mrs. Burke and stoped at Chesters, took tea. After tea, we went to Spences then to the Celler.

October 1864

SATURDAY, OCTOBER 1, 1864

It is the first of Oct. Very raw and cold. I have bin hom all day, not one of the girls have bin to see me but I enjoy father's society very much. I read to him and talk to him, makes the time pass.

Approximately 150 black men, including Emilie's pastor, Reverend Gibbs, gathered at the Wesleyan Methodist Church in Syracuse, New York, at the Colored People's Convention to discuss both the current and the future state of the race and to establish an agreed-upon program of action. They formed the National Equal Rights League and elected Frederick Douglass as chairman and John Mercer Langston, Esq., as president. As with most events during this time, history was being made as this was the first time that an organization was formed to focus solely on "promoting black equality." Biddle and Dubin, Tasting Freedom, *314.*

SUNDAY, OCTOBER 2, 1864

Rather dull day. I did not go out to church untill evening. Father went to church. I was so pleased to see him there.

MONDAY, OCTOBER 3, 1864

This morning, I spent over with Mary and Mr. F(oster). In the afternoon, Nellie and (I) went out, Hall was with us. In the evening, I went out to Maryes.

TUESDAY, OCTOBER 4, 1864

Cloudy but not raining. I went to see Meal off. Poor Meal, I was up there with her. Spent the day and evening out.

WEDNESDAY, OCTOBER 5, 1864

Still cloudy. I received a letter from Nellie yesterday saying she was going away on Thursday. She wants me to come home but I shant until Saturday, if not before.

THURSDAY, OCTOBER 6, 1864

In house all the morning. In the afternoon, I went up to Mrs. Sonders spent quite a pleasant time. I had Tom, gentlemen, to gallant me home. Little Alex was by. Warm gallant.

Gallant is said of a man or his behavior and means giving special attention and respect to women.

FRIDAY, OCTOBER 7, 1864

Clear, the first clear morning since I have bin here. Hale, Chester and I were out in afternoon after, I went to Spencers. Spent quite a pleasant time.

SATURDAY, OCTOBER 8, 1864

Lovely day. I stoped at Mrs. Harris and Chesters. I started for home about 20 to 1. Got there at 6 in the evening. We all went to see the torch light procession.

The national Union Party (the party of Lincoln and Johnson) held a rally at Independence Square.

SUNDAY, OCTOBER 9, 1864

Quite pleasant but very windy. I did not go to church in the morning. In the afternoon, Mr. Gibbs preached a very good sermon. I spent the evening at home. Vincent come up.

MONDAY, OCTOBER 10, 1864

Fine day. I have bin sewing away. To day I was to see Hazards, I expect to go there on Thursday. I went down to school. Very few out. Not more than a half dozen.

TUESDAY, OCTOBER 11, 1864

Quite pleasant. I received a letter from Ellen. This morning I answered it. I wrote to Sister. I have commenced my winter occupation. I did not go to meeting. I feel so very lonsome without Nellie. If she stayes all winter, I don't know what I shall do.

WEDNESDAY, OCTOBER 12, 1864

Raining all day. Clear in the evening.

THURSDAY, OCTOBER 13, 1864

Very pleasant. I went down to Mr. Livelys this morning. I did not get out until quite late in the evening. Lizzie and I went to a political meeting. It was very interesting.

FRIDAY, OCTOBER 14, 1864

Home as usal. On eight days, no word of Nellies coming.

SATURDAY, OCTOBER 15, 1864

I stoped home this evening, found Mr. Craige there. It seemed very strange not to stop (at) Blacks.

SUNDAY, OCTOBER 16, 1864

Very fine day. I went to church in the morning. Heard an excellent sermon. Stoped several places then went home for the rest of the day.

MONDAY, OCTOBER 17, 1864

Liz taken tea with me. Vincent spent the evening. He is as indefinite as ever. I went to Mr. Livelys. I was quite disappointed in my lesson. We had quite an interesting school.

TUESDAY, OCTOBER 18, 1864

Pleasant to day. Another meeting on hand tonight. I was disappointed. I did not get to prayer meeting but I had an opportunity to practice a little self denial. I need it very much. I huried home.

WEDNESDAY, OCTOBER 19, 1864

Crosed (off) a good deal to day. I feel almost sick. I expected the girls up this evening but they did not come.

THURSDAY, OCTOBER 20, 1864

I went to Mr. Livelys this morning. Home most of the afternoon. In the evening, I went to the concert, had to march.

FRIDAY, OCTOBER 21, 1864

I had a letter from Nellie on Thursday. Nann and Mrs. Hazard were in here a [Emilie stopped writing in the middle of the sentence]

SATURDAY, OCTOBER 22, 1864

Quite stormy all day. I stoped home in the morning. Nann did not get off. Liz Williams come with (while) I was there. She is looking very well.

SUNDAY, OCTOBER 23, 1864

Rather cloudy this morning. I did not go to church this morning. Nann and I went in the afternoon and in the evening, we went to Central (Lombard Street Central Presbyterian Church). Vincent went with us.

MONDAY, OCTOBER 24, 1864

Fine day. I have bin busy as usal. In the evening, I went to Mr. Livelys then to school. Oh how I miss Nellie. I feel lost and unhappy without her.

TUESDAY, OCTOBER 25, 1864

Clear. I must realy write to Nellie this evening. She will think all kinds of things. Meeting at our house. Pretty good meeting. Vincent come just as it was out. After meeting, I wrote a long letter to Nellie.

WEDNESDAY, OCTOBER 26, 1864

How I wish I could feel satisfied about some certian (certain) things. I am living in an uncertian (uncertain) state from time to time. I do not care to go out. I feel so lost.

THURSDAY, OCTOBER 27, 1864

I went to Mr. Livelys this morning. I am always glad when my lesson is done on Thursdays. I stoped at Hecs and Aunt Janes and at Bustils. Spent a dull evening at home. Vincent came about.

FRIDAY, OCTOBER 28, 1864

I come up here. I have bin exceedingly busy this evening fixing up our part of the house. I expected Kate Litle might be up here but she did not come.

SATURDAY, OCTOBER 29, 1864

I I did not get home as I usally do. I was to busy and the streets were to rowdy. The Democrats had the rowdy prossion (procession).

Like the Republicans, the Democrats typically held torchlight rallies to support their candidates. This event did indeed become "rowdy" as later reports showed that some- one was attacked after the procession. Daily Age, *November 19, 1864.*

SUNDAY, OCTOBER 30, 1864

Lovely morning. I went to church. Herd a very good sermon. I have a very happy feeling. I cant account for it. After church, Vincent and I stoped at Aunt Janes. Vincent come up in the evening.

MONDAY, OCTOBER 31, 1864

Quite cold to day. Nothing of intress occurd to day. In the evening, I went to Mr. Livelys then to school. We had a nice school, several strangers down.

November 1864

TUESDAY, NOVEMBER 1, 1864

To day is a holiday with most everyone. The colord soldiers are in and everything seems cheriful. I went to meeting. Quite a nice little meeting. After meeting, we went to see the Illumination at headquarters.

Less than a month after the National Equal Rights League was formed, local branch-es opened in both Philadelphia and Tennessee. In Philadelphia, "the elite of the elite" met and founded the Pennsylvania State Equal Rights League. Octavius Catto was elected as the secretary of the Philadelphia branch. In the audience, giving support and guidance was national president John Mercer Langston. Maryland formally adopted a new constitution that outlawed slavery in the state.

WEDNESDAY, NOVEMBER 2, 1864

I have had no letter from Nellie this week. She is never in a hurry to answer my letter.

THURSDAY, NOVEMBER 3, 1864

Cloudy I went as usal to Mr. Livelys. I cant see improvement. He thinks I do. Stoped in Bustills, intended (on) spending the evening (but) Meal was at our house. Vincent come for me. He comes as regular as can be. I dont see what he means, I havent (the) courage to sole [soil or console?] him.

FRIDAY, NOVEMBER 4, 1864

I received a letter from Tomy yesterday. He did not say anything about coming home.

SATURDAY, NOVEMBER 5, 1864

Here is the last of the weeke and no letter from Nellie. I think she has set me down as one of the small things, in her opinion. If I do not hear from her soon I shall act accordingly.

SUNDAY, NOVEMBER 6, 1864

Beutiful day. I was not out in the morning but I tried to spend my time profitable. In the afternoon, I went to church. Sunrise preached for us. In the evening, I stayed at home. Vincent come up, very dis(l)oyal.

I went to Mr. Livelys then to the meeting. We had no school. We had quite a nice time at the meeting. Vincent was there visiting again to day.

To day is the great election. I think Lincoln will gain the day. I did not go to meeting for fear something might happen. Ellen come home yesterday morning, did not come up to the National Hall this evening. I fear I will fight to hold that against her. I was delighted to see her, went to class. She spent the evening with me.

Abraham Lincoln did indeed gain the day and was reelected as president, defeating George B. McClellan by winning 212 of the 233 electoral votes, receiving 55 percent of the popular vote, and carrying twenty-two states.

It has bin a very spring week. I will not not get out to day.

I went down to Mr. Livelys. He did not give a nice lesson. Nellie was up. Vincent come up, he did not expect to see Nellie up here. I want to see how he will act now. Nellie has come home. Poor Egerton, I know he feels lost.

Nellie and I had a real triumph to day. I went to the lecture in the evening. It was very interesting.

Very busy all (day). I did not get home this evening.

Bitter cold day. I went to church in the morning. Heard a very good sermon. Stop(ed) at Mr. Gibbs after church. Spent the afternoon at home. Nellie come up. Vincent did not come up untill late.

Quite wintery. I went to Mr. Livelys then to school. Had pretty good school. Peterson come part the way home with me. Vincent will not be left behind.

Very wet and disagreeable. I went to meeting. Very few out, I am sorry to have to say. Vincent ever constant.

Dull and rainy. I have not bin out. I have bin quite industryes (industrious) this evening. I have sewed a great deal and and practiced quite much. Nellie was up.

THURSDAY, NOVEMBER 17, 1864

Very damp and disagreable to me. Had to go in town but the weather prevented. I spent quite an agreeable evening at home sewing carpet. Vincent there as usal.

FRIDAY, NOVEMBER 18, 1864

Raining all day, very fast. I left Vincent rather abruptly last night. It was quite late almost 12 [dego].

Here Emilie may have written "dego," cf. French degout, *meaning "disgust" or "disgustedly."*

SATURDAY, NOVEMBER 19, 1864

Dull this morning. Clear in the afternoon. I stoped home, a letter was awaiting from Tomy.

SUNDAY, NOVEMBER 20, 1864

Quite dull. I went to church in the afternoon. It rand (rained) quite hard towards evening. I spent the evening with Nellie.

MONDAY, NOVEMBER 21, 1864

Raining all day. Elijah J. came in here quite sick this afternoon. Frightend me much. He had not gone longe when Alfred come looking like a salor (sailor) indeed.

TUESDAY, NOVEMBER 22, 1864

I went down to Mr. Livelys. It raind very hard indeed then to school. I got very wet, cought a bad cold. Meeting at Mrs. Redds, I did not go. I was not well.

The Philadelphia Inquirer *reported that the rain was so heavy that it caused the Schuylkill River to rise.*

WEDNESDAY, NOVEMBER 23, 1864

Quite sick all day but had to iron wich did not improve my health. Barker come up and spent quite a pleasant evening with me. Nellie did not come.

Elijah J. was drafted into service and served as a private in the Sixth Regiment Company A of the U.S. Colored Troops. He was mustered out of service on September 20, 1865

THURSDAY, NOVEMBER 24, 1864

Quite cold to day. Always cold on Thanksgiving Day. I went to church in the afternoon, was disappointed. Mr Gibbs was not out. He was sick. Quite a number out. In the evening, we went to Mr. Lively's concert. Vincent taken me, Barker (and) Nellie. After the concert, we went to Lyonss. Next, Mrs. Nelson there we played the agreeable game.

FRIDAY, NOVEMBER 25, 1864

[No Data]

SATURDAY, NOVEMBER 26, 1864

Rainy day again. Alfred was up this afternoon. In the evening, I was quite surprised to see Vincent. He come up and spent the evening.

SUNDAY, NOVEMBER 27, 1864

Lovely morning. I went to church. A stranger from the Institute spoke for us. I was not very well. I did not get opportunity to hear much. Nellie come up early. We had quite a old time chat about matters and things.

MONDAY, NOVEMBER 28, 1864

Clear. I went to Mr. Livelys taken my lesson. Went to school then to Whites to a meeting. Very interesting meeting at Mrs. Whites. Quite a number out but I am sorry to say the meeting seemed quite cold and spiritless. Nellie did not go. Vincent was about.

TUESDAY, NOVEMBER 29, 1864

Quite warm. Busy as usal. Alfred come up and stayed a little while. I sent a letter to Tom on Sunday. Nellie did not come up this evening.

WEDNESDAY, NOVEMBER 30, 1864

The first day of snow. Winter, so called.

December 1864

THURSDAY, DECEMBER 1, 1864

Very pleasant. Nellie and I went out shoping. I succeeding in purching my dress. Spent part of the evening home alone then went down to Aunt Janes.

FRIDAY, DECEMBER 2, 1864

Went down to Aunt Janes. Alfred come up for me to go to the concert but I could not go. Very disagreeable out.

SATURDAY, DECEMBER 3, 1864

Very damp but not raining. I went home and stoped at Nellies. Barker was there.

SUNDAY, DECEMBER 4, 1864

Cold. I did not go out in the morning. Communion in the afternoon. Very happy meeting. We had several tables after church. We stoped at Aunt Janes in the evening and went to St. Thomases. Heard the great Mr. Cooper.

MONDAY, DECEMBER 5, 1864

Quite cold. I went to Mr. Livelys then to school. We had a very good school. After school, we appointed a committee to solicit donations.

TUESDAY, DECEMBER 6, 1864

Cold. I was down home a few minutes this morning. Meeting at Mrs. Smiths. More out than usaly come out. Vincent was about as usal. We went around to Shilohs Fair after meeting.

WEDNESDAY, DECEMBER 7, 1864

Very stormy. Vincent gave me coupel of tickets, one for Nellie. We went to the celebration. It certainly was a very grand afair. The singing and speaking was excellent.

The event was held at the National Hall on Market Street to celebrate the emancipation of Maryland. Reverend Gibbs was one of the main speakers.

THURSDAY, DECEMBER 8, 1864

Quite cold and windy. I went down to Mr. Livelys but he was so fatigued he could not give me a lesson. I went down to Mrs. Offerts and Burley and Le Counts. I come home about eight.

FRIDAY, DECEMBER 9, 1864

I only was out in the afternoon. Yesterday, Vincent spent the evening with me. He loves vists reagular but there is no understanding between us. Alfred was up this afternoon.

SATURDAY, DECEMBER 10, 1864

We had quite a snowstorm last night but it soon melts when when the sun makes his appearance. Nellie was up here this evening. It was disagreeable, I did not go down.

SUNDAY, DECEMBER 11, 1864

Very stormy. I did not go to church in the morning not at all usual thing for me. Ellen did not come up. Vincent come, spent the evening.

MONDAY, DECEMBER 12, 1864

Very cold but clear I went to Mr. Livelys. He was not home. He did not com to school. We had a sociable school.

TUESDAY, DECEMBER 13, 1864

Cloudy. Ellen come up and spent the day. Liz stoped before meeting. We all went together. Had a very good meeting. Quite a number out.

The subcommittee of the Ladies' Union Association met at the Masonic Hall to collect donations to send to Charleston, South Carolina. Although it appears as if Emilie recorded this on the 13th, the meeting actually happened on the 12th.

WEDNESDAY, DECEMBER 14, 1864

Home all day. No one come up. Very busy with my dress. Nellie did not come up.

THURSDAY, DECEMBER 15, 1864

I went down Livelys as usal this morning. Quite cold in the afternoon. Nellie and I went shoping. Stoped at Bustills. Spent the evening home.

FRIDAY, DECEMBER 16, 1864

[No Data]

SATURDAY, DECEMBER 17, 1864

[No Data]

SUNDAY, DECEMBER 18, 1864

Quite cold I was at church in the afternoon. It commenced raining right after church. I did not go to church in the evening. My throat being sore.

MONDAY, DECEMBER 19, 1864

Quite a rainy day. My throat very sore. I did not out to Mr. Livelys or to school. Quite a disappointment, Vincent stoped after school, gave me a ticket.

TUESDAY, DECEMBER 20, 1864

Quite pleasant. Was at meeting at Aunt Nancys. Excellent meeting, everyone seemed in the right spirit. After meeting, I went to the Fair. Very nice.

The fair seems to have lasted for two weeks, until December 29. The Ladies' Sanitary Commission raised over $1,200 (equivalent to $22,200) to assist the black soldiers.

WEDNESDAY, DECEMBER 21, 1864

Very disagreeable to day. Quite a snowstorm, I have not bin out. I saw several friends from Harrisburg promentomony (promenading), then I was (with) Miss. Spence.

THURSDAY, DECEMBER 22, 1864

Bitter cold day. I was not very well but I went down to Mr. Gibbs in the morning. In the afternoon, I went to Bustills and several other places. Barker was along with me.

FRIDAY, DECEMBER 23, 1864

Had a great deal of fun in the evening. We went to the Fair. I have bin busy all day trying to finish my dress. Vincent was up. I did not expect him after treating him so badly.

SATURDAY, DECEMBER 24, 1864

Very busy all day. I went out about 8. Went down home then to the Fair. I had an eggnauh, drinking in the evening. We had quite a nice time.

SUNDAY, DECEMBER 25, 1864

Christmas has come at last. Home in the morning. In the afternoon I went to church, herd a very good sermon. In the evening, we had several friends. We spent quite a pleasant time.

MONDAY, DECEMBER 26, 1864

Very stormy, raining all day. I went out in the afternoon but did not get far. Vincent was about as usal. We went down to school but did not stay. Nellie did not go out. She had the sore throat.

TUESDAY, DECEMBER 27, 1864

The last Tuesday in the year. I was not well but I felt it to be my duty to go to meeting. We had quite a pleasant meeting, few out.

WEDNESDAY, DECEMBER 28, 1864

Very damp. Vincent called for me to go to the concert. Alfred was up to see me. Nellie did not come this evening.

THURSDAY, DECEMBER 29, 1864

Very fine day. I attended to considerable business. In the afternoon, Vinc(ent), Nellie, and (I) went to call on Mr. Lively, then to the lecture, then to the Fair.

FRIDAY, DECEMBER 30, 1864

Beautiful day. Sue and Nellie stoped to see me. I have not had a visit (from) Sue for a long while. She spent the evening with Redding, was here a long time. Alf(red) here. I spent quite an agreeable day.

SATURDAY, DECEMBER 31, 1864

Quite a heavy snowstorm. Very disagreeable. It stoped snowing towards evening. We made donation to Mr. Gibbs this evening, wich was very gratefuly received.

Memoranda

I paid 5$ for Proyer for the organ.

This is equivalent to $92.50 in today's market.

I promised to go to the Sisters to see Ellie Chester with Meal. I must get some hair pommenade from Mrs. Bustill and soul pomoterne.

Here Emilie wrote "pommenade," cf. French "pommade" or English "pomade," which is a greasy and waxy cream that was used to slick down a woman's hair and help it to shine. It is not clear if soul pomoterne was another hair product (perhaps a brand) or if it was something else entirely.

I owe Em McCrell a visit, Em Johnson also.
I gave Aunt Jane my potograph. Barker has had some taken, I am good for one.
Meli Agusters was married on Sunday 12th.
Estelene Johnson was to see (me) this afternoon. She is very pleasant.
On Saturday 25, I visited the(re?) with Mrs. Wister. It certainly was worth going to. We visited all of the principle places of interest when I cam out. I had seen so much I hardly could recollect what I had seen. I saw a great deal of hansome work but I did not see any done by my colored people. There might of bin some things their, I did not see.
Martin was at our house on Sunday on July 1. I did not see him, I was up to Whites.
I received my dear brothers potographs last week Saturday 16th, 1864.

I must go and see my new Hall, the first opportunity.

Nellie paid me 7 wich was due me. I gave her 30$ to pay too mon in school.

Seven dollars is equivalent to $129.50, and $30 is equivalent to $555.

I must realy go and see Elizar Chester.

Thursday, October 13th: I commenced taken lessons of Mr. Lively to day.

Tuesday, November 1, 1864: To day has bin a great day. 6,000 slaves have bin declared free in the state of Maryland. It has bin generally ahseehed (assisted) here by our people. The head quarters for the colerd troops was butifully illuminated. The soldiers praded. Quite a holliday al around.

Nellie and I are to go to Whites on Thursday. Nothing happened to puniment (prominent).

Mrs. Bayard paid me $8 on the 17th.

This is equivalent to $148.

We are to have a grand donation party on New Year, are to meet at the Hall and proceed to Mr. Gibbses house.

The emancipation of Maryland was celebrated in grand style on the 7th of Dec 1864 at National Hall. They had band and a number of singers and several addresses. Everything was exellant.

I feel thankful that I have bin spared to enjoy another Christmas Day, Christmas Eve. I had several friends up here. We had quite a pleasant time. Christmas, being on Sunday, I went to church herd a very good sermon by one of the students from the Institute. In the evening, Foster, Vincent, Kate, and Nellie come up and we had quite a sociable time together.

Our dear pastor leaves us on the 20th for the South. I feel very sorry to part with him even for a short time.

A World of Women

Oh, if I had a kind friend
A friend that I could trust
It would be a source of joy to me
To know that I was blest
With one in whom I could confide
My secrets hopes and fears
And who would not in coldness turn
From me in furture years.

Diaries, Memoranda, 1863

At the end of every year, Emilie would summarize some of the major events that happened in her life and in the world in the back section of her pocket diaries. At the end of her 1863 pocket diary, in what seems to be an uncharacteristic practice for her, she wrote a poem. It is the only time within the three-year period that she did so, and since she spent a majority of her time in the company of others, a poem of longing for a friend seems to be out of place. Moreover the style and language in the poem that Emilie wrote about not having or needing to find "kind" friends is also uncharacteristic, as it is different from the style and language Emilie typically used during her daily entries. Perhaps she copied the poem from one of the daily newspapers or one of her women's magazines, as was commonplace at that time. Other than her daily entries, Emilie did not add anything to her books. She did not draw or doodle on the pages, and there are no grocery or to-do lists. She only recorded her daily activities, which is why the poem seems so out of place. According to her pocket diary entries, 1863 was not a particularly harsh or difficult year for her; in fact when comparing the three years, 1865 seems to be the worst—that was the year she met with and wrote about more hardships, personal disappointments, and sadness. In either case—whether she was writing about her feelings, trying her hand at poetry, or copying a poem that she liked—her pocket diary is where she chose to record it.

Diaries, Pocket Diaries, and Journals

The way that Emilie used her pocket diary, as an extension of herself, was very different from how pocket diaries were being marketed. Although they were originally marketed to businessmen on different social levels, the practice of keeping records seems to have been exclusive to the "middle and upper" ranks, and the design of the diaries reflected the habits of their clientele. Unlike diaries, which were designed for men to use for their private introspective writing, pocket diaries were originally designed and marketed as semi-private spaces to record public activities or family events. First introduced in London in 1812, pocket diaries were originally designed for merchants, with tide tables for the Port of London, a section for recording notes, and a page for recording cash accounts. They were introduced in America around 1850 and were advertised as "Blank Diaries," companions to the almanacs that were designed specifically for businessmen. Although the daily pages were blank, the books did include a list of eclipses, postage rates, and the daily sunrise and sunset times, as well as the distances between major U.S. cities and other commercially related information.[1]

The first pocket diaries were simple in their construction. They were designed as mini-books that were small enough to be carried and easily opened. Later versions, released around 1857, had tabs, loops, or locks in the front, which subtly affirmed that the pocket diary was beginning to assume a more private form. At the same time that pocket diaries assumed a more private look, they also began to be marketed to women as a place to record family events and traditions. There was a reciprocal relationship between women and their pocket diaries: the limitations of the pocket diaries, which allowed only brief daily comments, helped women shape their lives, while the structure of their lives then shaped how they used the pocket diary.[2]

Growing up in antebellum Philadelphia, Emilie Davis was uniquely situated to participate in the elite social and literary practice of keeping a daily pocket diary. She came of age during a time when boys and girls were instructed either in school or by their mothers to keep a daily record to "monitor their behavior, correct moral lapses, and use their time wisely" as they learned the "habits of order and regularity."[3] Further, girls were provided with etiquette instruction in how to use their daily records as a place to promote industry, count their daily blessings, and uphold their moral virtue. These musings, if shared, were done so only in privatized demarcated female spaces that were separate from and analogous to male public spaces. It is within these spaces that women began keeping records in the late sixteenth and early seventeenth centuries as family books to document everyday domestic experiences and as a private record for supporting and maintaining their husbands' activities.[4]

During the years that Emilie was writing in her pocket diary, the practice of maintaining more in-depth, introspective diaries was not widespread throughout America. It was not until 1889, with the American publication of Marie Bashkirtseff's diary, that American women were introduced to what the French called *le journal intime*, or the intimate journal.[5] Within their intimate journals, American women began to wax introspectively about the trivialities of their lives and unlike men they recorded both the mundane and the amazing. Events were recorded as they happened, and this act of writing placed diaries—their form, their content, and their history—"squarely within a tradition of women's writing and textual production." By participating in this practice, a woman's mind and body were then placed "squarely within the daily."[6] In this way the diary became a place where women could find their voices and assert themselves.

At the same time, men were being taught to use their journal (which derived from eighteen-century commonplace books) as a space where they could make a "record of the mind" rather than a recording of "what one does," which was what happened in a woman's diary. Cinthia Gannett argues that there is a tense relationship between the issues of dominant (voiced) language and muted (silenced) language that characterizes the gendered terms *journal* and *diary*.[7] By keeping personal diaries and consciously recording history from their personal points of view, a woman blurred and muted the line between her "public" sphere and her "private" sphere.[8] The blurring also gendered the diary as a woman's space, with men primarily using journals. Journals and diaries were, of course, similar types of books, but alongside gendered differences in their use, the word *journal* soon became associated with masculinity, whereas *diary* became associated with femininity. The pocket diary, as a woman's space, tended to include moment-to-moment autobiographical writing about what was happening in the world with the self as the center. The journal, as a male space, tended to follow a pattern of having periodic yet consistent writing about what was happening in the world with the self being decentered. In both texts it is the position of the self that informs the nature and the meaning of the writing. This demarcated gendered line between the journal and the pocket diary becomes even more complex and multifaceted when the issues of race and privilege are introduced, as these issues color the way the texts are analyzed and the way the lives of the writers are reconstructed. At the same time, the actual process of reconstructing the narrative in both texts is quite similar: in the journal, the work is completed on a micro level—with the researcher focused on discovering the personal history of the writer; and in the pocket diary, the work is completed on the macro level—with the researcher focused on telling the story of what was going in the world around the diarist. In both cases the story gets told in the spaces between what is written on the page and what the writer consciously chose to leave out. It is within these interstitial spaces that their stories are found.

A Sisterly Milieu

"Nellie stoped. She is still very disconsolate," Emilie wrote less than two weeks after her sister-in-law and their friend Mary Alfred died of tuberculosis. "I pittey her, for I have suffered the same." It was Nellie who came for Emilie when Mary was dying: "I went down to see Mary, found her very ill. I'm truly helpless. Stoped over home and told Sara. In the afternoon, Nellie come up for me, Mary was dieng." And though Emilie did not mention this, Nellie probably stayed with her during this time. Emilie's brother Alfred (Mary's husband) was a part of the Colored Troops and had already left for service. Emilie was attending both to Mary and to Mary and Alfred's one-year-old son, Frank. Nellie was there the following year when Emilie was attending to her sick nephew, Elwood; and when she was suffering from the worms: "My tormentors have come. The worms, I think, three on me this morning." Nellie was also there when Emilie, in December 1865, traveled to Harrisburg to bury her beloved older brother Alfred: "I started for Harrisburg this afternoon. Found father, Nellie, and the rest of the family. I had a very sad journey."[9] Within the pages of her pocket diary, Emilie wrote about these intimate sisterly moments.

The desire by nineteenth-century women to stay intimately connected, according to Carroll Smith-Rosenberg, led to the establishment of unique, highly structured same-sex kinship ties that males could not participate in, control, or dissolve. These were private spaces, built around "a generic and unself-conscious pattern of single-sex or homosocial networks" that were constructed and maintained by and for women and were not constrained by either distance or marriage. Furthermore, within this female world, women developed emotional richness and complexity because they bonded together closely during times of sorrow, grief, and loneliness. Their entire social world consisted of attending church, visiting, and being visited. Rosenberg contends that it is within these environments, where men have no emotional access or connection, that women, through supporting one another, developed a sense of inner security and self-esteem. Gannet adds that in the public sphere, women were taught to be listeners to and recorders of men; in the world of women, however, they were able to write for one another and share themselves openly with each other. This was the only space, public or private, in which women, if they chose to share, were able to do so.[10] Emilie spent a majority of her time in the company of women, and although she wrote of needing a strong friend to trust, she did—as reflected in her entries—have a large network of female friends. Her friendship with Nellie, in particular, seems to have been an integral part of her life. At once best friend, confidante, and *meilleur amie*, Nellie was the person that Emilie appears to have turned to for advice, support, and companionship. No other person, male or female, is written about as frequently or with as much tenderness or angst as Nellie. Emilie either visited or was visited by Nellie almost every single week and in some weeks, every single day. Out of the 1,086 days that Emilie wrote in her journal, she mentioned Nellie 504 times. In contrast to Nellie, Emilie mentioned her sister Elizabeth eighteen times; and her friends: Sue, 101 times; Rachel Turner, thirty-seven times; and Ellen Black, twenty-five times. Occasionally Emilie referred to Nellie, Sue, Ellen, and Rachel as the "girls," and she mentioned them twenty-two times. They spent a lot of time shopping, visiting, and attending meetings and church services. They were young and single and appear to have had a number of suitors or male companions though they spent a bulk of their time together.

They were not like most nineteenth-century married women who, according to Barbara Welter, were "slaves" to their homes. Emilie and her friends seem to have been able to express themselves and were not bound by the four cardinal virtues of piety, purity, submissiveness, and domesticity.[11] Although their activities may have been tempered within the public sphere, in their private spaces, they appear to have participated in an emotionally rich environment of sentimental affection. Sentimentalism, as a constructed method of female relationship, was designed "to evoke a certain form of emotional response, usually empathy," and in some cases, the trope of sentiment was present across racial and class boundaries.[12] This culture of sentiment intersected at the point where public and private spatial boundaries met, thus permitting women to establish a protocol to discuss public issues within a private protected space. Additionally, because there was a constant commingling of the private and political, women often had ongoing discussions on topics as varied as slavery and piety.[13] These environments (or private spaces) in which women openly engaged one another have long been the topic of debate and discussion.

In addition to her pocket diaries, Emilie also kept a friendship album, a photography album, and a sewing book where she kept pictures, designs, and swatches for future work. The practice of keeping and trading friendship and photograph albums was common among elite free black women. They were similar to scrapbooks in that they stored letters and watercolors inside the pages; their owners also typically wrote poetry, notes, and short stories on the pages. These books were usually shared with other families and were passed from friend to friend along the East Coast. Emilie shared her book and collected and traded photographs to fill it. Here she wrote, "I am quite interested about contributions for my book (album)"; "Lizzie gave me one of his pictures to day. My album is almost full"; and "I sent my book to Maggie Shags."[14] She received albums as gifts, and in one month in particular, both her brother and her male companion gave her one: "I saw Alfred (Davis) last night, he did not say he sent me the album, but I know he did," and "Vincent was up here this evening, he bought me a hansome album."[15]

Even though Emilie's albums (like many others) have not been found, there are four surviving friendship albums that were kept by nineteenth-century black women. The albums belonged to antislavery advocate Mary Virginia Wood Forten, the daughter-in-law of James Forten and the mother of writer and teacher Charlotte Forten; Amy Matilda Cassey, a founder of the Philadelphia Female Anti-Slavery Society (1833) and the Moral Reform Association (1836); and Martina and Mary Anne Dickerson, former students of Sarah Mapps Douglass. Within the pages of their friendship albums, elite black women typically shared their thoughts and concerns about private issues such as motherhood and child rearing, and public issues such as abolition, slavery, and freedom. They also used the space to remind one another about the responsibilities of their "appropriate" roles as women while at the same time openly challenging society's commonly held gender norms. This was an "unrestricted arena" that women used to support, admire, and stay intimately connected with one another. Men were invited to contribute to the albums—for example, James McCune Smith and James Forten Jr. are in Mary Virginia Wood Forten's album—but their entries focused mainly on contemporary political issues and did not have the level of intimacy and connection that the female writers shared.[16] Men were not a part of this closed community of women and may not have felt a connection to the album-keeping activity. When Frederick Douglass contributed to Amy Matilda Cassey's album, he noted, "I never feel more entirely out of my sphere, than when presuming to write in an Album. This suggestion of beauty, elegance, and refinement—whilst my habit of life passed history—& present occupation—have called into exercise all the sterner qualities of my head and heart."[17] Friendship albums belonged strictly to women who were in similar circles, which excluded not only men, but probably women who were not a part of these closely connected social communities.

Emilie's Gazetteer

Emilie inhabited a world of women, spending approximately 70 percent of her time in the company of women. "Beautiful day. Nellie was up and spent part of the day," Emilie told her diary on January 2, 1863; and "Nellie had an engagement and had to go home. I stoped home a few minutes, the girls were all there."[18] Since Emilie wrote of "going down" to visit her father and her friends, Nellie and Rachel, they probably lived in the lower sections of the Seventh Ward, near the shipyards. Sue appears to have lived outside of the city (maybe in Germantown?) though she visited the city on a regular basis, staying with either Emilie or Nellie. Although they probably had robust discussions when they were together, Emilie never recorded the content of their conversations. She made no mention of jokes that were shared, gossip that was discussed, or sorrows that were revealed. She simply made a daily recording of the mundane and ordinary events of her life. It is a reminder that life does not always happen in the big grand moments but that it happens in a sort of daily—even ordinary—repetition, as decisions are made, events unfold, and time passes.

Emilie was a faithful chronicler of her experience: when she traveled out of the city to live with families for short-term domestic work, her pocket diary went with her. When she went on overnight trips to visit her father after he moved to Harrisburg or to work as a live-in domestic in Germantown or to see the soldiers in Virginia, her pocket diary went with her. In "How Do Diaries End," Philippe Lejeune notes that in record keeping, discontinuity is a part of the diary's daily rhythm, and that it is the rare person who remains faithful and disciplined to the process. He goes on to outline some of the reasons why people record their lives: to express oneself through the process of releasing and communicating on paper and to liberate oneself from the weight of memory; to reflect, analyze, and deliberate in a process of psychoanalysis on paper; to freeze time and archive memories—that is, to collect and catalog the pieces of one's life; and to take pleasure in writing to give shape to the life that one lives by enjoying the oeuvre of one's writing life.[19] Because her entries were so short—roughly three to four sentences—Emilie was probably not reflecting on her life, enjoying the oeuvre of her writing, or participating in a form of psychoanalysis on paper. What seems clear, however, is that she was collecting and cataloguing her experiences in an effort to freeze time and record her memories.

She wrote about her life through a discourse that reflected both her training and her personality. Her decision to record her life attests to her sense of self-worth and her belief that she was living a life that was worthy of being documented and remembered. During a three-year period, from 1863 to 1865, at a time when the nation was preoccupied and in the midst of a Civil War, Emilie wrote more than ten thousand words per year about her private life. Because of the language that she used, her diary seems to have been used as a private space rather than as a public one. There are some specific characteristics that distinguish a private diary from a public one; most notable are that private diaries are typically written without extratextual information. Since they are writing for themselves, diarists such as Emilie Davis do not contextualize either the people that they come in contact with, usually writing just their first names or a pet name, or the places or events that they visit or attend. Diarists also tend to write into the allotted spaces without interpreting the information. They typically do not judge the quality of the event or the character of the people in their lives. Daily entries are also usually written in chronological order and, finally the diarists often fail to distance themselves from the text, lacking both an authorial image, and the depth and dimension of a biography or an autobiography.[20]

Emilie's pocket diaries actually have all these characteristics: she contextualized, and she wrote extratextual information; she used the allotted spaces, and she interpreted; she judged, and she had an authorial image; and she wrote in chronological order without separating one day from the next (except when she used the weather as a starting point). "I feel thankful I have bin spared so long; and if I should be spard in future, I will try and spend my time more profitable," Emilie told her pocket diary on February 18, 1863, her twenty-first birthday. It had been snowing throughout the weekend, and on that day, Emilie was unable to go out, and no one came to visit. In her words, it was "a very unpleasant day." On her birthday in 1864, she wrote, "I feel thankful that I have bin spared to see another birthday"; and she happily wrote, "Vincent came up her to meet me. It was almost eleven o'clock." In 1865 she again records that she is thankful to have been spared so long, but this year she solemnly adds, "I shall endeavor to devote my time in future more to the service of my maker with his help."[21]

Although pocket diaries were valued gifts, often given to wives by their husbands, Emilie as a single woman, purchased her own—another example of how writing in her pocket diary was, for Emilie, an activity of her own making. On January 2, 1864, she noted, "I staid home last night. Bitter cold day. I stoped in to see Nell, poor girl. She is very unhappy. Sue was there to day and two strang ladies. I ran out and bought *my* diary to day."[22] In addition to the other constants in her life (her family, friends, church, and school), her pocket diary was a constant. It was probably as much a part of her as anything else. Taken as a full document, the three years' worth of entries read less like a series of daily comments and more like a story. Even though the story is not obvious and seems to be both fragmented and sporadic, if one picks out a thread—say following the entries about Nellie or about sickness or about shopping—the story is there, and it is very rich.

It is also very patterned and consistent (sometimes in its inconsistency), as on February 10, 1863, when Emilie first mentioned that she was sick. Throughout the three year period, she mentioned being sick approximately every twenty-eight days, which suggests that Emilie was in some ways charting her ovulation and menstrual cycle. Although she never called it that, the regularity of the sickness coupled with her consistent notes about it supports this. During this time doctors were studying women's reproductive organs in an attempt to understand the changes that occurred in a woman's body between puberty, menstruation, and menopause.[23] Emilie did not record regular doctor's visits (visiting once in 1863 and twice in 1864), but it is reasonable to conclude that she was probably aware of and familiar with the changes that were happening in her body every month.

In some instances the story relies heavily on context clues, other entries, and some insight into how the relationships have developed to understand what is taking place. In March 1863, for example, two of Emilie's diary entries are needed to understand the story: March 29: "Sue was in. Cristy gallanted us to church but we had to march home. Nellie was furious." March 30: "I went down to school, we were down there untill nine o clock before any one came. Cristy came down, Nellie run off from him."[24] From these short excerpts and background information, much information about Emilie's life can actually be gleaned. Nellie frequently confided in Emilie about her relationship with Cristy. It is not clear, even though Emilie once referred to Nellie as Mrs. Cristy, whether or not they were married, particularly because he is not mentioned beyond April 1864. Both Nellie and Emilie seem to have had a contentious relationship with him. For Emilie it seems to have been based on the way that he treated Nellie: "Cristy still Frenchy, I do not know how to treat him. I certainly do not feel pittey some towards him"; "Cristy and her are on the outs"; and "Cristy still putting on French with Nellie. He has not bin there for foure weeks."

That night Sue was in town, and Cristy had given them a carriage ride to the church, but he was unable (or unwilling) to stay to give them a ride back to Emilie's house. It must have been a cold evening because they normally walked between the church and her house. Emilie wrote that *she* went to the school; that is, the Institute for Colored Youth, but the girls probably traveled together. School was held on Monday evenings, and there was a short period of time when the institute did not have a permanent teacher. When Cristy finally arrived at the class, either to teach it or to give them a ride home, Nellie, who was furious, ran off from him. It would not be until June 24, after Cristy and the other black volunteers had been sent back from Harrisburg, that Emilie records some news about the couple's relationship: "Nellie came up and staid until 10 o'clock go. We had a pleasant chat, as usal, about Cristy."[25]

As even this one entry illustrates, though Emilie's pocket diaries are small and her entries short, the contents nevertheless speak volumes about her experiences as an everyday working-class free black women. But they do not tell the entire story of the free black experience. For a complete understanding of this environment, other primary historical sources must be read alongside her entries to corroborate, qualify, and, in some cases, correct her story, with her diaries as the central element. Such primary sources include three diaries and one journal; all have been published in their entirety or in part, and all provide further insight into the free black community.

Quilted Narratives

One set of diaries was written by Charlotte Forten, a freeborn elite light-skinned mulatto who was raised in the home of her grandparents in Philadelphia, educated by private tutors, and one of the first northern teachers to work with the free men and women in South Carolina. Forten's diaries are the most comprehensive, as they were written over a thirty-eight-year period, 1858–92. The second one was written by writer and abolitionist Alice Dunbar Nelson and covers her activities in 1921 and 1926–31. Dunbar, at one time, had been married to Paul Laurence Dunbar, America's first nationally recognized black poet.[26] The third belonged to Ida B. Wells, who was born enslaved and went on to become a *feted* newspaper editor, columnist, and activist. Her diary covers three years from 1865–87. Forten's and Nelson's diaries document the experiences of nineteenth- and early-twentieth-century elite mulatto women, their challenges, and their lives, while Wells's diary articulates the experiences of a freed mulatto working-class woman.[27]

In addition to these diaries, Emilie's pocket diaries can also be read alongside the journals of Amos Webber, a Philadelphia working-class freeborn mulatto man.

His entries record his daily experiences as both a waiter and manager and provide insight into the working-class communities in Philadelphia and Worcester. Webber's journals span the years 1854–1904 and connect to part of Emilie Davis's life, since Webber and Elijah J. were both members of Carthagenian Lodge No. 901 of the Grand United Order of Odd Fellows benevolent society for mutual assistance and Webber's wife was a dressmaker.[28]

There are some obvious differences between Emilie Davis's pocket diaries and the published work of Forten, Wells, Webber, and Nelson. The writers lived in different cities and were of different ages, social status, marital status, skin color, and in Webber's case, gender. Yet at the same time, there are some similarities. In particular the writers can be compared and contrasted along the lines of their demographics, their education, and their occupations.

First, in terms of demographics, Emilie, Forten and Webber all came of age in free black Pennsylvania during the antebellum period—Emilie and Forten in Philadelphia and Webber in Attleborough, Bucks County. Emilie was born free in 1838, Forten in 1837, and Webber in 1826. Even though Emilie, Forten, and Webber were not living in the same city during the period of Emilie's pocket diary entries, they all lived in Philadelphia during the 1850s and early 1860s, when both Emilie and Forten were coming of age. Wells was born enslaved in 1862 in Holly Springs, Mississippi, and grew up during Reconstruction, and Nelson, born free in 1895, did not have firsthand knowledge of slavery but was well aware of what the experience had been like for enslaved and free people before the Civil War.

Next, Nelson, Forten, and Emilie were classified as mulattoes and therefore had access to some privileges afforded by their lighter skin color. Nelson, in particular, was so light that she sometimes passed for white, particularly when she traveled. It is not known whether Webber was classified as a mulatto, but he did have lighter skin, and in free black Philadelphia this probably afforded him access to social circles that he may have been barred from if he could have been racially classified as black.[29] Although Wells had darker skin than most mulattoes, her father was the "privileged son of his white master," and as Linda McMurray reminds us, this master/son privilege was an entry into the black southern aristocracy. At the same time, because of her skin color and her limited finances, Wells was fully aware that she was viewed as an outsider within the mulatto elite communities.[30]

One advantage that all the five writers had, probably in part because of their racial status, was the privilege of education. Emilie attended Philadelphia's Institute for Colored Youth and wrote of reading the Bible and teaching Bible class; Forten had private tutors and attended Higginson Grammar School in Massachusetts; Nelson graduated from Straight College (now Dillard University) and attended Cornell University; and Wells attended Freedman's School Shaw University (now Rust College) and Fisk University. Although Webber did not have much formal education, he did attend lower school at the Bethlehem Colored Methodist Church and learned the moral lessons of the Bible as well as how to read and write. All five writers were literate and educated, frequently mentioning books that they had read, events that they attended, and well-known figures that they came in contact with on a regular basis. Additionally, since they were all very active within their communities, they probably read the local newspapers, magazines, broadsides, and public speeches that were circulated in their neighborhoods.

Forten's and Wells's diaries in particular are also very similar to Emilie's in that the three women kept diaries while they were single and in their early twenties, and they seem to have viewed the world with an idealism that is lacking in Nelson's and Webber's work. One striking difference among the authors, however, is in their intended audiences. Wells's entries seem to suggest that she knew that she was moving in the direction of becoming a public figure, particularly since she was beginning to make her entry into both journalism and public speaking.[31] Additionally Wells, who often struggled financially, was enrolled in private elocution and dramatic lessons designed to hone her oratorical skills.[32] Alice Dunbar Nelson was a published author (her first book, *Violets and Other Tales,* was published in 1895), speaker, clubwoman, and activist who wrote a column for both the Washington *Eagle* ("As in a Looking Glass," 1926–30) and the Pittsburgh *Courier* ("From a Woman's Point of View" or *Une Femme Dit*, 1926).[33] Forten, as the granddaughter of James Forten (one of the richest men in America), knew that she was keeping her diaries for the public and not for herself. In contrast Webber—who began keeping his journal in response to the public request of James Pollard Espy (the head of the Department of Navy's scientific efforts) for civilians to record information on weather patterns—seldom wrote about his personal life. Instead he wrote generally about local and national events that he either attended or read about in the newspaper.[34] Neither Emilie nor Amos Webber were public figures, and in their cases, the author and the audience for their diaries were the same. They seem to have written freely, without editing themselves or their text.

Finally, the writers can be compared and contrasted along the lines of occupation.[35] Emilie and Webber possessed Du Bois's Grade II skills: Emilie occasionally worked as a seamstress and Webber as a caterer and manager, although unlike Emilie, Webber was able to maintain a steady income at the middle-class level. Nelson and Forten had Grade I skills as a writer and a member of the black elite respectively. Wells also possessed a Grade II skill as a teacher and journalist, and was on her way to becoming a part of the upper echelon of the black community. Wells's and Emilie's income levels were similar (both of them oscillated between the middle- and working-class income levels), whereas Webber and Nelson were property owners (rendering them middle class), and Forten had access to her family's money (making her part of the elite).[36] In fact Webber's and Forten's families were part of the four percent of black property-holding families in Philadelphia.

There are also some similarities and differences in the content of the five contemporary authors' diaries. First is the question of how the writers treated racially charged events. Wells, Forten, and Nelson were highly critical of America's racial policies and held strong views on slavery, freedom, and the black experience. Wells, in particular, had a passion for justice that is evident in her early entries, and one gets a clear idea of the path along which she will eventually tread.[37] This passion for justice is evident in Nelson's diary as well, but it is situated differently in that she spoke to the post-Reconstruction era, when the gains that were made during Reconstruction were being eroded. In contrast Forten, as a member of the black bourgeois, seems to have had a difficult time adjusting to being around formerly enslaved people who were "too black, too crude, (and) too African" and, in her words, the most "dismal specimen" she had ever seen.[38]

Second is the question of how the writers allocated space in their diary to discussions of private troubles versus public issues. Only Wells, who at sixteen years old had lost her mother and was taking care of her five siblings, wrote about living a life of misery or with any discomfort. Wells spent a considerable amount of time writing about her frustrations over her career, her relationship, and her struggles to raise her five siblings. Nelson, as the wife of a public figure, discussed at length her feelings for him, the troubles in the marriage, her concerns about her career, and her love for both men and women. And Forten, in her third journal (out of five), wrote often about her frustrations as a mulatto woman and her desire to "see in the world of slavery, discrimination, and despair, a reflection of *her* realm of beauty, harmony, and peace" (emphasis added); and "a cloud seems hanging over me, over all our persecuted race, which nothing can dispel"; and as a Christian woman, "I believe in the resistance to tyrants and would fight for liberty until death."[39]

Emilie, who kept a pocket diary rather than a traditional one, spent less time musing on public and racially charged issues than Forten, Wells or Nelson. Unlike Wells, Emilie does not offer any commentary about America's racial cloud nor does she view herself as being a part of the solution for solving the problems. Instead Emilie tended to focus on personal events. In December 1865, for example, when her brother Alfred died, she lamented for several days about her grief and sorrow: "I am so sorry I did not get to see him before he died." On the day of his funeral, she wrote, "This day I have looked forward to withe dread."[40] She was not always this open on the page, but she did use it to record her feelings, which is similar in so many ways to Forten, Nelson, and Wells.

This openness on the page that the four women reveal in their diaries is in contrast to Amos Webber. While the women often used their diaries as spaces in which to ruminate about their lives, their feelings, and their relationships, Webber generally limited his entries to issues that happened in the newspapers, around the neighborhood, or in the sky (his daily meteorological observations). He rarely included detailed comments about his personal feelings or his life. He mentioned his wife, Lizzie, only five times; when his brother died he simply noted, "Sam Webber died this morning about 2 Oclock"; and when his only son died, he simply wrote, "Harry J. Webber died last night. 10 mins before 12 O'clock midnight inflammation on the brain aged 5 years. 4 mo. 18 day." His son was buried in a cemetery that Webber passed on his way to and from work, but he chose never to mention his son in his journal again. Although this seems unusual when compared to the four other diarists, according to Nick Salvatore, his private, controlled, ordered sensibility was normal behavior for nineteenth-century men who had middle-class standing and aspirations.[41]

Unlike Webber, Emilie and the other women seemed to have viewed their pocket diaries as an extension of themselves, and thus the diaries were a comfortable place to work through and discuss personal issues. One factor that might have informed the different ways that Webber and Emilie wrote in their books was their marital status. Because Webber was married, he may have shared his most personal feelings with his wife. Additionally, since there are no weekend entries in his book and since on two occasions a coworker added weather information for him, Webber may have seen his journal as a public space, something he worked on only when he was in the office. Emilie was single and did all of her work alone (either cleaning up someone's house, watching their children, or making dresses), so her diary was like a silent companion always with her and bearing witness to her life and her experiences.[42] This may explain why Emilie chose not to keep a diary beyond 1865; maybe her life became more public or she entered into a serious relationship, perhaps with George Bustill White, whom she later married in December of 1866. Possibly her diary was no longer needed as a place to record her feelings or she was concerned about someone reading it and having her story being misunderstood. In either case, when the diaries that do exist are situated alongside other primary sources and alongside each other, Emilie Davis's story becomes a part of the quilted narrative that explains and illuminates the free black experience.

A World Expanded

Outside of her diaries and a few primary sources, Emilie Frances Davis is an invisible woman. Unfortunately she came of age during a time when the lives of women and black people were not seen as important enough to be recorded or remembered. If it were not for her diaries—her unconscious act of defiance against social erasure—her life today would have gone unnoticed. She was not the one on the stage giving speeches. She never wrote editorials for the newspaper or received any major awards. On the surface she was like thousands of women who moved through life without leaving anything of public value that ensured that their lives would be remembered. If one were researching any other time in history, her diaries may not be so significant and important; but, the fact that she wrote during a time when the nation was in the midst of an internal war, and at a time when the majority of people who looked like her could neither read nor write, makes her dailiness far from ordinary. From the material recorded in Emilie's pocket diaries, we see that, for a single free black woman, the line between her public life and her private life was permeable.

Emilie had some control over her own time, as evidenced by her work as both a short-term live-in domestic and a *modiste*. Her jobs did not dictate her time; *she* did. There were periods of time—anywhere from several days to several weeks at a time—when Emilie did not work and would spend the days shopping and visiting with friends. Other times she would work with families, cleaning their homes and taking care of their children. It was during the summers, when she worked as a live-in domestic outside of the city, that she seems to have earned quite a bit of money. She sent money home to both Elijah J. and Nellie to take care of family matters. "To day has bin a very stormy, dreary day. The rains was very heavy. I sent some money down for Nellie to disperse."[1] Leaving the city during the summer was very common among the free black elite community, as elites would often cancel all summer activities and travel to Cape May or Atlantic City from June to September.[2] Even though Emilie was not going on vacation, she still found a way to participate in this elite activity of leaving the city.

In April 1864 she traveled to Germantown to accept a situation with the Wister family. This was possibly a new family for her as she did not mention them before she took the job. "Lovely day I went out to Germantown to Mrs. Wister and engaged to go to her the first of June." Dr. Owen J. and Sarah Butler Wister were most likely the descendants of merchant John Wister, who made his fortune before the Civil War and was a part of Philadelphia's elite community. Dr. Wister worked in Germantown and in Philadelphia. On May 4 Sarah followed up, checking to confirm that Emilie was still planning to come, "Mrs. Wister called to see Mrs. Powell to day. I have promised to go out on the 7th of June." Since the Powell family was one of the families that Emilie worked with on a daily basis, they may have recommended Emilie for the job.[3]

When she finally arrived for work, she found Germantown to be "very pleasant"—unlike the year before, when she had worked with the Harris family in Harrisburg and she regularly complained about having to stay and about how much she missed her family. She seemed to be under incredible stress during that time: her father was planning to move, Mary was very sick, and Alfred was reluctant to enter into the military. "Mrs. Harris wants me to stay another week," Emilie noted after three months of work. "She has heard from Tawny, she wont be home for seven months." Two days later Emilie finally wrote, "I bid my dear friends farwell last night. I hav bin busy getting ready to go home, sent my things to day."[4] Despite the fact that she had the prospect of longer employment, Emilie preferred instead to return home. This year, though, Emilie seems to have enjoyed her time with the Wisters, taking care of their home and their son, Owen, and she was looking for ways to extend it.

"I have bin buisy with my dress"

At other times Emilie worked as a dressmaker, accepting jobs from clients who wanted her to make dresses and trim bonnets for them. She was a self-employed businesswoman who exercised complete control over her time and her money. By defining her as such, I add everyday black women to Wendy Gambler's definition of businesswomen.[5] As a dressmaker Emilie was able to copy, which means that she knew how to look at a dress and copy it, as well as how to follow a pattern. During the nineteenth century, there were three very popular ladies' magazines that highlighted fashion plates, dress patterns, advice columns, poetry, and articles: *Godey's Lady's Book* (or *Godey's Magazine and Lady's Book*), which was published in Philadelphia, had over 150,000 subscribers, a $3 yearly subscription cost, and was the largest circulated magazine before the Civil War; *Peterson's Magazine*; and *Graham's Magazine*.

The process of making a dress involved an extensive amount of time cutting the material. Dressmakers usually began by measuring and cutting out the pattern on muslin before cutting into the dress fabric. Muslin was a heavy cotton fabric that was sold plain and unbleached. For patterns it was cut to fit the body of the client, marked up with chalk or stitches, and held together by straight pins. It was an expensive fabric compared to calico: a muslin dress typically cost about five dollars (equivalent to $92.50) and a calico one cost about three (equivalent to $55.50). The price would also be higher if a client wanted a higher degree of fineness or if they wanted the fabric to have a printed, woven, or an embroidered pattern on it. Cutting out the body of the dress was extremely laborious, took almost as long as the sewing, and would typically be an all-day process. The cutting and fitting had to be completed before corsets or stays were designed. The top portions of nineteenth-century dresses were usually cut very close to the body, and the bottom portions were wide and layered. Since women wore pannier hoop skirts under their dresses to extend the width of the dress, the fabric had to be cut wide enough to comfortably accommodate for it. The cutting was completed in stages: the front was cut out first, then the sides, the centers, the collars, the material under the arms, the peplum (a short overshirt that is usually attached to a fitted jacket, blouse, or dress), and finally the linings. It took about twelve to fifteen yards of fabric to make a dress, and in addition to the cost of the fabric, dressmakers would charge approximately $50 (which is equivalent to $925) to complete the process. Dressmakers were also able to trim bonnets: milliners sold materials, fabric, and sewing materials, including plain bonnets, to clients, who would then take the bonnets to the dressmakers to add all of the trimmings.

Early model of Singer sewing machine (photo ca. 1940). Courtesy of Library of Congress.

Carte de visite: Woman in
a pannier style hoop dress
(between 1860–1870). Courtesy
of Library of Congress.

When sewing machines were introduced in 1855, dressmaking actually became more complicated because delicate trims were added to the dresses. That
same year *Godey's Lady's Book* noted of sewing machines, "every family in the U.S.
ought to have one." By 1860 the *New York Times* declared that the sewing machine
was "the best boon to women in the nineteenth century," and in less than three years
there were over seventy-five thousand sewing machines in American homes as the
"outside world of industrialization" comfortably collided with "the inner world of
the home." It certainly changed the lives of dressmakers, as sewing, when it was
by hand, was a "never-ending, time-consuming task for virtually every woman:
farm and city dweller, young and old, rich and poor."[6] For those who were able to
afford a sewing machine, even though the dresses had become more complicated,
their work became easier. In 1864, Emilie, along with many women around the
country, purchased her first sewing machine. She either paid for the entire amount

up front or she participated in Singer's hire-purchase or installment plan, with five dollars down (equivalent to $92.50) and regular monthly payments. Singer's rigid-arm sewing machine with an overhanging arm, a table, and a foot treadle sold for approximately $75 (equivalent to $1,387.50).

That Emilie, as a black woman, had this type of disposable income and was willing to spend it on a sewing machine is yet another indication of how successful she was as a dressmaker. She spent the first few days taking lessons on how to work the machine. She wrote, "I have had my first lesson on the sewing machine. Succeeded admirably. I worked all the afternoon." One week later she noted, "I have bin running the (sewing) machine nearly all day."[7] This purchase, even more so than her leather-bound journals or her penchant for ink, speaks volumes about Emilie's life and about her lifestyle. It also drastically shifts the current understanding of black nineteenth-century businesswomen. Emile invested her money in herself and in her talent. She was able to recognize how the market was changing (understanding that with the advent of sewing machines, the demand for ready-to-wear dresses would increase and those that were still sewing by hand would not be able to compete) and to capitalize on it.

In addition to her sewing machine and table, Emilie's sewing kit, depending upon how detailed she liked to be, would have consisted of some, if not all, of these items: straight pins in all different sizes and strengths; straight and curved sewing needles to be used either by hand or on the sewing machine; spools of thread in all different colors and weights; yards of linen, silk, fine fabric, and muslin; scissors (at least half a dozen); a steel pinking punch (to keep things from unraveling); irons of all different sizes and a separate fluting iron for ribbons; head forms for bonnets; buckram to stiffen the fabric; millinery wire; a fabric flower maker (to make bonnet decorations); ribbons, hooks, eyes, and buttons; linen tape for petticoats (to tie things closed); chalk or stickers to mark the fabric; a lamp and oil; and a work table (that was separate from the sewing machine table). Because Emilie was living in a room in a private home, she must have either kept everything packed up when she was not working and then transformed the room into her work space as needed; or alternatively she might have rented two rooms, with one designated as her work space.

Most of Emilie's dress clients were her family and friends. For example she noted, "Mary was up here in all the rain. I cut her dress, finally"; and "I taken Sues skirts off to furnes (finish)."[8] On days when Emilie worked on her dresses, she typically stayed in the house all day. Here, in 1863, she wrote, "It rained so I did not go out. I was very buisy with my dress. I cut the body out"; and "I have bin very buisy sewing all the evening." And in 1864 her client base began to expand beyond her immediate circle of friends: "I went down home and cut out a dress for Mrs. Burton."

One year later, in 1865, Emilie was hired to design and make the *crème de la crème* of a dressmaking enterprise: "Very busy, making Mary's wedding dress.

Sewing untill after 1'o clock." Since wedding dresses were made using the finest fabric and were usually very elaborate and detailed, dressmakers would normally charge two to three times their going rate. Emilie probably charged anywhere from $55 to $150 (equivalent to $1,017.50 to $2,775). Although she did not mention it throughout the month, the fact that she was able to complete the dress while still managing her domestic work would have been very difficult if she did not have a sewing machine at her disposal.[9] Even though women's and girls' clothing was not yet being marketed as ready to wear, Emilie did not have very many clients. It is not clear, save for the instances when she wrote a client's name, whether she was making a new dress every time she mentioned sewing or that she was finishing a dress. By 1865 she had joined a sewing circle and was building her scrapbook of ideas. She supplemented this with her domestic work, working steadily among her four families.

"I went to the party and enjoyed myself nicely"

In addition to a busy work life, Emilie also had a lively social life. Friends and acquaintances were very important to her, and it was common for her to record these moments in her diaries. In a typical week, Emilie had five to seven female visitors, two to four male visitors, and she made four to five social visits. These figures do not include her time spent at First African Presbyterian on Sunday mornings and evenings, her class time at the Institute for Colored Youth, or her time spent attending parties, meetings, and gala affairs. She spent about 90 percent of her time (at least the time she accounted for in her personal diaries) in the company of others. In 1863, in the final entries of the year, although Emilie was sick with a cold and a sore throat, she still chose to be in the company of others. On December 19 she complained about her throat and then consulted with a doctor about it. She had been working very hard throughout the month, trying to finish two dresses, collecting money to buy an organ from Mary Proyer (she paid this off in 1864), attending her club meetings (they were in the process of electing new officers), and cleaning houses. She complained again of being sick on December 20, catching a cold on the 21st, being sick all day on the 22nd, and not being able to talk on the 23rd. Yet from December 24 to December 31, she had twelve visitors and made four visits: "Very cold to day, Sue was here and bought our ribbons"; "Very fine day, but I could not enjoy myself, I had such a cold. Nellie and I went to Bustill and had some eggnaugh. We met Cristy. He went around to Aunt Janes with us"; "Vincent and Nellie come up and staid a little while with me"; "Raining all day, I did not get to church all day. Nellie and Liz come up after church"; "Sue was here this morning. Elijah J. stoped in the afternoon"; "Nellie was up here, spent the eveing. Vincent was up and staid a little while"; "I have bin quite sick all the week. Nellie and Tomy was up here. Nellie and (I) went out a little while, stoped into Bustills. Then went up to visit his family and helped to trim the childrens tree; stopped at Mrs Hills."[10]

Emilie's social calendar was frequently full, and it is within her pocket diary that she created and maintained a private space where she could record her life. It is within this space that she ranted when she was angry, complained when she was annoyed, and criticized if she felt that something needed to be said. It is not known whether Emilie was this direct in her relationships with people, but her pocket diaries seem to have been a place where she could write freely and without restraint. These were not public documents; rather, Emilie was writing for herself.

"Nellie and I, little Frenchy"

Some of her entries clearly reflect how she kept a record not only of daily events, but also of her feelings about something or someone. After spending an evening visiting her new friend Ruth, Emilie wrote, "In the evening, Harriet, Ephraim and I went over to Ruth. We met som of the homilzes (homeliest) people I believe I every saw."[11] Harriet and Ephraim either lived in or worked in Harrisburg. At the same time, while she was away, her family: Nellie, Mary Alfred, and Elijah J., would send her weekly letters to keep her informed about what was going on at home. In return Emilie would offer advice, talk about her day, and send money to Nellie or to Elijah J. to give to her father. Although Emilie stayed in frequent touch with her family, she was constantly reminded of how far she was from home. Here Emilie noted with frustration, "I had a letter from Elijah J., telling me he had spent all or nearly all of my money, very curoles (careless) guy."[12]

Additionally, Emilie mentioned when her friends did something that she did not like. Here when she felt that Cristy was mistreating Nellie, she wrote, "Cristy and her are on the outs. I am verry sorry, but I can not help it. I will have to take him to task when I go home." There is no indication that she took him to task because by the time she arrives home on October 2, she is surprised to find that "Cristy and Nellie are acting friendly yet." She would also note when her friends were acting in a way that she did not seem to agree with. One of the phrases that Emilie used quite often was "putting on the French." This phrase may have referred to others using French words (since that was a language taught at the elite black schools), or it may have referred to an attitude of snobbishness that she perceived them to have; or maybe Emilie's meaning was a combination of both: "Cristy still putting on French with Nellie"; or "I was out in the morning, Rachel's acting Frenchy"; and "John and Sue had French on."[13]

Emilie also wrote about attending lectures and readings, which was a commonplace leisure activity for the elite free black community. Because Elijah J. and Vincent were active members of the voluntary intellectual organization, the Banneker Institute, she regularly attended their sponsored activities. Founded in 1853, the Banneker Institute was a male intellectual network for black Philadelphia elites and their colleagues in Britain and Canada. Membership was by invitation only, required a 50-cent membership fee (equivalent to $8.50) and yearly dues of $2 (equivalent to $34), and consisted mostly of men who had graduated from or were affiliated with the Institute for Colored Youth. Although the Banneker Institute was one of the many black intellectual organizations in the city, its original membership was made up of young men with *known* demonstrable intelligence and disposable income: a factor that set the organization apart. These men, in many ways, were an "inclusive assemblage of one stratum of Philadelphia's black elite."[14]

Some of the other members included the wealthy Robert Adger Sr., whose wife, Mary Ann, was a member of the Ladies' Union Association with Emilie (and whose daughter, Lizzie, was one of her friends); Henry Barker Black, whose sister Ellen was one of the girls; and John Simpson, who served in various leadership positions within the Banneker Institute and whose sister, Mary was friends with Emilie. In fact Emilie attended Mary's wedding to Gideon H. Pierce and hosted the couple at her home for dinner on their wedding night: "Mary Simson (Simpson) was married this morning at 8 oclock, stoped at our hous for dinner then when home to Briasbury."[15]

Within the Banneker Institute, the few black women who were listed as contributing members—like Fanny Jackson Coppin (who became the principal of the institute in 1867) and Sarah Mapps Douglass—were either very well known or were the wives, friends, and sisters of the male members. Since most of Emilie's friends were connected to and probably involved with the Banneker Institute, Emilie was probably actively involved in the organization as well. In addition to the organization's weekly Thursday night meetings, members were expected to make regular intellectual contributions to the group. On Thursday nights the Banneker Institute hosted lectures, given by one of the regular members or a contributing member on topics of interest, and on rare occasions out-of-town speakers were invited to speak as well. Emilie usually attended the lectures, which cost around five to fifty cents per event, and wrote about them in her pocket diaries. She also attended other local readings and concerts that were held throughout the city.

On March 22, 1865, Emilie attended a lecture to benefit freedmen, sick, and wounded soldiers. The Honorable William D. Kelley, a former judge on the court of common pleas, hosted the event and delivered a speech, "The War, and the Rights of Humanity." The event's organizers included Jacob C. White Sr., Jonathan Gibbs, Cyrus H. Bustill, and James J. C. Bustill. The cost was 25 cents and featured music sung by the celebrated "Black Swan," Elizabeth Taylor Greenfield. Born enslaved in Natchez, Mississippi, Greenfield grew up in Philadelphia, where she took music and vocal lessons and later inherited her former mistress's estate. After retiring from singing and performing throughout the world (including singing for Queen Victoria at Buckingham Palace in 1854), Greenfield settled in Philadelphia, where she occasionally sang at events in and around the city.[16] After the concert and lecture, Emilie noted, "In the evening, we went to hear Judge Kelley's lecture. He lectured very well."[17] One month later Emilie attended a concert where one of her club members sang, but she had a different reaction: "We went to the Concert. It was very nice with one exception, Lizzie Brown sing miserable. The rest done well. Very good house."[18] Though it is difficult to know for sure, without knowing more about Emilie's typical patterns of interaction and communication, the honesty and bluntness of this entry seem to further suggest that Emilie used her diary as a private space, in which she recorded personal reactions, emotions, and feelings that she probably did not share with others in her life. Emilie had a number of close intimate relationships—with several family members and with male suitors. Even though Vincent was the most constant, Emilie had a number of male suitors vying for her attention.

"I do not know how I could get along without him"

Although she spent a majority of her time in the company of other women, when a male suitor did arrive, he often did so bearing gifts. They entertained her when she was not happy and escorted her to lectures, to the fair, or to the wharf. Other times they would come just to sit and visit. Since Emilie probably lived in a private home that took in boarders rather than in a boardinghouse, she was able to receive male visitors on a regular basis without being mistaken as a "woman of the town."[19] Because Emilie was single and because she had access to and spent time with the free black elite community, she was probably well aware of the customs and social standards of her time and knew that she needed to be protective of her image and how she was viewed in society. At the same time, she filled the pages with discussions of her social events and her numerous male suitors. "Vincent was up here this evening. He bought me a hansome album from a Philadelo (Philadelphia) present. I am deligted with it"; "I received a sweet little letter from Redding and his photog to day"; and "After school, George and I went to the Fair. He was very gallant."[20]

In 1864, it appears as if she began to see Vincent almost exclusively. First mentioned in January 1863, Vincent is mentioned 213 times in Emilie's diaries. He becomes "ever constant," and she is not sure how she would "get along with him." Though Nellie seems to be her *mon amour*, Vincent in many ways did hold a special place in her heart. When her brother died in 1865, it was Vincent who met her at the depot when she returned to the city, but it was Nellie who attended the funeral with her. Although Nellie and Vincent had close to the same number of visits that year, Nellie at 151 and Vincent at 120, Emilie talked about Nellie twice as much as she mentioned Vincent. In many ways, Emilie's writings about her friendship with Nellie, her concerns over Nellie's health, her time spent shopping and visiting with Nellie, or her sadness over Nellie failing to visit or write are all essential parts of her story. At the same time, both her fondness for and her frustration about Vincent are evident in her diary entries for December 1864, when she mentioned some of the difficulties: "Yesterday, Vincent spent the evening with me. He loves vists reagular but there is no understanding between us"; and "Vincent was up. I did not expect him after treating him so badly." One month later: "Vincent, he come and we re-consoled (reconciled) to each other."[21]

In 1866, after spending three years focused on Vincent and Nellie, Emilie nei-ther married Vincent nor chose to spend all of her time with Nellie; instead she married George Bustill White, the older brother of Jake White and a member of the Banneker Institute. In Emilie's diary George is never mentioned by last name. Here, in March 1863, Emilie and Cristy went down to the Institute for Colored Youth for class, and nobody but George showed up. Because Emilie mentioned five Georges in her dairies (George Fulner, George S., George Freeman, George White, and George Burrell), there is no way to know for sure which George ventured out that evening to class and later accompanied Emilie to the fair. "After school," Emilie wrote, "George and I went to the Fair. He was very gallant," (perhaps this gallant George was the same one who would later become her husband).[22]

"Concerning the several deaths"

In nineteenth-century Philadelphia, sickness was very common and could easily lead to death. Emilie recorded both the sicknesses and deaths of her friends, church members, and in some cases, family members. In 1864, at First African Presbyte-rian, there was such a concern about the increasing number of funerals that Rever-end Gibbs chose to address it from the pulpit. "A great many out in the afternoon," Emilie noted; "Mr. Gibbs preached a sermon concerning the several deaths wich has ocured in our church during the past month."[23] This sermon and gathering were probably very significant and emotional for Emilie, who had recently lost both her nephew and her sister-in-law.

In July 1863, when Philadelphia began drafting black men for the armed ser-vices, Alfred did not want to be drafted because Mary was suffering from breathing problems and coughing spasms. Emilie, who was spending the summer working with the Hazards in Germantown, wrote that she had received "A letter [from] Elijah informing me that Alfred had gone to Canada. I am very sorry. Mary is still quite sick."

Emilie, concerned, began to chart (either consciously or unconsciously) Mary's illness: September 2: "I have just finished a letter to Elijah J. and one to Mary Alfred. Poor girl she is so sick. I feel quite worried for her"; September 14: "Mary is still quite sick"; September 16: "Bad news about Mary heat the [health]." When Emilie returned to the city, she tried to help: October 9: "Poor Mary is not better. I expected to go with her to see a German doct"; October 10: "I went up to the doctors with Mary. He sayes he can do nothing for her. Her lungs is to far gone. How sad! I feel very anxious about her." Mary had tuberculosis, and at that time there was no cure for it. October 19: "I stoped to see Mary, she is still very ill. I fear she will not get over this attack."

As her health continued to decline, Alfred returned from Canada and applied (unsuccessfully) for an exemption. On the day that he left for service, Mary's health quickly deteriorated: October 28: "Mary is very ill to day. Alfred went on the ship today. I feel so badly about it to think he has to go away, just at this time when Mary is so ill." The next day Reverend Gibbs visited and probably prayed with Mary. This is also the last time that Alfred saw her alive: October 29: "Alfred was here to day. Mr. Gibbs was to see Mary this afternoon. He said she express a hope that her sins had bin forgiven"; October 31: "Mary is very ill tonight"; November 1: "I spent the rest of my day with Mary, she is very ill"; November 2: "I went down to see Mary, found her very ill. I'm truly helpless." And later that day, "In the afternoon, Nellie come up for me, Mary was dieng. I went down and staid with her." Sadly, on November 3, Emilie wrote, "She died last about 7 o'clock. She died very calm, she was ready. Alfred did not get to see her." One day later: "Poor Mary to be buried to day. No word of Alfred. Poor little Frank is left over alone."[24] Later Emilie noted that Elijah J. and Sarah took Alfred and Mary's son Frank home with them after the funeral. These are the types of everyday experiences—the *mundanities* of life and of coping and dealing with death and sickness—that Emilie recorded that provide further insight into some of the tensions that existed within the free black communities that did not have anything to do with the ongoing struggles for freedom and equality.

On January 24, 1864, less than two months after the family buried Mary, Elijah J.'s son, Elwood, became very ill. Surprisingly it took only one week between Elwood's first becoming sick and his death: "Elwood was very ill this morning. Elijah and Sarah are very ansious about him." The next day it appeared as if Emilie had moved back in with Elijah J. and Sarah to help with Elwood, as she noted: "I staid home all night with Elwood. He is very low. The fever has gone to his head. Poor little fellow. "He suffers very much." By Thursday, Emilie seemed to have resigned herself to the fact that Elwood was going to die, "Elijah J. has call in Doct Morris but I think it is to late for any earthly power to help him." "Elwood is still suffering but I think death will soon end his suffering." And on Saturday, after a long and tiring week, Emilie sadly recorded, "Elwood is dying. I hurried home and staid until he breathed his last. He died at 11 o'clock this morning. His spirit has gone to his Father, that quick."[25]

More than a year later, following the tragic deaths of two family members and the resignation of her beloved pastor, Emilie faced the shock of the assassination and death of a public leader. Leading up to April 1865, Emilie was actively working with the Ladies' Union Association raising money to send to the newly free populations and the black soldiers in South Carolina. She was on a subcommittee that had raised over $950 (equivalent to $17,575) in total donations. She was dating Vincent, attending night classes at the Institute for Colored Youth, making dresses, and celebrating the fact that the war had ended. Her writings began to take on a lighter, more joyous tone, "To day is the day we celebrate the Soldier's Parrade. A flag was presented to the Regiment by the Bannekers. Very plesenit. Everybody

24th Regt. U.S. Colored
Troops, "Let Soldiers in
War, Be Citizens in Peace"
(ca 1865?). Courtesy of
Library of Congress.

Engine "Nashville" of the Lincoln funeral train (1865, printed later).
Courtesy of Library of Congress.

seemed to have a holiday." It was April 14, and the 250 members of the Twenty-Fourth U.S. Colored Troops were preparing to go to help occupy Richmond, the former Confederate's capital city. The Twenty-fourth was made up of 987 black soldiers who were bright, talented, and educated: 780 of them could read, 457 could write, fifty-seven of them were clerks, forty-seven had attended the Institute for Colored Youth, eighteen were teachers, four were college graduates, three were licensed preachers, and one was a reporter. Octavius V. Catto was the main speaker, and he challenged the soldiers and reminded them of their motto, "Let Soldiers in War Be Citizens in Peace."They received their ceremonial battle flag, which had been purchased by the Banneker Institute and designed and painted by David Bustill Bowser. The blue silk flag depicted a black soldier ascending a hill with his arms outstretched in prayer.[26] These men were the best of the best. It was a grand affair attended by the entire community. These were Emilie's classmates, suitors, and friends, so she celebrated and rejoiced with them.

The next day she attended a meeting of her association, and it was during that meeting that they received the news that changed everything: "Very sad news was received this morning of the murder of the President. The city is in deep morning. We were at meeting of the association. It decided to posphone the Fare (Fair)." The city was in deep mourning. During the days surrounding Lincoln's death and burial, Emilie recorded the activities of herself, her friends, and the members of the community around her. "Everyone seems to partake of the solemnity of the times," she noted. "Everything has a solemn affect. The streets look mournful. The people are sad." It was announced that the president's body would travel back to Springfield, Illinois, by train, retracing his original 1,654-mile route to Washington. He was scheduled to arrive in Philadelphia on Saturday, and Emilie ventured out to be a part of this historic moment: "Lovely morning. To(day) is the day long to be remembered. I have bin very busy all morning. The President comes in town this afternoon. I went out about 3 in the afternoon. It was the grandest funeral I ever saw. The coffin and hearse was beautiful." Lincoln's body was lying in state in the East Wing at Independence Hall at Broad Street Station in downtown Philadelphia, and people lined up for miles to be able to "see" him. There were close to three hundred thousand people lining the streets from the Schuylkill to the Delaware River. In fact there were so many people on Saturday that Emilie could not get close. She tried again on Sunday morning: "This morning (I) went down to see the President but could not for the crowd"; and then again right after church: "Vincent and I tried to get to see the President. I got to see him after waiting four hours and a half. It was actually a sight worth seeing."[27]

Even more tragically, just over nine months later, on December 20, 1865, Emilie Frances Davis, after burying her sister-in-law and her nephew, and witnessing the procession of President Abraham Lincoln, sat down at her table and wrote, "I received very sad news to day. My dear brother Alfred died at 1 o'clock to day. I am so sorry that I did not get to see him before he died." Alfred had come home from the Civil War in November 1864, and though he continued to visit Frank, it is clear that he never took him from Elijah J. and Sarah. By November, it appears as if Alfred had moved out of the city and had become "quite sick." His health never improved, and Emilie continued to hear that he was sick, though she did not have an opportunity to visit with him before he died. One day after receiving the news, Emilie traveled to Harrisburg to meet Nellie and her father so that they could bury Alfred together. "No one but him that knows all things knows my feelings."[28]

Although Emilie chose not to share her feelings with anyone, she did write them down. Her pocket diary was her confidante, a place where she could be vulnerable and open and real and honest. Since her relationship with her pocket diary seemed to have been such a critical part of her life it is surprising to think that she may have stopped writing and recording her daily experiences. Perhaps the death of her brother was too overwhelming, or there were too many changes going on in the world around her; or maybe like the written work of so many nineteenth-century everyday black women, either her words have been lost to us, or they are (hopefully) sitting in someone's attic or basement waiting to be discovered.

Emilie Davis, 1865

The President was assasimated by som Conferderate villain at theathre . . .
the city is in the deepest sorrow. These are strange times.

Diaries, Miscellaneous, 1865

By the end of 1864, the country looked and felt different. African Americans were actively serving in the Union Army, proving more than once that they were indeed worthy sons of the nation; hundreds of thousands of enslaved men, women, and children had been freed by the soldiers or had taken it upon themselves to seek out and claim their freedom; Abraham Lincoln had been reelected; Emilie's church, First African Presbyterian, had accepted the resignation of their pastor; and her school and her association were continuing to mobilize their efforts to educate young men and women and to aid wounded soldiers. On a personal level, after dealing with the death of her sister-in-law in 1863 and the drafting of her brother, uncle, and several male friends in 1864, her nephew, Elwood (Bub), passed away, and she suffered from worms. Although her work as a domestic was not as steady, her work as a dressmaker improved once she learned how to use her sewing machine and she joined a sewing circle. In the midst of all of these national, local, and personal changes, Emilie seems to have been in a triangle of sorts between herself, Nellie, and Vincent, with quite a bit of tension between those two that was somehow connected to Emilie. The country was going into the fourth year of a war that had already claimed close to half a million black and white lives, a so-called "skirmish" that many thought was going to last only a few months. By the end of the Civil War, 427,286 white and black Pennsylvanians had answered the call and were serving in the Union forces. Although Emilie may have had several diaries after 1865, this is the last one to have either survived or been discovered. Her entries are particularly important given the national events—the end of the Civil War and passage of the Thirteenth Amendment, to name just two—that took place.

January 1865

SUNDAY, JANUARY 1, 1865

Beautiful morning. Very cold. I feel very thankful that I have bin spard while so many have bin called to their long home. I have come to see the beginning of the New Year. I spent the evening with Nellie.

Philadelphia's black community celebrated the second anniversary of the release of the Emancipation Proclamation with a celebration on Market Street hosted by the Banneker Institute.

Monday, January 2, 1865

Lovely day. Home all morning. Very busy, I wrote to Father and Sister yesterday and Tomy. Tonight it comes off, the long awaited Celebration by the Banneker Institute. It was very grand.

It is not clear whether Emilie is referring to the January 1 celebration hosted by the Banneker Institute or the January 3 concert hosted by the Financial Enterprise Association that was held at Sansom Street Hall.

Tuesday, January 3, 1865

Pleasant all day. Storming in the evening. I have bin sick all day. I did not get to meeting. I have not seen Nellie since last night. Redding was up. He goes away to day.

Wednesday, January 4, 1865

Sal was here this morning. She seems very glad to stop in. I am pitty her much. The Miss Christopher has called to see me. Vincent stop in.

Thursday, January 5, 1865

Very stormy. I went down to Mr. Livelys, had a very nice lesson. I went home. Mary Pierce was there. I did not get home in the evening. I went to Dagers to a Fair meeting.

Friday, January 6, 1865

Quite dull this morning. I received a letter from Tomy this morning. Mary Pierce taken dinner with me this afternoon.

Saturday, January 7, 1865

Quite stormy all day. Raining in the morning. Snowing in the afternoon. Very cold. Mr. Gibbs came home to day very sick. Mr. White went down this morning.

Sunday, January 8, 1865

Fine day. Cold, I am sorry to say that we had no meeting, not so much as a prayer meeting this morning. Doct Jones spoke for us in the afternoon. In the evening Mr. Farbeaux preached, very interesting.

Monday, January 9, 1865

Cloudy all the morning. Mary Clay called to see me. Nellie was here. I went to Mr. Livelys. He did not come to school. We went to see practiseing.

Tuesday, January 10, 1865

Raining fast all the morning. It slushed toward the evening. I went down home then to meeting. We had a very good meeting. Nellie did not go.

Wednesday, January 11, 1865

Clear and cloud. The girls come for me to go to the practicing. We all went up to the Hall. It was very nice. I did not go in the evening.

THURSDAY, JANUARY 12, 1865

Very pleasant. I went down to Mr. Livelys, he excused himself. I did not have a lesson in the afternoon. I went up to Mrs. Harrises and service at the Blocks. Mary, Nellie, and John and I spent the evening at Aunt Janes.

The Equal Rights League held a planning meeting at the National Hall on Market Street to raise money to build a home for the elderly.

FRIDAY, JANUARY 13, 1865

Lovely day but I have not bin out. Mary has bin here twice to day. She seems quite worried mind, I am discontenis (discontent) but she is more so.

SATURDAY, JANUARY 14, 1865

Very s(t)ormy. Has bin to stormy these three Saturday. I did not (go) out consequently I did not see any one. I am quite interested about contributions for my book.

Here Emilie refers to her friendship album as her book.

SUNDAY, JANUARY 15, 1865

Lovely morning only very windy. I have bin trying to meditate and fix my mind more on things that are beifentenl (beneficial), in future. Mr. Farbeaux preached for us this afternoon. He was interesting.

William Still arranged for a meeting with white civic leaders at the Concert Hall in Philadelphia to petition the state to change the railway policy.

MONDAY, JANUARY 16, 1865

Very pleasant. Quite cold. I was up to see Hannah Brown this afternoon. I went to Mr. Livelys, had a very good lesson. Went to school, very good school. Vincent, he come and we reconsoled (reconciled) to each other.

TUESDAY, JANUARY 17, 1865

Snowing all day. Cold of wintry evening. Nellie come up. I went to meeting. We had quite a spirited meeting. Few out at Mr. Farbeaux.

WEDNESDAY, JANUARY 18, 1865

Very cold to day. I have bin quite busy all day, as usal. I have had very good success with my book. Nellie did not get up this evening. Vincent come up and part of evening.

THURSDAY, JANUARY 19, 1865

Very cold. I went down to Mr. Livelys, had a very nice lesson. In the afternoon, I went out with my book. Stoped at Clayes and then Nellie and I went to Bustills. We spent quite an agreeable evening with Mary. Vincent was there.

FRIDAY, JANUARY 20, 1865

Clear and cold. Mary come up and spent the day with me. I looked for Vincent but he did not come. Nellie has not bin up here to stay any time this year.

SATURDAY, JANUARY 21, 1865

Very stormy all day. I did not get home as I intended.

SUNDAY, JANUARY 22, 1865

Cloudy. Very hard walking. I went to church morning and afternoon. I stoped to Elle Robinson. Vincent come up and spent quite an agreeable evening. Nellie did not go out when it was not my turn.

MONDAY, JANUARY 23, 1865

Very wet and raining. The streets are most impassable. I went to Mr. Livelys then to school. We had a very nice school, two new members.

TUESDAY, JANUARY 24, 1865

Very cold but clear. Working at Mrs. Thomases, not many out. Mr. Gibbs very sick. Mr. Derricks son, quite sick.

The members of the Philadelphia Female Anti-Slavery Society met and drafted a letter protesting the streetcar company's use of segregated streetcars.

WEDNESDAY, JANUARY 25, 1865

Clear and bitter cold. Mr. (Maumannon or Martin) lectures tonight. I expected to go but was disappointed. Vincent could not go. Nellie did not go.

Emilie was either referring to Meunomennie L. Miami, a lecturer and soldier who traveled through the North delivering a lecture, "The Meaning of War," or to Reverend James Sella Martin, who spoke at the Concert Hall that night about "The Friends of the Union in England."

THURSDAY, JANUARY 26, 1865

Exceedingly cold. I went to Mr. Livelys, had a very nice lesson. In the afternoon we went uptown. We spent quite a pleasant time. We come down in the cabs.

FRIDAY, JANUARY 27, 1865

Very cold this morning. Alfred went over to see Frank. He stoped and brought me my ring. Nellie was up in the afternoon. She seemed quite dull.

SATURDAY, JANUARY 28, 1865

Last evening, I went to hear John Smith read. Vincent taken me. I was quite delighted but caught a senal (sinal) cold from wich I have bin sick to day.

Emilie wrote that the event happened the previous night, but it actually happened on Thursday. The anniversary of the alumni association was held in Sansom Street Hall. The first address was delivered by John H. Smith and was entitled the "Model Statesman." Smith was a graduate of the Institute for Colored Youth and one of the founding members of Carthagenian Lodge No. 901.

SUNDAY, JANUARY 29, 1865

Butiful morning, not quite as cold. My hand is aching badly. I can hardly write. In the afternoon, I went to church. Doct. Jones spoke. Ellen treated me very cool, what for? I cant define.

MONDAY, JANUARY 30, 1865

Quite pleasent. My side is very painful this morning. I was not able to go out this evening. Vincent ever constant, stoped after school.

TUESDAY, JANUARY 31, 1865

Very damp all day. I have bin quite sick all day. In the evening, I waited patiently for Ellen to up to go to meeting but she did not come. I went out. We had quite a nice meeting.

With a House vote of 119 to 56, the U.S. Congress approved the Thirteenth Amendment to the U.S. Constitution to abolish slavery. The amendment was then submitted to the states for ratification.

February 1865

WEDNESDAY, FEBRUARY 1, 1865

Clear and cold. I have bin home all day. Ellen stoped a little while. Vincent was up. Pliny was here. We had quite a sociable chat.

THURSDAY, FEBRUARY 2, 1865

Quite pleasant. I went down to Mr. Livelys. Spent the best part of my time at home. In the evening, we spent with Mary B(rown).

FRIDAY, FEBRUARY 3, 1865

Quite pleasant all day. Ellen went to have her potographes (photographs) taken. Vincent come up and spent all the evening withe me. He is quite constant.

Pennsylvania became the seventh state to ratify the Thirteenth Amendment.

SATURDAY, FEBRUARY 4, 1865

Rather stormy in the morning. Mary stoped by in the afternoon. In the evening, I went down home. I have not bin out for sometime, was out early evening.

SUNDAY, FEBRUARY 5, 1865

Clear but very bidar (bitter) stay. I went to church in the morning. Mr. (William Johnson) Alston spoke in the afternoon. Vincent come up in the evening. He was very kind and affectionate.

Reverend William Johnson Alston, a freeborn black man from North Carolina, attended Oberlin College and was then serving as the pastor of the St. Thomas African Episcopal Church.

MONDAY, FEBRUARY 6, 1865

Very fine day. I went as usal to Mr. Livelys then to school. We had quite a nice lesson. After the lesson, I went to the Fair, Sewing. We had a grand time. I had to march.

TUESDAY, FEBRUARY 7, 1865

Very stormy. Ellen was up, quite awhile. In the morning, it stormed so I did not get to meeting. Vincent come up to say good by. He started for Harrisburg at about 6'o.

Vincent was probably on his way to the Equal Rights League of Pennsylvania meeting, which had been organized by Jonathan Gibbs, Jake White, and Alvin Green. It was scheduled to begin on Wednesday at 11:00 A.M.

WEDNESDAY, FEBRUARY 8, 1865

Clear and cold, The convention starts this morning. I sent a letter to Tomy to day and a note to Liz. Nellie did not get up, the walking is hard.

THURSDAY, FEBRUARY 9, 1865

Rather better walking than yesterday. Too cold to go to Germantown. I went to Mr. Livelys. Spent the afternoon at home. In the evening, Nellie and I called on Em Johnson. We spent the evening with Beck.

FRIDAY, FEBRUARY 10, 1865

Very interesting. I sent my book to Maggie Shugs. Nellie stoped here this afternoon. We had an old time chat about matters and things.

SATURDAY, FEBRUARY 11, 1865

Clear and cold. Very busy all day. I did not go home this evening. I was not very well. Vincent, I have not seen yet.

SUNDAY, FEBRUARY 12, 1865

Quite a heavy snowstorm this morning. I hope it will not prevent me from going to church this afternoon. I did not get to church all day. I went home in the afternoon, found Vincent there. They all scolded me for venturing out.

MONDAY, FEBRUARY 13, 1865

Clear and cold. I went down to Mr. Livelys then to school. Mr. Lively did not come after school. I went to the Sewing (Circle) and we had quite a nice time. Ellen treated me very cool. I cant understand, strange ocurrence.

TUESDAY, FEBRUARY 14, 1865

Meeting at Whites. Mary and I went up, very good meeting more than I expected.

WEDNESDAY, FEBRUARY 15, 1865

Very stormy, both snowing and raining. Very hard walking to day. Ellen did not get up. The celebration was postphoned indeffinately.

THURSDAY, FEBRUARY 16, 1865

Clear but very windy. I went down home. Ellen and (I) went to see Mr. Gibbs. He was much better. In the evening, we went to hear Frederick Duglass. Very interesting.

The Third Lecture of the Course between the Social, Civil, and Statistical Association of the Colored People of Pennsylvania was held at the Concert Hall. Frederick Douglass gave a lecture entitled "Equality before the Law," and both the "Black Swan," Elizabeth Taylor Greenfield, and the Post Band from Camp William Penn performed.

FRIDAY, FEBRUARY 17, 1865

Quite pleasant to day. I went over to see Mary but did not see her. Vincent come up and spent quit a while. I received a note from Ellen this afternoon.

SATURDAY, FEBRUARY 18, 1865

This is my birthday. I feel thankful that I have bin spard so long. I shall endeavor to devote my time in future more to the service of my maker with his help.

SUNDAY, FEBRUARY 19, 1865

Very fine day. I went down to church, very few out. Mr. White held for the draft. Very wendy, I did not go out in the afternoon. This evening, I have had a very solemn engagement with Vincent.

MONDAY, FEBRUARY 20, 1865

Beutiful day. I was out in the afternoon a little while. In the evening, we went down to school. I did not stay long. The sewing was at one house. I had quite a nice (Sewing) Circle.

TUESDAY, FEBRUARY 21, 1865

Clear not very well to day. Nellie stoped in the afternoon. I told her about Vincent. We went up to meeting. We had quite a nice evening meeting.

WEDNESDAY, FEBRUARY 22, 1865

Lovely bright day, not very well. I have something like the rheumatism. Busy all day. Hannah Brown stoped to see me. John Simpson has enlisted. I was quite disappointed this evening. I expected Vincent. He did not come.

Although Emilie stated that he enlisted here in February, service records show that he was drafted into service on October 21, 1864, and mustered out on September 9, 1865.

THURSDAY, FEBRUARY 23, 1865

Raining. I intended to stand for my photograph this morning. I did not go anywhere untill evening. We went to Shiloh. They had interesting meeting there. Nearly all the Sobbreth (Sabbath) school children are serious.

Founded in 1842 by Reverend John F. Raymond, Shiloh was located at the corner of Clifton and South Streets.

Lovely morning. I went to have my expression saved. I had quite a promenade on Chesnut St. Vincent come up in the evening. He seemed quite ansious about the draft.

Lovely morning, quite like spring. In the afternoon, it comenced raining and rained hard all the evening, consequently I did not get to pay usal Saturday night visit.

Very cloudy this morning. I did not go to church in the morning. Doct Joneses preached an excellent sermon in the afternoon. In the evening, I taken tea with Moncuers Foster at Nellies then went to church Shiloh.

Here Emilie wrote "Moncuers," cf. French monsieur, *a form of polite address for a man. Even though Emilie does not record it (she may not have attended), the Ladies' Union Association met to reorganize their mission, to focus on working on behalf of the freedman.*

Very pleasant to day. Nellie has the soore throat. No school this evening. I went to the lecture, very interesting.

*The Fourth Lecture of the Course between the Social, Civil, and Statistical Association of the Colored People of Pennsylvania was held at the Concert Hall. The main speaker was Frances Ellen Watkins Harper, a freeborn woman from Baltimore who was a well-known abolitionist, author (*Forest Leaves, *1845), prohibitionist, and suffragist. Her lecture was "The Cause and Effects of the War."*

The last of winter, we had a little snow and a little rain. We have had a very severe winter. Meeting at the Dr. Richardsons, very good meeting. After meeting, I went to the Sewing Circle.

March 1865

Pleasant this morning. Nellie is quite sick with her throat. Very busy all (day). Mary Wilson was married this morning.

Raining fast this morning. I went down to Mr. Livelys. It comenced raining before I got home. I went up and got my pictures. They are very good. I did not get far from home to day.

Still raining. Ellen's throat is better. I fear mine is getting soare. I have not seen anything of Mary since Monday. Vincent spent the evening with me. He is very affectionate. The grand celebration of the Union League came off last night. Very well attended.

After being debated for two years, the Enlistment Measure—which was designed to free the families of formerly enslaved soldiers who lived in the loyal border states— was finally signed into law by Abraham Lincoln.

The main speaker at the celebration of the Colored People's Union League was Dr. John S. Rock Jr., a dentist and doctor, and the first African American lawyer to be admitted to the bar of the United States Supreme Court.

SATURDAY, MARCH 4, 1865

Raining this morning. Clear in the evening, I went home.

SUNDAY, MARCH 5, 1865

Lovely morning. I did not go to church. I deprived myself to letherggie (lethargy). In the afternoon, the interesting servis of Communion taken place. Nellie was sick and did not get there. Vincent come up in the evening, spent quite a pleasant time.

MONDAY, MARCH 6, 1865

I went to Mr. Livelys and to school then to the Sewing Circle. Nellie was not able to be out. Very few at school.

TUESDAY, MARCH 7, 1865

Very fine day. Nellie is still not able to be out. Her throat is very bad. Meeting at Bustills.

WEDNESDAY, MARCH 8, 1865

Beatiful morning. Ellen better. It comenced raining in the afternoon. Very busy, making Mary's wedding dress. Sewing untill after 1'o clock.

THURSDAY, MARCH 9, 1865

The butiful day has arrived. This is Mary's wedding day. Very rainy all the morning. The sun offerrd for a little while. Cloudy all the evening. Mary looked lovely.

The Fifth Lecture of the Course between the Social, Civil, and Statistical Association of the Colored People of Pennsylvania was held at the Concert Hall. The speaker was John Mercer Langston, Esq., a graduate of Oberlin College (he passed the state bar in 1850), the son of a wealthy Virginia planter, and a practicing lawyer.

FRIDAY, MARCH 10, 1865

Very changeable all day. The groom called on me this morning in company with Vincent. He looked sober. I went down to see Mary. Had quite a holoday all day. Poor Nellie, she cant enjoy any of the fun.

SATURDAY, MARCH 11, 1865

Vincent was up last night. I stoped at Mary Simpson. She was out, then stop at home. Nellie better.

SUNDAY, MARCH 12, 1865

Lovely morning. Baptising at Shiloh, 44(?) to go under the water, all children. Jim Harris oftenness spoke for us this afternoon. In the evening, Nellie, Mary, and I took tea with Mrs. Simpson. Spent quite a pleasant evening, expect Vincent he was not well.

> *This entry is very confusing because Emilie is either saying that forty-four children were baptized (which seems like a large number of people to be baptized at one time) or that the Forty-fourth Regiment, which was the First Calvary of Pennsylvania Volunteers (they were first mustered into service from July to August in 1861), was preparing to go out to sea (hence "under" the water).*

MONDAY, MARCH 13, 1865

Lovely day. I had several callers. The Chief was here and Nellie, Mary P., (and) I met withe a disappointment in the evening. We did not have any school. Good many out.

> *The Congress of the Confederate States passed and President Jefferson Davis signed the "Negro Soldier Bill," authorizing the enlistment of enslaved men as soldiers. The bill required the consent of the owners and was designed to enlist up to three hundred thousand black men ages of 18–45 with the same pay, clothes, and rations as white soldiers. Even though one unit was organized, they never actually fought in the Civil War.*

TUESDAY, MARCH 14, 1865

Very fine day. Mary was here. She had bin out buying her outfit. Meeting at Mrs. Mills. Very good meeting. After meeting, we stoped at Rachels. Alf(red) come home withe me.

WEDNESDAY, MARCH 15, 1865

Very fine day. Nothing of note happening. Mary was up and spent the evening. She goes to camp tomorrow. I am sorry to say, Vincent not about.

THURSDAY, MARCH 16, 1865

Very fine day. I went to Mr. Livelys then to school. We did have any lesson. I did not go to the (Sewing) Circle, it being late when school let out.

FRIDAY, MARCH 17, 1865

Quite like spring. Nellie come up and spent the afternoon with her mother then Vincent come up and spent the evening with me. Hannah Brown stoped a few minutes to see me.

SATURDAY, MARCH 18, 1865

I have pain in my side again. I received four letters from Tomy and his picture. I was home this afternoon.

SUNDAY, MARCH 19, 1865

Lovely morning. I went to church. Mr. Gibbs preached a powerful sermon. He leaves as of this week. In the afternoon, an Indian from west spoke for us. Vincent was up ~~this~~ last evening.

MONDAY, MARCH 20, 1865

Fin day, nothing of interest going on. I went to Mr. Livelys as usal, very interesting lesson. At school, few out only one man.

TUESDAY, MARCH 21, 1865

Pleasant to day, busy as usal. Horace Greely lectures to night. Meeting at Rachels tonight, very feeling meeting. Mr. Guy spoke very solemn. Mr. Gibbs started last night.

Horace Greeley was an abolitionist, a newspaper editor for the New York Tribune, *a reformer, and a politician. He delivered a lecture entitled "Self-Made Men."*

WEDNESDAY, MARCH 22, 1865

Quite changeable all day. Hannah Brown stoped in this morning. Em McCrell, Judge Kelley lectures tonight. Vincent stoped after the lecture. He is very affectionate.

The lecture/concert was designed to benefit freedman and sick and wounded soldiers.

THURSDAY, MARCH 23, 1865

Pleasant. I went to Mr. Livelys. He was sick. I did not take my lesson. I went out shoping, met with good success. In the evening, we went to hear Judge Kelley's lecture. He lectured very well.

FRIDAY, MARCH 24, 1865

I bout (bought) my shoes yesterday. Mary went to Camp yesterday. Nellie promised to come up but did not come. Mon cher Vincent come after the lecture. He is quite nice.

Mary probably went and visited the black soldiers at Camp Penn. Here Emilie calls Vincent her "ma chere," cf. French "ma chere," meaning "my love."

SATURDAY, MARCH 25, 1865

Cloudy. Mary was here shoping as usal. Nellie was here a minute. She is bonnet hunting. I stoped home a litt(te) while, took my bonnet.

SUNDAY, MARCH 26, 1865

Very raw and cold this morning. I did not go to church in the morning. We had an excellent sermon in the afternoon. Quite a number out. I taken tea with Mary. Vincent come in about 8. We went home and spent the rest of the evening. Vincent has enlisting on the brain.

MONDAY, MARCH 27, 1865

I (had) very nice lesson this evening. Quite a good school, after school I went to the day seminary. Keep Vincent waiting a half hour in the cold. He was very amiable.

TUESDAY, MARCH 28, 1865

I have bin walking a great deal to day. Went to meeting, after meeting I went to Marys.

WEDNESDAY, MARCH 29, 1865

I feel quite excellent this morning. I have considerable amount before me to do. After I was done ironing, I went down to Mary Proyers. Nellie did not come up this evening.

THURSDAY, MARCH 30, 1865

Raining all day, very disagreeable. I had a great deal of walking to do. I did not go to Mr. Livelys. Nellie and (I) went to meeting alone, Scotts in the evening. We went to hear the lecture. Sarah Shimm was there looking like Sarah Thomas.

FRIDAY, MARCH 31, 1865

Very wet and disagreeable all day. Vincent come up abut the eleventh hour.

April 1865

SATURDAY, APRIL 1, 1865

Lovely morning. Home all day. In the evening, I went down home. Nellie and (I) went out shoping. Elijah J. is quite sick with a cold.

SUNDAY, APRIL 2, 1865

Beutiful morning. I went to church. We heard a very good discourse from all of the sergents. In the afternoon, Doct Joneses held forth. Vincent ever constant, was up in the evening.

MONDAY, APRIL 3, 1865

Beutiful day. I have bin quite busy all day. In the afternoon, I went down to Ellens, to rejoice over the good news. Richmond has fallen. The city is wild with excitement. Flags are flying. Churches are open to day. I have bin running errendres (errands). In the evening, I went to meeting at Mrs. Gibbs. We had a lovely meeting. Quite a number out.

TUESDAY, APRIL 4, 1865

Cloudy to day. Home all day. Nellie come up in the evening. We had quite an old time chatt.

WEDNESDAY, APRIL 5, 1865

Raining. This morning I went to Mr. Livelys. In the afternoon, I paid my long talked of visit to Germantown. Quite a pleasant visit. In the evening, I went to Sarah Shimms. Vincent brought me my ring last night. It is very hansome.

THURSDAY, APRIL 6, 1865

Raining all day. I was out shoping. Vincent here in the evening.

FRIDAY, APRIL 7, 1865

Lovely day. I have bin out several times. This morning, I stoped home. This evening, Elijah J. is still Frenchy. Nellie and I went shoping as usal.

SATURDAY, APRIL 8, 1865

[No Data]

SUNDAY, APRIL 9, 1865

Pleasant but cool. I did not go to church in the morning. In the afternoon, Mr. Adams preached for us. I spent the evening at home.

After more than four years of fighting and the death of over half a million black and white soldiers, the Civil War effectively ended when General Robert E. Lee surrendered his Confederate Army to General Ulysses S. Grant at Appomattox Court House in Virginia.

Grant allowed Confederate officers to keep their side arms and permitted the soldiers to keep their horses and mules. This day also marked the end of the American system of slavery that had existed in the country since approximately 1657 and had enslaved millions of captured Africans from the cradle to the grave. Even with the Union's victory, it would still take the combined efforts of the Reconstruction Amendments, the 1954 Brown v. Board of Education decision, the civil rights movement, and almost one hundred years before the long arm of justice would complete its pendulum swing toward righting the scales of equality, citizenship, and ultimately acceptance into the American society for the black population

MONDAY, APRIL 10, 1865

Raining all day. In the evening, it slacked off very little. I went to Mr. Livelys, he did not not come to school. Egerton come up here with Ellen.

TUESDAY, APRIL 11, 1865

Quite pleasant. I have bin very busy all day. This evening, I was too tired to go to meeting. Vincent did not come up this evening.

President Abraham Lincoln gave his final public speech on the White House balcony, where he spoke of "molding a new government" by "providing the vote to literate blacks and black veterans."

Although very little is known about how everyone in the crowd responded, much has been said about the reaction and response of one guest in particular. Confederate sympathizer and actor John Wilkes Booth, standing in the audience, was heard to have muttered, either in obvious frustration or in an indication of his future plans, that that was the last speech Lincoln would ever make. Horton and Horton, Hard Road to Freedom, *181*

This has bin quite a stiring week. Very good news from the army. I have bin working hard to get my dress done.

Very pleasant. Miss Mamie started for Baltimore this morning, inconsequently I
did not get to take my usal lesson. Spent part of the evening home.

To day is the day we celebrate the Soldier's Parrade. A flag was presented to the
Regiment by the Bannekers. Very plesenit. Everybody seemed to have a holiday.

After planning for months to either kidnap or assassinate the president, John Wilkes
Booth snuck into the Ford's Theatre in Washington, D.C., went up to the president's
box, and shot him in the head. He then jumped onto the stage and managed to allude
capture for ten days. Booth was later executed for his crimes, but his deed, by his hand,
had been done.

The 250 members of the Twenty-fourth U.S. Colored Troops marched from Camp
Penn to Broad and Locust Streets to receive their ceremonial battle flag. Biddle and
Dubin, Tasting Freedom, *321*

Very sad news was received this morning of the murder of the President. The city
is in deep morning. We were at meeting of the assossination (association). It decided
to posphone the Fare (Fair).

At 7:22 A.M., President Lincoln died from complications from his gunshot wounds, and
Andrew Johnson was inaugurated as the seventeenth President of the United States.

Emilie was at the Masonic Hall attending a subcommittee meeting of the Ladies'
Union Association of Philadelphia. They were planning a fair for April 17 to collect
donations to send to the black soldiers in Charleston, South Carolina. With the news
of the president, they rescheduled until May 15.

Very fine day. Everyone seems to partake of the solemnity of the times. Doct Jones
spoke for us.

To day was set apart for a general holiday but seems to be a day of mourning. I went
to Mr. Livelys then to school. Working was not very likely.

Nothing special on hand to day. I had meeting at eight. Very good meeting. After
meeting Nellie and (I) went to Sarah Shimms. Vincent invisible.

WEDNESDAY, APRIL 19, 1865

To day is a general holiday. The churches are open and the day has every appearance of Sunday. The President is concidered buried to day. I was out in the afternoon. We did not have church, Mr. Gibbs being away. Vincent was up a little while, as usal.

THURSDAY, APRIL 20, 1865

Everything has a solemn afect. The streets look mournful. The people are sad. I went to Mr. Livelys in the afternoon. I did not get far for from it. Rained all the afternoon and evening. I spent the evening withe Nellie.

FRIDAY, APRIL 21, 1865

Cloudy and very dork (dark) morning. The funeral procession pass through tomorrow. I have not bin out to day. I am tired of the st(reet). Vincent was up this evening, He is so full of business.

President Lincoln's body left Washington, D.C., by train to retrace the 1,654-mile route back to Springfield, Illinois.

SATURDAY, APRIL 22, 1865

Lovely morning. To(day) is the day long to be remembered. I have bin very busy all morning. The President comes in town this afternoon. I went out about 3 in the afternoon. It was the grandest funeral I ever saw. The coffin and hearse was beautiful.

President Lincoln's body was lying in state in the East Wing at Independence Hall at Broad Street Station in downtown Philadelphia.

SUNDAY, APRIL 23, 1865

This morning (I) went down to see the President but could not for the crowd. Mr. Robinson spoke for us in the afternoon, Very interesting sermon, after church, Vincent and I tried to get to see the President. I got to see him after waiting four hours and a half. It was actually a sight worth seeing.

MONDAY, APRIL 24, 1865

Very pelesant. I did not go to Mr. Lively. We went to the Concert. It was very nice with one exception, Lizzie Brown sing miserable. The rest done well. Very good house.

Lizzie Brown served as the secretary of the Ladies Union.

TUESDAY, APRIL 25, 1865

Very fine day. I stoped at Em Johnsons a little while. Nellie and I went to see Sarah Shimm then to meeting. Very good meeting. After meeting, we went down town.

The National Lincoln Monument Association was formed and held their first meeting in Washington, D.C. The goal of the organization was the raise money to build a statute horning Abraham Lincoln.

WEDNESDAY, APRIL 26, 1865

Quite in arm to day. I have this soore throat as a likely Sunday adventure.

THURSDAY, APRIL 27, 1865

Nothing of interest to day. Nellie come up this evening. She has not spent an evening with me for some time.

FRIDAY, APRIL 28, 1865

Very much like summer to day. Very pleasant. I went down to Mr. Livelys in the afternoon. Nellie and I went out shoping. I went down to Bustills a little while. In the evening, I spent at home.

SATURDAY, APRIL 29, 1865

Very pleasant. I have bin quite busy all day. I expected to go to Anna Dickinson's lecture but was disappointed. Vincent could not go, he come up in the evening as usal.

Anna Elizabeth Dickinson was scheduled to deliver a lecture on Friday night at the Academy of Music entitled "Women, Work & Wages," but with the death of the president, she decided to eulogize him instead.

SUNDAY, APRIL 30, 1865

Busy as usal. The city is not in such a stir as it was last week. I did not get out this evening, it commenced raining about four. Sue was here this morning. Beutiful morning. After the rain, I went to church. We had prayer meeting. Mr. Farbeaux spoke beautifully. We had preaching in the afternoon. I stoped to see Mrs. Gibbs. Nellie come up with me but would not stay. Vincent was up.

May 1865

MONDAY, MAY 1, 1865

Quite a dull day for the first of May. Raining all day, quite hard. I heard some good news from Father yesterday. This evening, I stoped at Mr. Livelys. We went down to school together. Not many out.

TUESDAY, MAY 2, 1865

Pleasant all day. The 6th Regiment went away this afternoon. I did not get to see John. Meeting at Adgers, quite a good number out. We stoped at Sarah Shimms.

The Sixth Regiment was scheduled to leave for southern service.

WEDNESDAY, MAY 3, 1865

Quite warm. I have bin very busy. Nellie come up this evening. Vincent was invisible this evening. Kate Little was here yesterday.

THURSDAY, MAY 4, 1865

Lovely day. The examination comes off to day. I did not go in the morning. I went in the afternoon, very interesting. After the examination, we went to the sisters. Nellie and I, little Frenchy.

The Institute for Colored Youth held its annual examination for graduating seniors.

FRIDAY, MAY 5, 1865

Dull this morning. I went to the alumni, it was very grand. I have rather a heavy heart to day. I received a letter from Sister wich made me feel quite sad this evening, account of being ~~disspotenion~~ disappointented.

SATURDAY, MAY 6, 1865

Raining this morning. Mary stoped here this afternoon. In the evening, I went down home. Ellen and I stoped at Aunt Janes.

SUNDAY, MAY 7, 1865

Lovely morning. I did not go out in the morning. I sent a letter Sister on Friday. Quite warm in the afternoon. Doct Jones spoke in the evening. I went to St. Thomas. Quite a few affairs at Millies this evening.

MONDAY, MAY 8, 1865

Raining all the morning. In the evening, I went to school. Very nice lesson. After school, I went to Fair meeting. Very wet. I missed Vincent, had to come home by myself.

TUESDAY, MAY 9, 1865

I feel very heavy all day. The house is so much confusion that it worries me. Meeting at Offerty. Nellie did go. After meeting, Mele, Vincent, and (I) stoped at Bustills, stoped at Nellies. She had gone to bed.

WEDNESDAY, MAY 10, 1865

Nellie stoped here a minute this morning. She is over run with worry. I have bin in working very hard all day. Vincent did not get up.

THURSDAY, MAY 11, 1865

Clear. This morning, I went down home. In the afternoon, I did not go out. Stoped at Sowahes. It commenced raining very hard. I did not get to Smithes readings.

FRIDAY, MAY 12, 1865

Ellen was to come up this afternoon but did not come. In the evening, I went to the meeting. Very interesting.

SATURDAY, MAY 13, 1865

Very busy all day. Ellen was up this afternoon. I did not get home this evening. Something unusal. Sarah was quite sick this evening.

SUNDAY, MAY 14, 1865

Beutiful day. I went to church in the ~~evening~~ morning. In the afternoon, we had a French lecture on Mr. Catto's concerns at home. In the evening, I spent pleasantly at home.

MONDAY, MAY 15, 1865

This is busy day. The Fair commences to day. I have bin working hard all the afternoon. At the Fair, in the evening.

TUESDAY, MAY 16, 1865

Very busy. Did not get to the Fair this morning. I went down home. Sarah was better. Sister come down this morning. I went out with her. She staid all night withe me.

This is Emilie's first documented visit from her sister Elizabeth.

WEDNESDAY, MAY 17, 1865

Very busy all day. I went out with Alfred. It is very warm. In the evening, we went to the Fair. Sister went home about 10.

THURSDAY, MAY 18, 1865

Quite a change in the weather. Quite cold, I have bin out all the all the afternoon. Very little seeing the boyes.

FRIDAY, MAY 19, 1865

Warm as usal. Cool, I have not bin to the Fair to day. Vincent wa(s) up this afternoon. There was quite a riot don on Eleventh an Lombard this evening between the blacks and whites.

This is the first entry in three years where Emilie chose to use the word black *rather than* colored.

SATURDAY, MAY 20, 1865

Quite showery all to day. I went up the Fair about 7. Quite lively this evening, great time. Sue Raneller was here.

SUNDAY, MAY 21, 1865

Quite rainy, showering and a rainy day. I went to church in the afternoon bteen prayers. In the evening, Professor Bellamy lectured at the church. I got very wet coming home.

MONDAY, MAY 22, 1865

Quite cloudy all day. No school at all. The Fair is all the go now. Quite a good attendance this evening. Vincent on hand. Egerton very scarce. Virgil about.

TUESDAY, MAY 23, 1865

Very busy all day. I went up the Fair expecting to go to meeting but was sorely disappointed, Very busy all the evening, very good sales.

WEDNESDAY, MAY 24, 1865

I am all most worn out. Very busy to day, I did not get to the Fair untill evening. I have not bin home since Sunday. Sarah was up to the Fair yesterday. I went down (a)bout home, found Rich there. Sarah is furious at Mele. Mills grand explosion on hand. Very busy this evening, sales pretty good, plenty everything.

THURSDAY, MAY 25, 1865

[No Data]

FRIDAY, MAY 26, 1865

Pleasantis for tonight is the grand concert. It came off poorly. We had a crowded house, done very well at the tabbules (tables).

SATURDAY, MAY 27, 1865

Tonight I am happy to say is the final of the Fair. I have got a bad cold by the experation (expiration), I was there working with holy passion.

SUNDAY, MAY 28, 1865

Very cloudy all day. I have bin quite under the weather all day. I did not go to church in the afternoon. Vincent not come up in the evening.

MONDAY, MAY 29, 1865

Quite pleasant. I have bin busy as usal, I was agreeably surprised to day. Just as I was going up stairs, Tomy come walking in. He has bin discharged. In the evening, Nellie and I went to school. Only a few out. Meeting at Mrs. Harisons. Quite a good turn out. Nellie was not there.

TUESDAY, MAY 30, 1865

Very warm all day. I have bin working, very tired after I was done. I sat down to console myself with the idea, I would not go out. Mary Black come for me to go to the committes meeting. I have had no rest for somtime. We realized over $1000.

This was equivalent to approximately $18,500 dollars in today's market.

WEDNESDAY, MAY 31, 1865

Clear from the rain, melting warm to day. I have bin putting away my winter clothing. Spent the evening at Blacks, had quite a party on a small scale.

June 1865

THURSDAY, JUNE 1, 1865

I quite a nice time, very warm. No prospects of my going away this summer. Alfred was up here a few minutes. Vincent was here.

FRIDAY, JUNE 2, 1865

Very warm. I have bin out in the sun a great deal. Mrs. Powers received news that Mrs. Byers was dead. The news is very mournful. I was home a minute.

SATURDAY, JUNE 3, 1865

Pleasant. I feel very sad. I will not be able to go to church to day. It is sacrament Sunday but I must learn to bear disappointment for we meet with many in this world.

SUNDAY, JUNE 4, 1865

To day has bin a trying day. I have bin very much worried. Did not get to go to school or to the meeting. Vincent did not stop.

MONDAY, JUNE 5, 1865

Very busy all day. Quite disappointed. I did not get out and especially to meeting wich I was very anxious to attend. Vincent did not stop this evening. I shall be cross with him when he comes.

TUESDAY, JUNE 6, 1865

Another busy day. Mrs. Hazard comes home to day. She looks badly. I ran home a minute this evening owing Alfred is quite sick.

WEDNESDAY, JUNE 7, 1865

I have not had time to answer Sister's (Elizabeth) letter for it worries me very much but I cant help it. I went down home few minutes in the evening.

THURSDAY, JUNE 8, 1865

I went down home a few minutes in the evening.

FRIDAY, JUNE 9, 1865

Very busy putting away the light clothing. Raining very hard in the evening. Vincent come down. He is ever constant.

SATURDAY, JUNE 10, 1865

Quite pleasant. I have bin out shopping. Nellie was here a minute. I stoped home a few minutes.

SUNDAY, JUNE 11, 1865

Lovely day. I went to church in the morning. Mr. Gibbs preached in the afternoon. We had a Scotchman. He spoke well. Home in the evening. Vincent about.

MONDAY, JUNE 12, 1865

Quite warm, busy all day as usal. In the evening, I went down to school. Mr. Lively did not come after school. Nellie and I went out to the meeting at Mrs. Adams. We had quite an exciting meeting and very pleasant.

TUESDAY, JUNE 13, 1865

Nothing of interest to day. Tomy was up and stayed a long time. Meeting at Elijah J.'s, very good attendance. Not either of the Blacks attended. I went to Alexander (VA) yesterday with the committee.

WEDNESDAY, JUNE 14, 1865

This morning I went out with Sarah and Mrs. Adams to purchase things for the soldiers. We met with good success.

Although the Civil War had ended, the Ladies' Union continued to raise money for soldiers who were still stationed in the South.

THURSDAY, JUNE 15, 1865

Very pleasant. We started about 1/3 pas nine for the warter (water). The boat left at ten. We had a pleasant trip up the river. Arived at White Hall about 12. I shall ever remember White Hall. Oh, we did not get time to distribut the things as we wished but we enjoyed our selves very much.

Emilie probably visited Whitehall Manor, which is located on the western edge of Loudon County, Virginia. The area was originally known as Snicker's Gap, and it is where the Battle of Snickersville took place in October 1862.

FRIDAY, JUNE 16, 1865

Very pleasant to day. Father was here this evening paid me quite a pleasant visit. Vincent was up, his visits are mostly pleasant. I went down home to hear the the news. Meal arrived last night. Alf(fred) bought me a letter yesterday from Anna, all well.

SATURDAY, JUNE 17, 1865

[No Data]

SUNDAY, JUNE 18, 1865

Very fine morning. I did not go out in the afternoon. I went to church. Mr. Gibbs spoke. It seemed quite natural to hear him in the evening. We went to Em Johnsons and Liz Browns, neither of them home.

MONDAY, JUNE 19, 1865

Fine day. Mary Simpson was up here and spent the day. In the evening, I went to school. Not many out. Mr. Lively did not stay long. Taylor and Minton were down after school. We went down to Sarah Thomases.

Theophilus J. Minton was a student at the institute.

TUESDAY, JUNE 20, 1865

Very warm to day. Meeting at Blackes, very nice meeting. Quite a number out.

WEDNESDAY, JUNE 21, 1865

Very warm to day. Quite busy as usal.

THURSDAY, JUNE 22, 1865

Clear very warm. Nellie and I went out shoping. Got caught in the shower. In the evening, we went in town. German professor Stringes and the Duglasses were with the party.

FRIDAY, JUNE 23, 1865

Warm as ever. My prospects of being in town all summer, very certain at present. Vincent was up in this evening. He is very constant.

SATURDAY, JUNE 24, 1865

Very warm. Prospects of a very warm summer. After working very hard, I had to dress and go several erands. I stoped at hom and at Nellies. I have not bin out for several Saturdays in the evening.

SUNDAY, JUNE 25, 1865

The sun is very hot this morning. I went to church an Mr. Gibbs held forth. In the afternoon also. Very few out, the heat being so great. Vincent was up in the evening. We had quite a pleasant chat about matters and things.

MONDAY, JUNE 26, 1865

Quite rainy all day. We went down to Mr. Livelys. He played for us and sang. It was quite late when we got to school. School closed last night for the summer.

TUESDAY, JUNE 27, 1865

Meeting at Whites, curant alley. I did not go down town. Quite a nice meeting. Not many females out.

WEDNESDAY, JUNE 28, 1865

Quite warm. Busy all day. Alf(red) was up this morning. He goes away tomorrow. He went out to see Frank to day. Nellie and Sarah Douglass went with the school.

THURSDAY, JUNE 29, 1865

This is the warmest day we have had. I think Lizzie Adger was by in the evening. Nellie and (I) went up to Whites. Quite a pleasant visit. We staid quite late.

Lizzie Adger was one of the fourteen children of Robert and Mary Ann Adger.

FRIDAY, JUNE 30, 1865

Very warm I have bin sewing all day. In the evening, we had quite a thunder storm. It did not seem to cool the air. Ma cher Vincent was here. He was quite affectionate.

July 1865

SATURDAY, JULY 1, 1865

To day feels like August, very sweltering. I down home a few minutes. We had a shower wich was quite refreshing.

SUNDAY, JULY 2, 1865

Lovely morning. I did not go out. We had a very interesting speaker in the afternoon. Liz and I went around to Sarah Thommas. Nellie was not out all day. She was not well. Vincent was. I spent the evening at home.

MONDAY, JULY 3, 1865

Very warm. I was out shoping this afternoon. In the evening, I went down to Mr. Livelys than to the Ladies Union. We had quite a nice meeting. Dariy Party out in power.

This is the great day. It has bin pretty quite (quiet). I did not go to meeting. Mary Simpson is quite sick. Vincent come up about 10. I went out to see the Illumination. It was very pretty.

Very busy all day. I stoped in to Nellie to say good by to (her) Mom, she goes tomorrow.

Very warm. I went down to Nellies and staid all the afternoon. In the evening, I went down to Bustills. Vincent come up later, spent rather a dull evening.

A another very warm day. I think it is the warmest day we have had. We had a very little shower, it did not do much good.

Pleasenter than yesterday but still warm. Vincent was up last night. This evening, I went down home and to Nellies.

Very pleasant. This morning, I went to church. Mr. White exorted in the afternoon. We had preaching. The public has met withe a sad loss in the death of Dr. (James H.) Wilson. He died yesterday at 6 'o clock in the morning.

According to his death certificate, James H. Wilson died of acute dysentery.

Lizzie sent for me this evening. She is to be married on Thursday night. I went to the meeting. Very satisfactory. Nellie was there. We concluded to continue as we are untill fall.

Cloudy all day. Tom was here to say goodbye. He goes to seek his fortune. I had a letter from Alf(red) on Saturday.

Meeting last night at Milles. Very interesting. Nellie or Liz was not out. I received a note from my darling, the first I have received since I too. Very plesent evening, not so warm.

Pleasant all day. I went out shoping a little. Stoped at Lizzie Brown. Sarah Shimms not at home. Spent part of time at Nellies. In the evening, I went to the wedding. We had a very pleasant time. Vincent did not get there untill after the ceremony.

FRIDAY, JULY 14, 1865

Very pleasant all day. I did not go around to see the bride. Vincent come up in the evening. He is very sweet.

SATURDAY, JULY 15, 1865

I had a letter from Will. Last Thursday, Nellie was up here this morning and ate breakfast with us. Wonderful. In the evening, I went down home. Tom come home again. I went to purchase something for the bride.

SUNDAY, JULY 16, 1865

Very windy this morning. I did not go to church. I answered Alfred's letter. In the afternoon, had an excellent sermon. I spent quite a pleasant evening in Meles.

MONDAY, JULY 17, 1865

Raining all morning. Clear in the afternoon, I stoped at the bride but did not see her. Mrs. Brown was in town yesterday. I did not go out in this evening,

TUESDAY, JULY 18, 1865

Clear and cold. I have bin busy as usal. Meeting at Aunt Marys, very full house. After meeting, we went part way home with Mrs. Harding. Mr. Thomas Amos was at meeting from Africa.

> Reverend Dr. Thomas Amos was a minister and a teacher who had been born in Monrovia. Liberia, who served as the pastor of First African from June 1889 to May 1891.

WEDNESDAY, JULY 19, 1865

Nellie comes up home with me after meeting. Pleasant in the day and the evening. We had quite a heavy shower. Nellie did not get up. Vincent has not made his appearance since Sunday night.

THURSDAY, JULY 20, 1865

Very warm in the afternoon. Nellie and (I) went on a regular tour of visits. We stoped at Morgans and Clayes. Vincent did not come untill late.

FRIDAY, JULY 21, 1865

Quite warm all day. Nellie come up in the afternoon, she staid part of the evening. She ran off soon after Vincent come. He paid a pleasant visit as usal.

SATURDAY, JULY 22, 1865

Very warm. I have bin in the street all the morning shoping for Mrs. Powell. In the evening, I went down home and to Nellies.

SUNDAY, JULY 23, 1865

Very pleasant this morning, I went to church. No preaching. In the afternoon, we had a powerful sermon, Dr. Sherman (W. D. W. Schureman) spoke for us. Vincent come up. He is very pasem (passim).

Dr. Schureman was a minister with the African Methodist Episcopal Church and was working to raise monies to build a church in Baltimore.

MONDAY, JULY 24, 1865

Very warm, busy all day. In the evening, I went to annual meeting of the Association. We elected our old President, changed three of our officers.

Amelia Mills served as the president of the Ladies' Union Association; Amina Morgan was the vice president; S. L. Brown served as the corresponding secretary; and Emilie's aunt, Sarah Davis, served as the treasurer.

TUESDAY, JULY 25, 1865

Very warm and very busy. Meeting at Elises. I had a hard work to make up my mind to go but through the influence of Pop Guy, I went. I did not regret it. We had quite a nice meeting. Quite a number out.

WEDNESDAY, JULY 26, 1865

Quite warm tody. I have bin busy dressmaking this week. Vincent make his appearance after this evening.

THURSDAY, JULY 27, 1865

The sun is schorching (scorching) hot to day. I had some shoping to do in the afternoon. I went down Lombard St. Stoped at Rachels, Maryes, Bustills, and Aunt Janes. Spent the evening with Nellie.

FRIDAY, JULY 28, 1865

Exceedingly warm, I have bin out all the morning. The sun is melting. Jim Scott was here this evening. Vincent come up late. Very affectionate.

SATURDAY, JULY 29, 1865

Not quite as warm as yesterday but warm enough. I have bin out as usal. In the evening, I went down home. Sarah did not get out.

SUNDAY, JULY 30, 1865

Very pleasant morning. I have not bin to church. I spent part of the time in reading the scriptures. In the afternoon, I went to church. Mr. Amos preached. After church, I went up with Liz. I spent quite an agreeable evening.

MONDAY, JULY 31, 1865

Quite pleasant. The ladies went away this morning. I went down home in the evening. Stoped at Nellies.

August 1865

TUESDAY, AUGUST 1, 1865

Very pleasant. No celebration on hand to day. Very busy this morning. I went down home. Sarah did not go meeting at Milles. Very good turn out.

WEDNESDAY, AUGUST 2, 1865

Quite warm to day. I have bin busy sewing all day. Nellie come up in the evening. George Freeman come in with his guitar and enlivened the evening.

THURSDAY, AUGUST 3, 1865

Quite warm. Harlin and I started for Touerdael (Torresdale) this morning but did not get off until the afternoon. We had a serious time before we found Mrs. Brown then had to walk from Keninstown (Kensington) in the evening.

Torresdale was a neighborhood in the Northeast section of Philadelphia, along the Delaware River. Kensington is located between the lower Northeast and North Philadelphia.

FRIDAY, AUGUST 4, 1865

Quite warm. I went down to Nellies this morning. She is thinking about going to Germantown to morrow.

SATURDAY, AUGUST 5, 1865

Pleasant this morning. We had quite a refre(shing) spring shower in the afternoon. Nellie did not got to Germantown. I did not go down town this evening.

SUNDAY, AUGUST 6, 1865

Showery all day. I did not go out in the morning. I was not well in the afternoon. I went to church, heard the Drops. In the evening, spent in with Nellie. The widower was there. I helped to entertain him. I have bin quite sick all day.

MONDAY, AUGUST 7, 1865

Vincent stoped a very few minutes this evening.

TUESDAY, AUGUST 8, 1865

Quite pleasant. Nellie stoped in this morning. Liz was here a few minutes. I answered Marye's letter. Yesterday Mr. (Jeremiah W.) Asher was buried this afternoon. Very large funeral.

Reverend Jeremiah W. Asher was a chaplain with the Sixth Regiment Infantry U.S. Colored Troops and died as result of attending to soldiers who were suffering from malignant fever. In addition to dying on the field, soldiers died as a result of infection from their wounds and diseases.

WEDNESDAY, AUGUST 9, 1865

I went to meeting at Mr. Farbeaux. Vincent left for Harrisburge this morning. I was out this morning, made several calles. Home all the evening.

The Pennsylvania State Equal Rights League held their meeting from August 9 and 10. The Philadelphia delegates included Jacob and Jake White, Charles and James "J.C." Bustill, Jonathan Gibbs, David Bustill Bowser, William and Octavius Catto, John Simpson, James McCrummell, and Alfred Green.

THURSDAY, AUGUST 10, 1865

Not well all day. I did not go out in the evening, untill evening very reluctantly then stoped at Nellie, staid there all the evening.

FRIDAY, AUGUST 11, 1865

Quite pleasant. This morning I have busy all the morning. In the afternoon, I was quite sick. I did not go to meeting. I miss Vincent very much. The Convention wade last night.

"Wade" is an obsolete term meaning "to proceed."

SATURDAY, AUGUST 12, 1865

I received a letter from Vincent this morning. He expectes to come on Monday. Nellie and I went to Germantown on this afternoon. I felt very weak after I got up to hous.

SUNDAY, AUGUST 13, 1865

Lovely day and and a lovely spot. We are out. Nellie and I hadeu (had a) long walk before breakfast. We did not get to church. We read the bible together. We engaged ourselves.

MONDAY, AUGUST 14, 1865

Finally this morning, we were up before five. Started for the Cares about quarter of 6. We arrived home about 7. We spent quite an agreeable visit.

TUESDAY, AUGUST 15, 1865

Very pleasant, Vincent did not come last night. I was so disappointed. Meeting at Mrs. Gibson. I waited patiently for Vincent but he did not come.

WEDNESDAY, AUGUST 16, 1865

Quite pleasent. I have bin busy all day. This afternoon, I took a walk. Stoped at Bustills and the other many placed. Went home and could not get in. Vincent come last night about 10.

THURSDAY, AUGUST 17, 1865

Rather cloudy this morning. I ran down to Nellies a few minutes. Vincent was here this morning. I did not go out this afternoon.

FRIDAY, AUGUST 18, 1865

Very pleasant. I have bin sewing all the morning. I went down to Nellie about 2, spent the afternoon very pleasantly. In the evening, I went to the lecture. Mr. Amos spoke very feeling. I was much pleased with him.

SATURDAY, AUGUST 19, 1865

Very busy sewing all day. Nellie was up this afternoon. I stoped there in the evening.

SUNDAY, AUGUST 20, 1865

Very warm. I went to church in the morning and in the afternoon, also. Heard a very interesting discours both times. Spent the evening at home as usal. Vincent come up late.

MONDAY, AUGUST 21, 1865

Very warm. Busy all the morning. In the afternoon, I paid several calles. In the evening, I went to the meeting but we did not have much of any.

TUESDAY, AUGUST 22, 1865

Cloudy all the morning. It comenced raining in the afternoon. Rained all the evening. I did not get to meeting.

WEDNESDAY, AUGUST 23, 1865

Beutiful morning. Nellie stoped in. Mary has not come up yet. Home all day. Vincent come up, spent the evening.

THURSDAY, AUGUST 24, 1865

Quite coole. Celestine, Mary, Clay stoped here this morning on their way to Arlington. Nellie and I went to Mr. Livelys. He was not home. We paid several calles. I spent quite agreeable evening at Nellies.

FRIDAY, AUGUST 25, 1865

Very pleasant to day. Home as usal on Friday. Vincent did not come up consequently, I was alone all the evening.

SATURDAY, AUGUST 26, 1865

Very warm. All busy as usal. Not of not pasing in an unsettled mind about matters and things. Mary is expected this evening. Nellie come up, we went for my guitar.

SUNDAY, AUGUST 27, 1865

Lovely and clear. Very warm, I went up to church. In the morning and afternoon, Pop Guy spoke in the morning. Dr. Blackburn in the afternoon. We had an excellent sermon. Vincent up in the evening.

MONDAY, AUGUST 28, 1865

Really very warm. I discovered Anna's letter to day. This evening, Nellie and I went Mr. Livelys. Very pleasant time. Mary come home to day.

TUESDAY, AUGUST 29, 1865

Cloudy all morning. The grand picnic come off to day. I did not attend. We received the sad news of the death of (Theolpilus T.) Peterson. This evening, meeting at Riders. Very happening meeting, not a great many there.

This may have been Corporal Theolpilus T. Peterson who was a soldier with Company H, Twenty-fourth Regiment of the Unites States Colored Troops (USCT) and died in Berkville, Maryland.

Quite warm, busy as usal. Jake stoped in here a minute this morning. Home all day. Vincent was up quite late. He seems quite affected about Peterson's death.

Very warm all day. Redding was hear this morning. He looks well. I stoped at Lizzies in the evening. I spent the best part at Nellie.

September 1865

Mary went to Em (Warwich) party. She looked well. Quite like summer to day. Nellie was in this evening. Vincent come up very early spent the evening.

Very warm, showering in the afternoon. In the evening, clear. I went down home to Bustills saw Mrs. Mesly from Harrisburg.

Very warm all day. Rainy in the afternoon. Communion in the afternoon. Very solem. Emma Amos taken in church. Lovely evening.

Emilie's use of the phrase "taken in church" is hard to understand; perhaps Emma was baptized, or she became a believer, or she had the "spirit of God" fall upon her.

Exceedingly warm to day. We had one of the heavyest rains I think I ever saw this afternoon. It poured for an hour. It clear off in the evening. I went to meeting.

The Philadelphia Inquirer noted that this one-hour rainstorm was so heavy that visibility was low and water flowed through the streets.

Very warm all day. In the afternoon, I started for Whites. Stopcd at Nellie. She went up with me. We stoped at Rachels, Bustills, and Bettyes. Not many at meeting. Mr. Weighes was very gallant.

Very warm, home all day. Went down to Nellies. Went down to see Mary's mother.

Clear all day. I went out a little while with Nellie. We went down to Mrs. Potters and Mary Duglass and Mary Jones and Mary Brown.

Mrs. Potter was probably the wife of retired Reverend Alonzo Potter, a graduate of the Institute for Colored Youth. Mary V. Brown was an 1864 graduate of the institute and served as the vice president of the Ladies' Union Association.

FRIDAY, SEPTEMBER 8, 1865

Raining pretty much all day. Little cooler, I did not go to meeting, not being very well. Raining very hard all the evening. George Freeman was up here.

SATURDAY, SEPTEMBER 9, 1865

Raining. Nellie was up early this morning with her bonnet. I went home in the evening and met her friend from Concord.

SUNDAY, SEPTEMBER 10, 1865

Cloudy all day. I went to church, Harison spoke for us. He spoke well. In the afternoon, Mr. More spoke for us. Quite a number out. Vincent was up, he was robed (robbed) on Saturday night.

MONDAY, SEPTEMBER 11, 1865

Very warm this morning. Clear in the evening, we had a meeting covering the reopening of the school. We decided to comence on the first Monday in October.

TUESDAY, SEPTEMBER 12, 1865

Exceedingly warm. We went up to meeting. Quite a large number out. Very interesting meeting. Not well to day.

WEDNESDAY, SEPTEMBER 13, 1865

Very busy all day. The Festival comes off for the children. I went down about 7, quite a number of children and adults were there. All seemed to enjoy them selves.

THURSDAY, SEPTEMBER 14, 1865

Very warm. I did not go out untill evening. Julie and I went to hear Blind Tom. I was much pleased with the performance. Exciting. We had to sit upstairs wich made me furious.

Thomas Green Wiggins, "Blind Tom," was a seeing-impaired, autistic pianist. While in Philadelphia, Blind Tom had two performances at Philadelphia's Concert Hall— located on the corner of Chestnut and Twelfth Streets, one for the public and one invitational performance for Philadelphia's most esteemed musicians and scientists (which was organized so that they could access his musical skills and talent). Born on the Wiley Edward Jones plantation in Harris County, Georgia, but later sold to Colonel James Neil Bethune, Esq., Wiggins learned how to play the piano from one of Bethune's daughters (Mary Bethune was a classically trained pianist, having studied under George W. Chase, the highly respected New York–trained pianist-composer-conductor). Wiggins traveled the world as a pianist, singer, orator, and composer. Even though American slavery ended in 1865, Wiggins was known as a man who was continually enslaved as his plantation owners signed him to indenture contracts that lasted up until his death in 1905. Although he made millions of dollars for his owners and his managers, Wiggins's family lived in abject poverty, and he died penniless.

FRIDAY, SEPTEMBER 15, 1865

Another warm day. Poor Frank Duglass died this morning at 12a. Last night, I went to meeting. Cant say it done me much good as I went to sleep. Nellie did not go, very few out.

Frank was probably the nickname for Frances Douglass, who died of phthisis pulmonalis (tuberculosis).

SATURDAY, SEPTEMBER 16, 1865

Not quite as warm as yesterday. Meal come last night. Sarah and Connie did not come to night. Quite a disappointment.

SUNDAY, SEPTEMBER 17, 1865

Lovely bright day. I was out all day. Went to Sunday school and to church. Nellie was not all day. I went out to Duglasses after church. I was at Bustills to supper. I spent the evening with Nellie.

MONDAY, SEPTEMBER 18, 1865

Clear this morning. In the afternoon, it cloud up. Quite a storm. It rained so I did not get to go to Frank Duglasses funeral.

TUESDAY, SEPTEMBER 19, 1865

Beautiful morning, after the rain, Nellie was up this morning, Liz stoped in the evening. We went down to Mr. Livelys then to meeting. We had a very interesting meeting last night. Mr. Amos lead. Connie was there.

WEDNESDAY, SEPTEMBER 20, 1865

Very pleasant. Home all day. In the afternoon, Nellie come up and spent part of the evening. Vincent did not come.

THURSDAY, SEPTEMBER 21, 1865

Lovely day. I did not go out untill late. Spent the evening at Nellies. Vincent very lively.

FRIDAY, SEPTEMBER 22, 1865

Lovely morning. I have bin busy all day. In the afternoon, Nellie and I went out to see the Duglasses and Martha W. In the evening, I went to lecture. Sarah come home last night. Long waited for, come at last.

SATURDAY, SEPTEMBER 23, 1865

Very much buetfull day. I stoped home in the evening.

SUNDAY, SEPTEMBER 24, 1865

Quite pleasant all day. I attended church all day. Vincent was not at church. In the morning, he was quite sick. He went home early.

MONDAY, SEPTEMBER 25, 1865

Very cloudy. I went down to see Mr. Johnson. It very hard all the morning. I did not go out. Vincent did not come. His face is bad.

TUESDAY, SEPTEMBER 26, 1865

Very pleasant to day. I received a note from Vincent. His face was better last night. Meeting at Mrs. Hills, few out. Nellie was not there. Vincent was not out, he's fine but not better.

WEDNESDAY, SEPTEMBER 27, 1865

Very pleasant. I am looking for Vincent tonight. Nellie and Barker come up. Vincent not out. His face is much wouse (worse).

THURSDAY, SEPTEMBER 28, 1865

Pleasant to day. I did not go untill late. Vincent did not come down. I went around to Bustills. Heard the news about the grieving widow. Barker come home with me.

FRIDAY, SEPTEMBER 29, 1865

I received a note from my one, he is better but not able to be out. Home all day. Liz Brown stoped at the door this evening.

SATURDAY, SEPTEMBER 30, 1865

Lovely day. Barker and Nellie went to Concordville this after(noon). I went home this evening. Connie is quite sick.

Concordville is located twenty miles west-southwest of Philadelphia and is a small unincorporated community in Concord Township, Delaware County, Pennsylvania.

October 1865

SUNDAY, OCTOBER 1, 1865

Lovely morning. I did not go to church in the morning. I went down to Sunday School in the afternoon. Quite a number out. Vincent was out. Looking very pale, he was.

MONDAY, OCTOBER 2, 1865

Quite enjoyable to day. Ellen and Barker come home this morning. In the evening, I went to Singing School (Association). Very few out. Vincent better.

The Singing School Association was a choir at First African Presbyterian Church.

TUESDAY, OCTOBER 3, 1865

Pleasant all day. Meeting at Mrs. Hawkins. Nellie was there. Very good meeting. Mrs. Egerton there. Vincent not down.

WEDNESDAY, OCTOBER 4, 1865

Very busy ironing. Nellie was up. Vincent come up early and spent the evening. He seemed quite well.

THURSDAY, OCTOBER 5, 1865

Quite pleasant. I was out very early & done some shoping and visiting. Elijah J. come after me to come home untill morning. He started for Baltimore tonight.

FRIDAY, OCTOBER 6, 1865

Connie very sick all day. I went down to the store this afternoon. In the evening, I went to ~~met~~ the lecture.

SATURDAY, OCTOBER 7, 1865

I went down to the store this morning. Stoped at Bustills' Central Depot. Finished my bonnet this morning and done several other important things.

SUNDAY, OCTOBER 8, 1865

Lovely morning. I did not get to church. Connie is so cross. In the afternoon, we herd an excellent sermon. We heard Elijah J. was very sick in Baltimore. We expected him home last night. He arrived this afternoon, looking very weak.

MONDAY, OCTOBER 9, 1865

Singing School was splendid this evening and returnned volunteers were there an enlivened school with there voices.

TUESDAY, OCTOBER 10, 1865

Very pleasant. I was hom this afternoon. The sick was better, not at meeting.

WEDNESDAY, OCTOBER 11, 1865

Lovely day. Quite warm. Very busy all day. Nellie did not come up. Vincent either. I spent the evening in practicing.

THURSDAY, OCTOBER 12, 1865

Very bright to day but still blustery. I did not go far from home. In the evening, I went to Bustills and Becks. Mon Craige come down this evening and Vincent come late.

Here Emilie called Craige mon, *cf. French "mon," meaning "my."*

FRIDAY, OCTOBER 13, 1865

Lovely morning. Quite cool. I expected to go to the lecture this evening but was disappointed. Mr. Gibbs is home. Nellie did not come up. Mon Craige come up and spent the evening. Vincent was up.

SATURDAY, OCTOBER 14, 1865

Very cool and damp. Comenced raining in the afternoon. I was out, stope at Nellie. Had quite a long talk with Occe.

SUNDAY, OCTOBER 15, 1865

Very dull. I did not go out in the morning. Mr. Gibbs preached in the afternoon. Spent quite a pleasant evening in Nellies.

MONDAY, OCTOBER 16, 1865

Beautiful morning. This is the grand parade with the fireman, I went to see them had quite a fine view of them. In the evening, I went to school. Mr. Lively did not com.

> *The grand parade of the firemen took place in downtown Philadelphia, with more than twenty thousand firemen in over one hundred companies marching in procession.* New York Times, *Tuesday, October 16, 1865.*

TUESDAY, OCTOBER 17, 1865

Very fine day. I have had quite a reception of ladies to day. There were 6 ladies here this morning. Meeting at Mrs. Sulinous, quite a number out. It was very discouraging. I did not see Vincent.

WEDNESDAY, OCTOBER 18, 1865

Raining all day. Very busy as usal at work. Mon Craige and Mr. Farbeaux call this evening. He is very fine looking.

THURSDAY, OCTOBER 19, 1865

Dull morning. Very blustery all day. I did not get any(where) other than home and Ellens. Spent quite a pleasant evening. Nellie was in our house. Harris was up. Nan did not come home.

FRIDAY, OCTOBER 20, 1865

The girls were here this morning. Liz went home this afternoon. Miss Harris was here. Nan also. Vincent come up and spent the evening. Nellie was not up.

SATURDAY, OCTOBER 21, 1865

Very bright day. Very busy all day. I went down home awhile in the evening. Elijah J. not very well.

SUNDAY, OCTOBER 22, 1865

Lovely morning. I went to church, we had no preaching. Very few out. Doct Joneses spoke in the afternoon. Beutiful sermon. I saw our old friend Nan this afternoon.

MONDAY, OCTOBER 23, 1865

Pleasant to day. I was out in the afternoon. Nellie come up before school time. We had a very interesting school, not as many out as last Monday night. Mon Morris come with me.

> *In what appears to be an unusual pattern for Emilie, she referred to Morris by the term* mon, *cf. French "mon," meaning "my."*

TUESDAY, OCTOBER 24, 1865

Cool this morning. Meeting at Mrs. Harrisons, quite a nice meeting. Vincent, home on tonight.

Beautiful day, the girls and I went over Jersey to Peterson's furnereal. It was very solemn furnereal. He was buried with military honors. The Banneker(s) was represented.

It is not clear whether Emilie is referring to Theolpilus T. Peterson, who died on August 29; if so, perhaps they had to wait to have a military funeral.

Very fine day. I did not get out untill late in the evening. Nellie and I went to Bustills and Aunt Janes. Nellie gave me a folly in about not spending Thursday evenings with her. She made me feel very bad concerning the past.

Cloudy all day. Raining in the evening. George Freeman stop in a few minutes. Vincent was up, Liz Brown was here.

Quite (quiet) this morning. I heard very discourageing news on Thursday night concerning Mr. Gibbs. He is going to leave us altogether.

Quit(e) cold and windy. I did not go out in the morning, not well. In the afternoon, Mr. Gibbs gave me a very interesting account of the freeman down South. I spent the evening with Nellie.

Very pleasant to day. In the evening, I went to school. We had a very nice time. Mr. Shore was down.

Raining all day. It cleared off toward evening. I went to meeting. We had quite a refreshing time. Quite a number out.

November 1865

Beutiful day. Last Wednesday went to funeral, this evening we are going to Miss (Rebecca J.) Coles wedding. St Thomases church was litterly packed. The guest looked beutiful.

Raining all day. I went down home and amuse myself by unpacking my winter clothing. Nellie and I went down to Becks in the evening.

Vincent was up last night. He was very pasem (passim). Cloudy this morning, comenced raining all the afternoon. Vincent did not come up this evening.

SATURDAY, NOVEMBER 4, 1865

Another rainy day. Pouring all day, I have not bin out since Thursday. I did not go home this evening. Sue was up here this morning. She looks badly.

SUNDAY, NOVEMBER 5, 1865

Very cold and windy. I went to church all day. Mr. Gibbs preach his farewell sermon this afternoon and church is without a pastor. He leaves on Wednesday for the South. Vincent was up, spent quite an agreeable visit.

Although Reverend Gibbs preached his farewell sermon, the resolution that allowed him to leave the church was not formally accepted until March 2, 1866.

MONDAY, NOVEMBER 6, 1865

Quite cold. Very busy all day. No school. We went to see Mr. Gibbs, not home. We then went to Bustills then the serstys (sisters) meeting. We had considerable fun after wich we went the Ladies Union. Nellie, I am sorry to say lost her fur cote.

TUESDAY, NOVEMBER 7, 1865

Sue was here this afternoon. I started for meeting but did not get there. Went to see Mr. Gibbs. Stoped longer than I intended. We had a long talk. I feel very sorry he has left us. It might of bin prevented. He has bin treated rather shodily. Mary stoped a minute.

WEDNESDAY, NOVEMBER 8, 1865

Sue spent the evening.

THURSDAY, NOVEMBER 9, 1865

Lovely day. I was out shoping. I was very fortunate in making a good bargain. Got a hansome coat. Spent the afternoon at home and the evening with Mrs. Simson.

FRIDAY, NOVEMBER 10, 1865

Cloudy this morning. Quite cold, nothing of interest happening to day. Busy as usal. Nellie did not come up, Vincent either. I heard last night Alfred was quite sick.

SATURDAY, NOVEMBER 11, 1865

Clear and cold this morning. Mele started for Harrisburg to day. I stoped at Nellie this evening. Barker was there.

SUNDAY, NOVEMBER 12, 1865

Lovely morning. Very cold. Mr. Gibbs is in town. I hope he will speak for us to day. Dr. Gaites spoke this afternoon. Mr. Gibbs in the morning. Stoped at Bustills and Mr. Gibbs, spent quite an agreeable evening at Nellies.

MONDAY, NOVEMBER 13, 1865

Very pleasant to day. Great many are going to Harrisburg. Vincent is going. Sarah and Fine. I would like to (be) one of the number but I yield to circumstances. Nellie was up to.

Sue spent the afternoon with me. Meeting at Bundys, not one of the girls out.

Quite warm this morning. The Harrisburg folks arrived to day. They were quite disappointed in the reception. Vincent did not come down.

Very much like spring to day. Nellie and I took a little promenade, several visits, spent the time quite agreeably. Spent part of the evening at home and part with Nellie.

Very dull this morning. Tony Simpson was married last night. Vincent did not come up. I miss him much.

Very pleasant to day. Ellen stoped in a few minutes. I went down home a few minites then to Nellies. Kate did not come out according to promise.

Cloudy. I went to church in the morning. We went to see Mrs. Turner and Aunty Hollys. Sick in the afternoon. Did not get to church. Kate come up and spent quite an agreeable evening.

Very stormy all day. I went to school. Very good lesson, Very few gentleman there.

Raining this morning. I received a letter from Anna this morning. Alfred is quite sick. Elijah J. is very sick. I had a great deal to worry about. I did not get to meetings.

Quite (quiet) home to day. Very busy, Nellie and Rachel was up. I went down home this evening. Elijah is quite ill. I feel very ansious about him.

Clear and cold. I was down home a few minutes this morning. Elijah J. better. No word from Alf(red). I feel very ansious about him. Vincent did not get down until late.

Quite cold. Elijah J. still continues to improve. Nellie spent part of the day and all the evening. Sue was in a few minutes. I have bin very unhappy all this week. I am so worried and sick, I hardly know what to do. I know I ought not to give up to bad feelings. I try to look on the bright side. I cant help feeling sad. I try to say thy will be done.

SATURDAY, NOVEMBER 25, 1865

[No Data]

SUNDAY, NOVEMBER 26, 1865

Lovely morning, not at church. I went to church in the afternoon. Mr. Gaits preached. I did not like him as much as the first time.

MONDAY, NOVEMBER 27, 1865

Clear and cold. I have not heard from Alfred as yet. I feel quite worried about him. Elijah J. is recovering slowly. I went down to school, not many out. Vincent not there.

TUESDAY, NOVEMBER 28, 1865

Rather pleasant to day. No word from home. Elijah J. better. Meeting at (M. Gertrude) Offits, very few out. I stoped home after meeting. Cody still was at meeting.

M. Gertrude Offit was an 1864 graduate of the institute.

WEDNESDAY, NOVEMBER 29, 1865

Very much like snow to day. I have not bin out. Liz was up. Nellie spent the evening withe me, remarkable.

THURSDAY, NOVEMBER 30, 1865

Clear and pleasant. Lizzie and I went to the ex-field's office then went home. I received a letter to day. Alfred is still quite sick. In the evening, we went to Concert Hall to see the Militonid(?) Tableaux. It was very fine.

December 1865

FRIDAY, DECEMBER 1, 1865

Very horible to day. Not very cold. Nellie and I paid visit to Maryes orphans hom(e). They looked very lonly.

SATURDAY, DECEMBER 2, 1865

Very pleasant. Quite busy all day. Mary was up this afternoon. I went home in the evening. Elijah J. is better. Alfred is still very ill.

SUNDAY, DECEMBER 3, 1865

Lovely morning. Quite like spring. I was at church in the morning and afternoon. Tim was received in to church. It was Communion. After church, Nellie and I went to see Miss Mele. We spent a happy time with the old lady.

MONDAY, DECEMBER 4, 1865

Pleasant. Sue was up this morning. She looks like a married lady. In the evening, we went to school. Very nice lesson. Stoped at Maryes, John (Simpson) had her locked up and the key in his pocket.

TUESDAY, DECEMBER 5, 1865

Colder than yesterday. Did not go to meeting. Nellie and I went to Mr. Lively's school, did not stay long.

WEDNESDAY, DECEMBER 6, 1865

Clear and cold. I sent a letter home yesterday. Nellie was up this morning. Very busy all the evening. Vincent stoped at a late hour.

After almost 208 years, the Thirteenth Amendment to the U.S. Constitution (which was passed by Congress on January 31, 1865) was ratified, and the American system of perpetual slavery (that "peculiar institution") finally ended.

THURSDAY, DECEMBER 7, 1865

Very rainy day. Very unusal for Thanksgiving Day to be dull. I went to hear Mr. Catto preach at St. Mary St. In the afternoon, stoped at Bustills with Vincent. Spent the evening withe Nellie.

FRIDAY, DECEMBER 8, 1865

Clear and cold. I was down home. Elijah J. was out a little ways. Mary was up in the evening, helped me trim my bonnet. John come up for her.

SATURDAY, DECEMBER 9, 1865

Very cold. It commenced snowing. In the afternoon, quite a snowstorm. I did not go out as usaly. No letter from home to day.

SUNDAY, DECEMBER 10, 1865

Beutiful day. Not cold, very windy. I went to church in the afternoon. Quite a number out. Stoped at Bustills after church. I spent the evening with Sue.

MONDAY, DECEMBER 11, 1865

John an George behaved in theire usual style. Clear. Mary was up this morning. We went to school, Egerton was here.

TUESDAY, DECEMBER 12, 1865

Rainy all day. Meeting at Elijah J.s. We had very nice meeting, few females out. After meeting, Nellie and I went down to Mary. John come up with us.

WEDNESDAY, DECEMBER 13, 1865

Clear all day. Raining in the evening. Mary was up in the evening. John come for her. Nellie did not make an appearance.

THURSDAY, DECEMBER 14, 1865

Clear and very cold. We have a donation party for the freedmen to day at the Hall. I have bin there all the afternoon and evening.

The subcommittee of the Ladies' Union Association met at the Masonic Hall to collect donations to send to Charleston, South Carolina.

FRIDAY, DECEMBER 15, 1865

Still very cold. Nellie went to Germantown this afternoon. We sent the boxes to day. Vincent did not come down as I hoped.

SATURDAY, DECEMBER 16, 1865

Still very cold. Was out a little while this afternoon. Nellie did not come in the day. She is quite a misery.

SUNDAY, DECEMBER 17, 1865

Quite cold this morning. Chris Field spoke for us this morning. Mr. Gaites in the afternoon. The church was quite clod (cold) all day.

MONDAY, DECEMBER 18, 1865

Cold and dull. School in the evening. Very nice lesson. Quite a number out.

TUESDAY, DECEMBER 19, 1865

Wet and disagreeable. Meeting at Browns, few out. Nellie did not go, stoped there after meeting. Vincent was down.

WEDNESDAY, DECEMBER 20, 1865

Cold. I received very sad news to day. My dear brother Alfred died at 1 o'clock to day. I am so sorry I did not get to see him before he died.

THURSDAY, DECEMBER 21, 1865

Very cold to day. I started for Harrisburg this afternoon. Found father, Nellie, and the rest of the family. I had a very sad journey.

FRIDAY, DECEMBER 22, 1865

Very cold. This day I have looked forward to withe dread. Poor Alfred was buried this afternoon. No one but him that knows all things knows my feelings. If it is the Master's will I hope I never will have another day like yesterday.

SATURDAY, DECEMBER 23, 1865

Very cold. I have not bin out since I have bin her(e). Frank and Harriet were here last night.

SUNDAY, DECEMBER 24, 1865

Snowing and raining. Very disagreeable. I spent the morning in reading to Father. We spent a quiet Sunday together. I hope we not spend many hours such. In the morning, I went to church.

MONDAY, DECEMBER 25, 1865

Very dull. I started for home this morning. I was quite disappointed in the way I was received at home. Vincent ever constant was the Depot. I went down home but did not stay. I spent the evening home. Vincent was up. Nellie went to hear Blind Tomy.

TUESDAY, DECEMBER 26, 1865

Very disagreeable. I have not bin out. Nellie stoped after meeting.

WEDNESDAY, DECEMBER 27, 1865

Still dull weather. I have bin very busy all day. Julie very kindly helped me. Mary and John were up this evening. Vincent was here, also spent quite a pleasant evening.

THURSDAY, DECEMBER 28, 1865

Raining all day. Very dull. I went down home in the afternoon. Spent part of the time in Nellies. Spent the evening home, quite pleasant. Vincent did not come untill late.

FRIDAY, DECEMBER 29, 1865

Clear and cold. The first clear day we have had this week. Busy all day sewing. Vincent come up in the evening.

SATURDAY, DECEMBER 30, 1865

Quite a heavy snowstorm. I sent a letter home on Thursday. Mele started for Harrisburg to day. Clear in the evening. I went down to Nellies. She has the soar throat.

SUNDAY, DECEMBER 31, 1865

Very cloudy this morning. I went to church. Very few out. Mr. Weaver spoke for us. I stoped at Marys after church. She looks quite comical sailing around. This year closes withe many changes, who knows what the next year will be. I feel very thankful that I am alive and well. Nellie and Mary are bothe sick. Vincent spent part of the evening with me. We went to Watch meeting.

Miscellaneous

Jan 1, 1865 Mr. Gibbs preached his farwell sermon to day. His text was from 20th of Acts 32 verse and "Now Bretherne, I commend you to God."

A grand reception was given on the 11th of Jan for Mr. Briarsbank, the antislavery sufferer.

Vincent went to Harrisburg on the 7th of Feb to attend the Convention.

Feb 20th John Simpson has at last enlisted. Mary is quite distressed.

Mary S. married March the 9th, 1865. An eventful wedding, Mr. Gibbs married them.

March 19th Mr. Gibbs preached a very impressive sermon from the text, "The King's Business Requires Hast Some Times, Large."

April 15th, 1865 The President was assasimated by som Conferderate villain at theathre. He die Saturday morning the 15. The city is in the deepest sorrow. These are strange times. The body of the President passed through on the 22nd of April.

Sunday, Dec 26th, 1865 Sue's baby born this afternoon. I was there in the morning after church.

All is well that ends well.

785 Jock Avenue

739 South Fourth St.

Epilogue

A WORLD WHERE THINGS ARE WELL

On October 18, 1914, at the weekly meeting for the trustees and elders of First African Presbyterian Church, an issue was raised about how the standard and quality of the Sunday School classes had gone down. After some discussion, the committee decided that changes needed to be made and that during this time of transition and reorganization, the trustees and elders needed to teach the classes. One of the first to volunteer was William B. Gaillord, who volunteered both himself and his wife. She was a lifetime member, very knowledgeable about the Bible, in good financial standing; and she owned a seat in her own name.[1] Emilie Frances (Davis) Gaillord was forty years old at the time, and like her mother and her father, she had grown up at First African surrounded by family and friends. She was probably present at the meeting, but like most married women during this time, her husband was able to speak for them both. She may have been sitting in either the Davis or the White family pew. Since her seat was in her name, she had probably purchased it on the family pew. Emilie Gaillord was the third child, second daughter of George Bustill and Emilie Davis White. She was named after her mother, and although Emilie Davis's name is spelled Emily on all of her legal documents, she gave her daughter the spelling that she preferred.

Connecting the Dots

On December 13, 1866, one year after Alfred died and Vincent was "ever constant," Emilie Frances Davis—a seamstress, domestic, and diarist—married George Bustill White. On her marriage certificate, her name is spelled Emily; perhaps it was misspelled, or maybe that change was indicative of all of the changes that had taken place in her life over the last year.

By the end of 1865, Emilie was in a serious steady relationship with Vincent that had been slowly building over three years. In the first year, he visited twenty times, and from the earliest entries, it appears as if Emilie had some feelings for him. "Nellie and Rachel over, went to the concert," Emilie wrote, "It was good, every one seemed pleased. Barker cam home with me, and Vincent with Rachel and Ellen (Black). I felt quiet displeased with Vincent." This was in March, and before then Vincent had visited only twice and had escorted her to the Douglass lecture at Mother Bethel. By July Emilie had become quite fond of him: "Vincent came home with me. What I would (do) if he was not about, I do not know." In 1864 he visited fifty-five times, but by the end of the year, Emilie was expressing some real concern over the uncertainty of their relationship: "Yesterday, Vincent spent the evening with me. He loves vists reagular but there is no understanding between us." By the end of 1865—having visited Emilie eighty-four times throughout the year, traveling to see her when she worked outside of the city, giving her a handsome ring, writing her notes and letters, and being present in her life—Vincent was "ever constant," "kind," and "very affectionate." Emilie called him her "mon cher" and seemed delighted that his presence was "passim."[2]

As a reader I was intrigued by their relationship and was quite certain (hopeful, really) that they had eventually married. I searched both the 1870 and 1880 U.S. Census Reports hoping to find Emilie and Vincent. When I did not find them, I decided to try to find all of Emilie's suitors to see if she may have married one of them. Henry Barker Black was mentioned twenty-one times and was an ideal candidate, as his sister Ellen and Emilie were such good friends. Both George Freeman (mentioned three times) and George Fulner (twice) were not discussed in any great length but were also possibilities. What is intriguing is that out of the five Georges mentioned, George Bustill White was never mentioned by his full name. Since Emilie did mention the White family, since she wrote about seeing Jake and George together (Jake was, of course, Jacob White Jr.), and since George was a member of Emilie's Singing School Association, I concluded that he was one of the Georges that she wrote about. When I discovered that Emilie had married George, my analysis about her life and her experiences changed. All of my initial conclusions about what I thought had happened to her were incorrect.

Forensic Herstorical Investigation

Very little is known about Emilie's life after 1865, and readers will walk away with more questions than answers. Part of the joy of being a forensic herstorical investigator is knowing that the story will continue to evolve as future scholars begin to piece more of Emilie's world together starting at the point where my story ends. In the last couple pages of her 1865 pocket diary, Emilie appears to have struggled with a number of personal issues, noting that "these are strange times." First, President Lincoln was assassinated in April, and Emilie traveled downtown, along with three hundred thousand other people, to view his body. She sadly noted, "To day was set apart for a general holiday but seems to be a day of mourning." Next, her older brother Alfred became very ill in November and relocated to Harrisburg, perhaps to a hospital for black soldiers and veterans. When he died in December and she received the news, she lamented, "I am so sorry I did not get to see him before he died." And on the day of his funeral, after helping her father and Nellie to bury him, Emilie, deeply saddened, wrote, "If it is the Master's will I hope I never will have another day like yesterday."

Finally, Emilie's pastor, Reverend Jonathan Gibbs, who comforted her when she lost her sister-in-law Mary and her nephew Elwood, announced that he was relocating to South Carolina (He had formally resigned in 1864 but had continued to attend and preach at the church.) to work with the formerly enslaved communities. Upon hearing the news, Emilie wrote, "I heard very discourageing news on Thursday night concerning Mr. Gibbs. He is going to leave us altogether."[3]

There was a heaviness in Emilie's final diary entries in 1865 that was not present in her earlier work. Perhaps this may have been why she decided not to keep another pocket diary (assuming she chose to stop writing a diary and not that they have been lost) or even why she may have chosen to marry George. Still, at the end of her 1865 pocket diary, Emilie turned to the very last page and wrote "All well that ends well."[4] (She later inserted the word "is.") Her first diary entry discussed the release of President Abraham Lincoln's Emancipation Proclamation, and her last one ended with her writing about how the country was in mourning because he had been assassinated. Throughout that three-year period, Emilie wrote close to thirty thousand words documenting both her experiences as a black woman and the experience that many everyday black women had during this time.

For the first two years, Emilie's pocket diaries provide a ground-level, insider's view of free black life in Philadelphia, as she recorded, in a form of repetitious dailiness, her life and her experiences. Once President Lincoln is assassinated and Emilie began to write about that experience, her 1865 diary begins to provide an even more expanded view of the free black experience as a whole. It becomes a prism that refracts the feelings and experiences of free blacks during this difficult time of mourning.[5]

One year later, the one man whom she rarely mentioned in her diaries is the one that she chose to marry, either for love or for social status. They had their first son, Jacob C.—named after both his grandfather and his uncle—in 1867. Two years later they had Maria, followed by Emilie F. in 1873.[6] By 1877 they had two more children, George Jr. in 1875 and Carry in 1877. In the 1880 U.S. Census, Emilie F. Davis White listed her occupation as a housekeeper, which was akin to being a stay-at-home mom. Emilie, who was listed as domestic in 1850 and 1860 taking care of other people's home and children, now spent her days doing this only for herself. Although she was probably still active in her Association and with the church, she was also a young mother and wife. The life that she recorded from 1863–1865 was completely different from her life as the daughter-in-law of one of the wealthiest men in Philadelphia. Even though her husband is listed as a barber, which was a Grade II skill, he had access to money and property through his father. He was a graduate of the Institute for Colored Youth and a member of the Banneker Institute (which had been founded by his brother). When his father purchased five and a half acres of land and opened Lebanon Cemetery (the only black-owned cemetery that was not attached to a church), George probably worked with him to manage the property. For Emilie, the life of leisure and comfort that she had always wanted (or at least that is the picture she paints in her pocket diaries), she finally achieved.

Readers will leave Emilie's story with more questions than answers: What happened to Vincent and Nellie? What was the distressing news that her sister mentioned in the letter but Emilie never discussed in her diary? What happened to Alfred and Mary's son Frank? What happened to Emilie in 1866? What happened to her father and her sister? What was her life like with George? Was she happy? And even more important, are there any copies of Emilie Davis's other diaries that are waiting to be discovered?

Ending Well

On December 26, 1889, after more than twenty-three years with George, Emilie died from an infection in her lungs and her kidneys. She was 51 years old, a mother of five, and a grandmother of at least one. She was buried at the family plot at Lebanon Cemetery and was joined there by her husband ten years later. Eden Cemetery acquired Lebanon in 1903, the records (for the most part) are still intact. At least three of Emilie's children and one of her grandchildren are buried at Lebanon: Emilie (d. 1959), her husband William (d. 1955), and their daughter Florence (d. 1909); George Jr. (date of death unknown); and Maria (d. 1905).

Emilie's system of daily record keeping may have ended on December 31, 1865 but her life continued on. By putting her words onto paper, she ultimately controlled both her story and how it was told. Although her life was not exceptional, the fact that her words have survived and been preserved makes her an exception to the rule and allows her life and her story to be read, analyzed, and used as one of the stitches that help to fill the gap between the elite and the enslaved woman's experience. The gap, though it is not full, is not as empty as it once was. Emilie's voice and life have finally been added to this space and for now, at least, all is indeed well.

WHO'S WHO

MARY ANN ADGER was married to Robert J. Adger and was the mother of fourteen children (including Bell, Lizzie, James, and Robert Jr.). She was a member of the Ladies' Union Association.

ROBERT M. ADGER SR. was born enslaved in Charleston, South Carolina. Although his mother was born free in New York, in 1810, while visiting friends in South Carolina, she was captured and enslaved. Adger's family was eventually freed after their plantation owner died and friends filed legal papers. Adger relocated to Philadelphia in 1845 and worked as a nurse and as a waiter at Old Merchants Hotel, and he owned a furniture business on South Street above Eighth Street, in the Fourth Ward. He served as an elder and a member of the board of trustees at First African Presbyterian church. Adger was one of the signers of the 1863 "Call to Arms" circular.

(DR.) THOMAS AMOS was a minister and a teacher who had been born in Monrovia, Liberia—his parents were among the first black missionaries sent from America to work in Africa. They had been sent abroad by the Presbyterian Church. When Amos's father died, he returned to America and studied at Ashmun Institute (now Lincoln University). He served as the pastor of First African Presbyterian from June 1889 to May 1891. After leaving First African, Amos served as the head of Ferguson Academy in Abbeville, South Carolina.

(DR.) JAMES J. GOULD BIAS was born enslaved and worked as a bleeder, a cupper, a dentist, a practitioner of phrenology (the detailed study of the shape and size of the cranium, which is supposed to indicate character and mental abilities). He was a Mason and a Methodist preacher. Bias was also a founding member of Carthagenian Lodge No. 901 of the Grand United Order of Odd Fellows and had worked with Charles Tourney, a white minister who helped runaway slaves escape north to Baltimore. Bias was married to Eliza Anne, who worked with him as his medical assistant and on the Underground Railroad.

EBENEZER BLACK was a cleaner, a dyer, the corresponding secretary at First African Presbyterian Church and the owner of several real estate properties in and around Philadelphia. Black was one of the signers of the charter for the Philadelphia Library Company of Colored Persons along with James Forten Jr. (the eldest son of sailmaker James Forten Sr. and the father of Charlotte Forten); boot maker and amateur musician Morris Brown Jr. (his father was Bishop Morris Brown Sr. of the African Methodist Episcopal Church); and well-known barbers Daniel B. Brown, William S. Gordon, and Thomas Butler. Black was also one of the signers of the 1863 "Call to Arms" circular.

ELLEN BLACK was one of Emilie's closest friends. They sang together on the Singing School Association choir at First African and were both members of the Ladies' Union Association. Her father was Ebenezer Black.

HENRY BARKER BLACK was Ellen's brother and a member of the Banneker Institute, an elite men's intellectual organization. In 1866 he lived at 612 Barclay Street.

DAVID (BOUSE) BUSTILL BOWSER was an ornamental portrait painter who had studied under his cousin Robert Douglass Jr. (Douglass attended the School of Design and the Pennsylvania Academy of Fine Arts; he was well known for painting and selling lithographs of William Lloyd Garrison in an effort to raise money for the abolitionist movement); a former steamboat barber who had worked on steamboats on the Mississippi and Red rivers; a grandmaster and grand secretary of Carthagenian Lodge No. 901 of the Grand United Order of Odd Fellows 1872–92; and the grandson of Cyrus Bustill—one of the founders of Philadelphia's Free African Society. Bowser was one of the signers of the 1863 "Call to Arms" circular and a member of the African Protestant Episcopal Church of St. Thomas', Philadelphia.

ELIZABETH (LIZZIE) HARRIET STEVENS GRAY BOWSER was a seamstress and a member of the Ladies' Union Association. Bowser was married to David Bustill Bowser and had three children: Raphael, a painter; Mary; and Ida Elizabeth Bowser Asbury, who was a music teacher, a violinist, and the first African American woman to earn a degree from the University of Pennsylvania. In 1860 the family lived in the Twelfth Ward at 841 North Fourth Street.

HANNAH BROWN was married to John Brown, and they had a seven-year-old daughter, Lizzie. The Browns lived in Ward 10 of the East District.

LIZZIE BROWN served as the secretary of the Ladies' Union Association in 1865.

MARY V. BROWN was an 1864 graduate of the Institute for Colored Youth and lived at 87 Locust Street. She served as the vice president of the Ladies Union Association and was known for hosting elaborate soirees to raise money for regimental flags to be made and shipped to the black regiments.

GEORGE BURRELL was one of Emilie's closest male friends and a member of the Banneker Institute.

William T. Catto served as the pastor of First African 1854–59. He was born in Charleston, South Carolina, to Fanny Shields (she was freed by her plantation owner, Matthew Shields, before he died); was an established member of the free black Philadelphia elite (he relocated to Philadelphia in 1848, after establishing himself as an activist and a minister); and was the father of activist Octavius Catto. He was married to Sarah Isabella Cain, a descendant of a respected South Carolina mulatto family.

Octavius V. Catto was born free in Charleston, South Carolina. In 1858 he was both the valedictorian and the commencement speaker for the Institute for Colored Youth. After studying in Washington, D.C., Catto returned to the institute to work as the assistant to the Yale- and Dartmouth-educated principal of the school, Professor Ebenezer Don Carlos Bassett. Catto later became the principal teacher of the male department. He was a member of St. Thomas and the Banneker Institute, where he served as secretary. He was an outspoken activist who had helped to organize the 1863 "Call to Arms" circular and helped to integrate the Philadelphia streetcar system. He was either involved with or engaged to Caroline Le Count and was childhood friends with Jake White.

Alfred Davis was Emilie's older brother and lived in Pottsville with his wife, Mary, and his son, Francis (Frank). He worked as a waiter and was later drafted into the U.S. Colored Troops.

Charles Davis was Emilie's father. He was born in Maryland and was married to Helena Davis.

Elijah Joshua Davis was Emilie's uncle. In 1860, he lived at 916 Rodman Street, between South and Lombard, with his wife, Sarah; his son, Elwood (Bub); his nieces, Emilie and Elizabeth; and, his nephew, Thomas. He worked as a waiter and was later drafted into the Sixth Regiment Company A of the U.S. Colored Troops. Davis was one of the lodge leaders of Carthagenian Lodge No. 901 of the Grand United Order of Odd Fellows and was a member of their subcommittee of management. Davis was also one of the signers of the 1863 "Call to Arms" circular.

Elizabeth Davis was Emilie's younger sister. She was five years younger than Emilie. The 1850 U.S. Census notes that she attended school, and in the 1860 U.S. Census, she is listed as a seamstress.

Helena Davis was Emilie's mother and was married to Charles Davis. She was mentioned in the 1850 U.S. Census but was not mentioned in Emilie's diaries.

Mary A. Davis was Emilie's sister-in-law, Alfred's wife. In 1860 her occupation is listed as nurse.

SARAH DAVIS was Emilie's aunt, Elijah J.'s wife. She served as the treasurer of the Ladies' Union Association.

THOMAS (TOMY) DAVIS was Emilie's younger brother and a soldier in the U.S. Navy.

WILLIAM HENRY DORSEY was the oldest child of caterer Thomas J. (an escaped slave from Maryland) and Louise Tobias (a freeborn Philadelphia woman). He listed himself as an artist in the Philadelphia city directory and was a custodian of the American Negro Historical Society. Dorsey collected over 388 scrapbooks and 914 biographical files, which included paintings, portraits of notable blacks, coins, autographs, catalogues, books, letters, and artifacts. He married dressmaker Virginia Cashin in 1859, and they had six kids: Thomas Rembrandt, Van Dyke, Toussaint Overture, Virginia, Ira, and Sadie.

SARAH ("ZILLAH," "ELLA") MAPPS DOUGLASS was the daughter of Robert and Grace Bustill (and a granddaughter of Cyrus Bustill), a women's rights antislavery activist, a Quaker, an accomplished painter, a published poet (publishing under pen names "Zillah" and "Ella"), and the head of the preparatory department at the Institute for Colored Youth. She studied anatomy at the Female Medical College of Pennsylvania and Pennsylvania Medical University during the 1850s. She founded an all-girls school in 1820 that was subsidized by the Philadelphia Female Antislavery Society. The school eventually merged with the institute in 1859. In 1833 Douglass was one of four black women (along with the Forten sisters: Harriet Purvis, Sarah, and Margaretta) to sign the charter for the Female Anti-Slavery Society of Philadelphia and later was elected to serve two terms as the treasurer at the second and third antislavery conventions. She served as president of the Female Literary Association in the 1830s and helped to found Gilbert Lyceum, a polite literary group, in 1841. She married William Douglass in 1855.

SARAH DOUGLASS was the daughter of William J. Douglass and the stepdaughter of Sarah Mapps Douglass. She was a teacher at the Institute for Colored Youth and a member of the Philadelphia Female Antislavery Society.

WILLIAM J. DOUGLASS was born and raised in Baltimore and was tutored by black emigrationist Daniel Coker in Latin, Greek, and Hebrew. Douglass was first ordained as an African Methodist Episcopal (AME) minister and worked as a pastor of a church in Baltimore before relocating to Philadelphia to become the rector of African Protestant Episcopal Church of St. Thomas', Philadelphia, for close to thirty years before he retired. He was first married to Elizabeth, and they had twelve children before she died in 1853. He married Sarah Mapps less than a year after his wife passed and went on to become a prominent, well-known speaker on slavery and African colonization.

First African Presbyterian Church was founded in 1807 by John Gloucester Sr. and was the first and only black Presbyterian church in the country and the fifth black church in the city. From 1811 to 1813, the congregation grew from 123 members to 300 hundred. It sat at the corner of Seventh and Shippen (now Bainbridge) Streets, which was four blocks from Emilie's 1860 address. It is currently located at 4159 West Girard Street.

Hiram Fry attended the 1858 Second Presbyterian and Congregational Convention held at the Central Presbyterian Church on Lombard Street in Philadelphia. He represented the Reading Presbyterian Church.

Anna Amelia Harris Gibbs was an elite free black woman from New York and was married to Jonathan Gibbs. They had three children, Thomas Van Renssalaer (who later cofounded and was the vice president of Florida A&M College), Julia Pennington, and Josephine Haywood. They later divorced sometime between 1863–64.

Jonathan Gibbs was the fourth pastor of First African Presbyterian Church. He was officially installed on January 29, 1860, and served until 1865. Prior to working at First African, Gibbs was the pastor of the Liberty Street Presbyterian Church in Troy, New York, and had attended the 1858 Second Presbyterian and Congregational Convention in Philadelphia. He was one of the signers of the 1863 "Call to Arms" circular. Gibbs was first married to Anna Harris, and they had three children. He later married Elizabeth, and they had one daughter, Anna, who died in infancy. Gibbs and Elizabeth later relocated to South Carolina and then to Florida, where he was eventually appointed secretary of state, becoming the first black person to serve in this position.

James A. Gloucester was the founder of Siloam Presbyterian Church in Brooklyn, New York. The church served as a stop on the Underground Railroad, and in 1850 John Brown stopped by en route to Harpers Ferry.

Jeremiah Gloucester graduated from the Presbyterian Synod of New York and New Jersey and served as the pastor of the Second African Presbyterian Church located on St. Mary's Street between Sixth and Seventh Streets.

John Gloucester Jr. was, a Presbyterian minister, and a student at Ashman Institute (now Lincoln University).

John Gloucester Sr. was born enslaved in Tennessee on the plantation of Gideon Blackburn, an evangelical preacher. Growing up, Gloucester made a name for himself converting whites and blacks to the church. In the early 1800s, after Blackburn freed him, Gloucester traveled with Blackburn to preach in Philadelphia.

Gloucester remained in Philadelphia, founded First African, and traveled through-out the North and abroad to raise money from various supporters to purchase his wife and his four sons: Jeremiah, John Jr., Stephen, and James.

STEPHEN GLOUCESTER founded Lombard Street Central Presbyterian Church in 1842, after his brother's church, Second African, burned down. He was also a member of the Banneker Institute along with Ebenezer Bassett. He was a member of the committee of twelve, along with James Forten, Absalom Jones, and Richard Allen, to vote on the issue of African colonization. (The first vote was no, and the committee vowed then to "never voluntarily separate themselves from their brethren in slavery.")[1]

ALFRED B. GREEN was a quartermaster at Camp William Penn and was a member of the Banneker Institute. He was one of the signers of the 1863 "Call to Arms" circular. He was the son of Reverend Augustus Green, an AME minister who relocated to Canada because of the Fugitive Slave Act, later writing and publishing *A Discourse for Our Time*. The pamphlet extolled the benefits of living in Canada and urged black Americans to consider moving there. Alfred had originally been arrested in 1860, when he attempted to help rescue Moses Horner, a free man who was seized under the Fugitive Slave Act in an effort to take him to the South.

ELIZABETH TAYLOR GREENFIELD was born enslaved in Natchez, Mississippi. When her mistress moved to Philadelphia, Greenfield moved as well and was raised and tutored by a Philadelphia-based Quaker woman. When her mistress died in 1844, Greenfield inherited her estate. As an opera singer, Greenfield had an astonishing three-and-a-half-octave range and an active career in England (she once sang for Queen Alexandra) and America and was known around the world as the "Black Swan."[2]

MARY GREW attended the Second Anti-Slavery Convention of American Women held in 1838 and was a member of the Philadelphia Female Anti-Slavery Society.

THE HUTCHINSON FAMILY SINGERS were one of the most popular singing groups of the 1840s. Specializing in four-part harmony, the group sang about slavery, women's rights, and temperance. The group frequently traveled with Frederick Douglass, performing at the events where he was scheduled to speak.

THE INSTITUTE FOR COLORED YOUTH (now Cheney University) was established in 1852 on a bequest from Quaker Richard Humphreys and was located at 915 Bainbridge on Seventh and Lombard Streets, two blocks from Emilie's 1860 address. Although it is the oldest African-American institution of higher learning, degrees were not granted until 1914, when it adopted the curriculum of a normal school (teacher training).

Rochel Johnson was a washerwoman who lived at 807 Locust within walking distance of Emilie's home.

Mary Jones was a washerwoman who lived at 511 South Tenth Street within walking distance of First African.

Redding B. Jones was unanimously elected and served as the pastor of First African Presbyterian Church 1873–79. He previously worked as a community pastor in the Seventh Ward. Although he was very popular with the First African congregants, Redding was asked to leave the church because the elders were concerned that he was becoming too involved with the "holiness" fad. Jones was a theology student at Ashmun Institute (now Lincoln University).

William D. Kelley was a former judge on the Philadelphia court of common pleas and an ardent supporter and speaker for the antislavery movement.

The Ladies' Union Association of Philadelphia was formed on July 20th, 1863, for the purpose of administering exclusively to the wants of the sick and wounded colored soldiers. Members included Mary Brown, Caroline Le Count, Ellen Black, Lizzie Bowser, Sarah Davis, and Emilie.

John Mercer Langston was an honors graduate of Oberlin College, the son of a wealthy Virginia planter, and a practicing lawyer. He passed the state bar exam in 1850 and was admitted to the Ohio bar in 1853. Langston was married to Caroline and was the author of *Selected Lectures and Addresses* (1883).

Caroline (Carrie) Rebecca Le Count was an 1863 graduate of the Institute for Colored Youth, a descendent of the Le Count family—one of the elite black families in Philadelphia—and was involved with activist Octavius Catto. Her father, James, was a cabinetmaker-turned-undertaker who sent all three of his children to the Institute for Colored Youth. Le Count was the corresponding secretary of the Ladies' Union Association and a part of the subcommittee. She taught at the Ohio Street School in 1865, and by 1868 she had been promoted to principal.

Addison W. Lively was born in Virginia around 1820 and was a member of Shiloh Baptist Church, a musician, and the director of the church's choir. He was also Emilie's guitar teacher.

Pliny Locke was the son of Ishmael and Mary Locke from Camden, New Jersey. He graduated from the Institute for Colored Youth, class of 1867, and was the father of Alain Locke, America's first black Rhodes scholar.

Theophilus J. Minton was a student at the Institute for Colored Youth and was known for his diligence and good conduct.

MOTHER BETHEL AFRICAN METHODIST CHURCH was one of the first black churches in America. It is located at the corner of Sixth and Lombard Streets (which is now considered to be the oldest continuously black-owned parcel of land in the country).

NELLIE was Emilie's confidant, companion, and *meilleur amie*. From 1863 to April 1864, Nellie dated Cristy, Emilie's teacher. Although Nellie was mentioned 504 times and Cristy was mentioned 38 times, I have been unable to locate any biographical information on them.

MARY CORNELIA SIMPSON was married to Gideon H. Pierce of Bridgeton, New Jersey and was the sister of John Simpson.

JOHN SIMPSON was a private in the Third Regiment Company D of the U.S. Colored Troops. He was drafted on October 21, 1864, and mustered out on September 9, 1865. He was one of the signers of the 1863 "Call to Arms" circular.

WILLIAM STILL was a noted abolitionist and a "conductor" on the Underground Railroad. He lived at 410 Sixth Street within walking distance of Mother Bethel Church. Still served on Philadelphia's Board of Trade and had helped to establish a Young Men's Christian Association (YMCA) for the black community. He worked as a clerk and janitor for the Pennsylvania Anti-Slavery Society and then as a clerk for the Pennsylvania Abolition Society (PAS). In 1867 he was elected—along with Octavius Catto, Ebenezer Bassett (the principal of the Institute for Colored Youth), Stephen Smith, William Whipper, and Jacob White—for membership into the PAS. They were the first black members of the PAS, along with Frederick Douglass and Robert Purvis.

VINCENT was Emilie's suitor from 1863 to 1865 and was mentioned 213 times in the diary. Since Emilie did not mention his last name or any identifying information about him, I have been unable to locate any biographical information on him.

GEORGE BUSTILL WHITE was one of six children of Jacob C. and Elizabeth White, Sr. He was a graduate of the Institute, a barber, and a member of the Banneker Institute. He married Emilie in 1866 and they had five children: Jacob C. III, Maria, Emilie F., George Jr., and Carry.

JACOB (JAKE) CLEMENT WHITE JR. was born and raised in Philadelphia and both attended and later became a teacher at the Institute for Colored Youth. He was the son of Jacob White Sr. and grew up working in his father's cemetery as a secretary and a manager. Early on, White took after his father and ventured into business and education: in 1854 he founded Benezet Joint Stock Association (with stock selling for $25 and returning dividends into 1885); in 1861 he served on the Haitian Bureau of Emigration. In 1863, he was one of the signers of the "Call to Arms" circular and a youth leader at First African. One year later, he was hired as the principal and the only teacher at Robert Vaux Elementary School (becoming the first black principal in Philadelphia). White served as the secretary of the Pythians Base ball Club, the city's second (and most popular) black baseball team; helped to found the American Negro Historical Society; and later worked as a consultant to W. E. B. Du Bois (1890).

Jacob Clement White Sr. was one of the wealthiest men in Philadelphia and was one of the founders (along with Sarah Mapps Douglass) of Gilbert Lyceum. He also served as First African's Sunday School superintendent (under one of his closest friends, Reverend William Catto) and was the first president of their board of trustees. White worked as a barber, a bleeder, an unlicensed physician, and a store owner. In 1847 White bought five and a half acres of land at Ninth and Lombard and opened Lebanon Cemetery, one of the few black-owned burial grounds (and the only one that was not attached to a church). He also owned property in Providence. He was married to seamstress Elizabeth Miller White, and they were members of Second African Presbyterian Church. Elizabeth was also a member of the Female Vigilance Committee. The Whites lived at 100 Old York Road.

NOTES

Editorial Methods

1. *Diaries of Emilie Davis* http://www.libraries.psu.edu/psul/digital/davisdiaries.html (Accessed 7 January 2013); "Memorable Days: The Emilie Davis Diaries." Villanova University. http://davisdiaries.villanova.edu (Accessed 20 July 2013).

2. Sterling, *Speak Out in Thundertones*, 61–65; Diaries, February 17, 1863.

3. Du Bois *The Philadelphia Negro*

4. Diaries, January 2, 1863.

5. Diaries, January 3 and July 13, 1863; and Miscellaneous 1863.

Introduction: A World Discovered

1. Laurel Thatcher Ulrich writes that the process of moving from invisibility to visibility occurs when women's work moves from the household into the marketplace. I submit that the same process takes place when a nineteenth-century working-class free black woman makes a conscious decision to record and preserve her experiences, particularly since "far more women were accustomed to using needles than pens." "Of Pens and Needles," 202, 205.

2. Motz, "Folk Expression of Time and Place," 138.

3. Nash, *Forging Freedom*, 251.

4. Decosta-Willis, *Memphis Diary*, 9.

5. In 1997, *Education World* noted that over fifty-five books had been published about the Civil War, an average of one a day since the War ended in 1865. *Education World*.

6. For more on immortality, Afrocentric womanism, and the focus on preservation, see Temple, "The cosmology of Afrocentric womanism."

7. This idea that language was a cultural artifact and had social value was first expanded on by Pierre Bourdieu, who argued that the greater amounts of linguistic capital a person possessed then the more power they had within their society, because linguistic fluency translated into social advantage. Bonfiglio, *Race*, 12.

8. Lorde, "Poetry Is Not a Luxury," 38.

9. Hull, "Researching Alice Dunbar-Nelson, 318; Marwick, "Two Approaches to Historical Study, 9; McCarthy, "A Pocketful of Days," 277n5.

10. Panniers were undergarments that were used to extend the width of the skirts at the side while leaving the front and back flat.

11. Ulrich, "The Ways of Her Household," 53.

12. McCarthy, "A Pocketful of Days," 283–84.

13. In addition to providing instructions on how to keep a daily record, Cobbett also gives advice for the lover, the husband and father, the youth, and the citizen. McCarthy, "A Pocketful of Days," 87.

14. Prior to 1863, lead pencils were manufactured exclusively in Germany. It was not until 1865, with the adoption of a U.S. tariff and the creation of automatic machinery, that pencils were manufactured in America. "History of the Lead Pencil"; beginning in 1850, fountain pens—which consisted of iridium-tipped gold nibs, hard rubber, and free-flowing ink—were widely produced and distributed throughout the U.S.

15. Sterling, *We Are Your Sisters*, 237.

16. "Peter Wood on Inheriting Mother's Slave Status."; Given that this law that shifted inherited status from the father to the mother ran counter to the English law, one wonders how many mixed race children were being born every year that would necessitate this type of change. Giddings, *When and Where I Enter*, 33–35; Hine, *African-American History*, 79.

17. Sterling, *We Are Your Sisters*, 242–43.

18. Diaries, January 1, 1863.

19. Hershberg et al., "The 'Journey to Work,'" 142; Weigley, "The Border City," 379, 381.

20. Du Bois, *Philadelphia Negro*, 58–59.

21. Salvatore, *We All Got History*, 19; R. Lane, *William Dorsey's Philadelphia*, 72.

22. The information about Emilie and her family has been compiled from the 1850 and 1860 U.S. Census, the McElroy's Philadelphia Directory for 1860, and Emilie's 1863–65 pocket diaries.

23. Connolly, "The Disappearance," 33.

24. Diaries, January 22, 1863, May 6, 1863, May 9, 1863; Gambler, *The Female Economy*, 11–13.

25. Du Bois, *Philadelphia Negro*, 6–7.

26. D. Newman, "Black Women," 289.

27. D. C. Hine, *Hine Sight*, 7.

28. Lapsansky, "Friends, Wives, and Striving," 5–6, 11–13.

29. Lindenmeyer, *Ordinary Women*, xvii–xix.

30. Lorde, "Poetry Is Not a Luxury," 38.

31. King, "Out of Bounds, 128; Berlin, *Slaves without Masters*, xiii.

32. Quoted in Gilbert, *Narrative*, i–xxvi.

33. Stevenson, *Journals*; Hull, *Give Us Each Day*; Decosta-Willis, *Memphis Diary*.

34. Quoted in Gutman, *Black Family*, 36.

35. In "Rape and the Inner Lives of Black Women," D. Hine uses the phrase "culture of dissemblance" to describe how enslaved women collectively created and maintained alternate self-images that helped them to function and bear the weight of racial and sexual oppression in mainstream America. I suggest that this type of collective image creation and masking also happened in the area of literacy. D. Hine, *Hine Sight*, 42–43; Hunter, *To 'Joy*, 40.

36. Blassingame, "Using the Testimony," 480–85; For more information on how the interviews are viewed within the sociolinguistics field, see Kautzsch, *The Historical Evolution*, particularly 13–16, 23–26.

37. Kautzsch, *Historical Evolution*, 23–26.

38. Temple, "Theory of Immortalization," 4; Lerner, *Black Women*, 569–70; Bennett, *Before the Mayflower* (1984), 152.

Chapter 1: Emilie Davis, 1863

1. Bennett, *Before the Mayflower* (1984 ed.), 191.

Chapter 2: A World Imagined

1. Walters, *We Have This Ministry*, 6, 28.

2. There are contradictory reports on how many children Gloucester had, with some reports stating that he had four sons and other reports stating that he had six children. Four of his sons are mentioned in at least two sources, Walters's *We Have This Ministry* and an unpublished report of the history of First African Presbyterian Church. It was equivalent to $22,200.

3. Du Bois, *Philadelphia Negro,* 211–17; $1,538 is equivalent to $28,453, $900 is equivalent to $16,650, $650 is equivalent to $12,025, and $3,338 is equivalent to $61,753.

4. R. Lane, *William Dorsey's Philadelphia,* 61.

5. Instead of working at First African, Cornish relocated to New York to cofound *Freedom's Journal,* the first black newspaper, with John B. Russworm.

6. On August 1, approximately twelve hundred free blacks marched through downtown Philadelphia to celebrate the anniversary of the abolition of slavery in the British West Indies. They were attacked by an Irish mob that proceeded to vandalize the homes of black residents and burn several black-owned establishments, including Second African and Smith's Hall on Lombard Street. With numbers somewhere in the thousands, the mob, according to Frederick Douglass, had the "ferocity of wild-beasts" and black people left the city heading to Bucks County and New Jersey. Salvatore, *We All Got History,* 22–23.

7. Lapsansky, *Neighborhoods in Transition,* 120–24

8. "A History," 1–2.

9. Diaries, July 24, January 29, and April 5, 1863.

10. Du Bois, *Philadelphia Negro,* 87; Nash, *First City,* 181.

11. Du Bois, *Philadelphia Negro,* 138, 149; Nash, *First City,* 181.

12. Diaries, March 29, May 7, and May 28, 1863; September 20, 1864.

13. Ibid., January 19 and January 26, 1863.

14. Ibid., March 16 and November 19, 1863.

15. *Walker's Appeal, in Four Articles; Together with a Preamble, to the Coloured Citizens of the World, but in Particular, and Very Expressly, to Those of the United States of America, Written in Boston, State of Massachusetts, September 28, 1829* http://docsouth.unc.edu/nc/walker/walker.html (accessed July 20, 2013).

16. Royster, *Traces of a Stream,* 61.

17. Gambler, "Tarnished Labor," 186–88, 194–95.

18. Diaries, Memoranda section, 1863, and September 18, 1863.

19. Du Bois, *Philadelphia Negro,* 310–20; R. Lane, *Roots of Violence,* 41.

20. By 1880 the figures had shifted down to approximately two to four dollars per week ($37.50–$74.00). Wright, *Negro in Pennsylvania,* 58; R. Lane, *William Dorsey's Philadelphia,* 60–62.

21. South Carolina was the first to leave the Union and was quickly followed by Mississippi, Florida, Alabama, Georgia, Louisiana, Texas, Virginia, North Carolina, Tennessee, and Arkansas—coincidentally, the states that had the largest enslaved populations in America.

22. Garcia et al., *Creating America,* 481–84, 520.

23. Basker,"This Government Can Not Endure," 6.

24. Bennett, *Before the Mayflower* (1984 ed.), 191.

25. Guelzo, *Lincoln's Emancipation Proclamation,* 134–35.

26. Blight, *A Slave No More,* 157.

27. Douglass, *In Memoriam,* 44–45.

28. Tillery, "Inevitability," 138–39.

29. P. Foner, *Frederick Douglass,* 3, 9–10.

30. Remond also joined Douglass on the American Anti-Slavery Society's Hundred Conventions project, which was a six-month tour of meeting halls; Martin R. Delany previously published *Mystery,* a successful weekly newspaper that highlighted black issues and women's rights; he coedited the newspaper. In 1868 Frances "Frank" Rollin, a freeborn writer and teacher from Charleston, South Carolina, wrote Delany's autobiography, *The Life and Public Services of Martin R. Delany.*

31. *An Appeal from the Colored Men,* 6

32. Royster, *Traces of a* Stream, 46.

33. Bennett, *Before the Mayflower* (1984), 198–99, 496; Stauffer, *Giants,* 16–17.

34. Lincoln Qtd. in Bennett, *Before the Mayflower* (2007), 179–80; for more on Lincoln's contradictions around freeing the enslaved population to save the Union, see E. Foner, *Our Lincoln,* particularly pages 135–85; and Bennett, *Forced into Glory;* Stauffer, 17.

35. Bennett, *Before the Mayflower* (1984), 198.

36. Dorothy Sterling, *We Are Your Sisters,* 243. Author's note: Even though I am aware of the criticism around using enslaved interviews without removing the obvious edits from the interviewees (the deliberate use of "eye" dialect, that is using "dem" and "dose" instead of "them" and "those"), I am choosing to use them as they were printed.

37. Dwight Lyceum (DL) Moody was an evangelist and preacher who founded Moody Church, the Northfield School, and the Mount Herman School in Massachusetts; the Moody Bible Institute; and Moody Publications; F. Douglass, *Life and Times,* 429.

38. Higginson later led the First South Carolina Volunteer Regiment, which was the first organization of black soldiers fully authorized by the War Department. He stated that his troops ranked among the best in the army: "Instead of leaving their homes and families, they are fighting for their homes and families; and they show the resolution and sagacity which a personal purpose gains." Katz, *Breaking the Chains,* 164.

39. Higginson, *Army Life,* 41; Katz, *Breaking the Chains;* Higginson's regiment and was stationed in Beaufort, South Carolina, and one of the northern teachers on the base was Charlotte Forten, a freeborn woman, who wrote that Higginson was "the one best fitted to command a regiment of colored soldiers." Stevenson, *Journals,* xv.

40. Sterling, *We Are Your Sisters,* 243.

41. F. Douglass, *Autobiographies,* 782.

42. Bennett Jr., *Before the Mayflower* (2007), 185; F. Douglass, *Autobiographies,* 792.

43. Hershberg, "Free Blacks," 375; Bennett, *Before the Mayflower* (1984), 200, and (2007), 197.

44. For a thorough listing of the types of activities that free black communities were involved in throughout the North and South, see Christian, *Black Saga,* 63–195.

45. Bennett, *Before the Mayflower* (2007), 183.

46. Binder, "Pennsylvania Negro," 386.

47. Bennett, *Before the Mayflower* (1984), 492, 186.

48. Diaries, February 15, June 28 and June 30, 1863; July 16, 1864; May 16, 1865.

49. Ibid., October 30–31, 1863, and January 29–30, 1864.

50. Hershberg and Williams, "Mulattoes and Blacks," 396.

51. E. Foner, *Who Owns History*, 157.

52. Ibid., 397. This shift in color designation was not exclusive to Philadelphia, it also happened in Ohio. In 1860, the family of Joseph Willson, the author of *Sketches of Black Upper-Class Life in Antebellum Philadelphia by "A Southerner"* (1841), was described as white and enjoyed access to the colored aristocracy. By 1870 the family members were reclassified as "Negroes" and experienced a slight economic downturn. Winch, *Elite of Our People,* 58.

53. R. Lane, *William Dorsey's Philadelphia*, 59.

54. Hershberg and Williams, "Mulattoes and Blacks," 397–99. For more on how the term "mulatto" was used in the Afro-Cherokee communities, see Mills, *Ties That Bind.*

55. The other large free black communities were located in New York City and in New Orleans. Hershberg, "Free Blacks," 368; Martin, "Banneker Literary," 304.

56. Hershberg and Williams, "Mulattoes and Blacks," 392–434.

57. Du Bois, *Philadelphia Negro*, 6–7.

58. Because of its concentrated wealth, talent, and prestige, Emma Jones Lapsansky contends that the Seventh Ward was very much like Harlem during the 1920s. "Friends, Wives, and Striving," 10.

59. Du Bois, *Philadelphia Negro,* 375; Lapsansky, "Friends, Wives, and Striving," 7; Sterling, *We Are Your Sisters*, 112.

60. This color stratification, in both the North and the South, did not end with the Emancipation Proclamation, or even Reconstruction; in some areas, like Washington, D.C., and Mississippi, color distinctions remained in place until World War II ended and unfortunately it remains part of the discussion in the black community today. Hershberg and Williams, "Mulattoes and Blacks," 423; R. Lane, *William Dorsey's Philadelphia*, 277.

61. Diaries, August 23, 1863.

62. Ibid. This is the only time that Emilie used the word "white" in her three years' worth of entries.

63. At the same time, throughout the South, many states had passed restrictive Slave Codes, which made it a crime to teach black people how to read and write. This legislation, which lasted from 1705 to 1865, also greatly restricted their movement and was the precursor to the harsher and more restrictive Black Codes. Legislated during Reconstruction, the Black Codes stayed in place from 1865 to 1877 and were designed to reinstitute slavery by restricting the rights of newly freed men, women, and children under vagrancy and apprenticeship laws. The Black Codes later evolved into the Jim Crow "separate but equal" laws, which began in 1877 and stayed in place well into the twentieth century. The phrase "separate but equal" comes out of the 1896 *Plessy v. Ferguson* U.S. Supreme Court decision, which allowed for the establishment of separate white and black facilities as long as they were "equal." In 1954 the Supreme Court case *Oliver L. Brown et al. v. the Board of Education of*

Topeka, which was a combination of five different court cases, overturned this decision. The Court ruled that separate facilities were not equal. One year later they ordered all public facilities to "integrate with all deliberate speed." Even after the *Brown* decisions, it was not until after the modern-day civil rights movement that schools, businesses, churches, and universities (to name just a few public and private spaces) began to fully integrate and allow people of all races to participate. Whitehead, "Impact"; Hershberg, "Free Blacks," 380.

64. Bacon, *Statistics,* 3–6.

65. Lapsansky, "Friends, Wives, and Striving," 9; Bacon, *Statistics*, chap. 3, 3–6 passim.

66. Although Wheatley is best known as a poet (she published her first book of poetry at the age of six, when she was living in London), she frequently corresponded with her friends by letter. Some letters have survived and substantiate her reputation as a perspicacious writer. Here she wrote to a friend in New Port, Rhode Island, in July of 1772: "I can't say but my voyage to England has conduced to the recovery (in a great measure) of my Health. The Friends I found there among the Nobility and Gentry. Their Benevolent conduct towards me, the unexpected and unmerited civility and Complaisance with which I was treated by all, fills me with astonishment. I can scarcely Realize it. This I humbly hope has the happy Effect of lessening me in my own Esteem. Your reflections on the sufferings of the Son of God, & the inestimable prive of our immortal Souls, Plainly dem[on]strate the sensations of a Soul united to Jesus." Qtd. in Woodson, *Mind of the Negro*, xviii; Majors, *Noted Negro Women*, 21.

67. Bennett, *Before the Mayflower* (1984), 78–80.

68. Diaries, March 18, 1863, March 24, 1863, and March 26, 1863. For more on the Hutchinson Family Singers, see Gac, *Singing for Freedom*.

69. The 1850 Fugitive Slave Act also nullified the writ of habeas corpus for black Americans and denied them of the right to have a trial by jury and the opportunity to take the stand, placing the power in the hands of plantation owners and federal marshalls. N. Taylor, *Frontiers of Freedom,* 154–55.

70. Christian, *Black Saga,* 60–61.

71. Diaries, January 1, 1863.

72. Ibid., January 1, 1864.

73. Ibid., July 21, 1863. Although Emilie records it on the 21st, the official records for the Ladies' Union Association states that the meeting happened on the 20th.

74. *Report of the Ladies' Union Association*, 7–8; Diaries, December 13, 1864.

75. Salvatore, *We All Got History*, 71; Lapsansky, "Discipline to the Mind," 88–89.

76. Salvatore, *We All Got History*, 60–66.

77. Diaries, July 17, 1863, and July 23, 1863.

78. *Report of The Ladies' Union Association*, 7–8; Diaries, May 12, 1865.

79. Le Count was also well known for her work in education. In 1881 she organized an open petition against Henri Halliwell, the secretary of Philadelphia's board of education, based on his remarks about black teachers. Halliwell felt that they were inferior and unable to "submit to the course of studies and discipline of the regular public schools." Fanny Jackson Coppin and Jake C. White Jr. (among many others) signed her open, published protest letter. R. Lane, *William Dorsey's Philadelphia*, 126, 149–50, 153–55.

80. *Report of the Ladies' Union Association*, 3–4

81. For more on cultural and linguistic capital, see Bonfiglio, *Race*.

82. Giddings, *When and Where I Enter,* 53.

Chapter 3: A World Created

1. Baltzell, *Philadelphia Gentleman,* 6.

2. Quarles, *Black Abolitionists,* 10; Lapsansky, "Friends, Wives, and Striving," 4–6; For more on color classification within the free black Philadelphia community, see Hershberg and Williams, "Mulattoes and Blacks," 392–434.

3. Jones, "Race and Gender," 222.

4. Du Bois, *Philadelphia Negro,* 34–36.

5. Hershberg, "Free Blacks," 372; R. Lane, *William Dorsey's Philadelphia,* 277.

6. Although the bill was never ratified, less than five years later, free black Philadelphians were denied the right to vote. This law stayed in place until the ratification of the Fifteenth Amendment in 1870. Sterling, *We Are Your Sisters,* 126–27.

7. Blockson, *Pennsylvania's Black History,* 97–98.

8. Casway, "Octavius Catto"; Hershberg and Williams, "Mulattoes and Blacks," 392; R. Lane, *William Dorsey's Philadelphia,* 305–6. For more on Catto, see Biddle and Dubin's *Tasting Freedom.*

9. When Emilie mentions Mr. Catto in her diary, she was probably referring to the father William, rather than to Octavius.

10. Allen helped to organize the AME Church and served as its pioneer bishop and in 1829 was elected as the president of the first national African American convention. For more on Allen, see Newman's *Freedom's Port* and Nash's *Forging Freedom.*

11. *Philadelphia (PA) Public Ledger,* 19 March 1863, p. 1, col. 2.

12. Bennett, *Before the Mayflower* (1984), 496.

13. Lapsansky, "Friends, Wives, and Strivings," 4; Committee, "Men of Color, to Arms!"

14. Taylor, *Philadelphia,* 188–89.

15. Diaries, March 17, 1863.

16. Given the type of meeting they were having and the people that were present, I believe that this was the home of William Still rather than Mary Still, an older member of First African. Founded by Quakers in 1784, the Pennsylvania Society for Promoting the Abolition of Slavery and for the Relief of Free Negroes Unlawfully Held in Bondage (commonly referred to as the Pennsylvania Abolition Society, or PAS) worked for the abolition of slavery and for blacks that were illegally enslaved.

17. Still, *Underground Rail Road.*

18. Taylor, "(1863) Rev. Jonathan C. Gibbs."; Whitehead, "'Rise in the Scale of Being.'"

19. Diaries, May 11 and May 2, 1863.

20. Ibid., March 8, 15, and 29, 1863.

21. Binder, "Pennsylvania Negro Regiments," 386.

22. Diaries, June 16 and 17, 1863.

23. Born in Putnam County, New York, Couch graduated from the Military Academy in 1846, along with George B. McClellan and Thomas J. "Stonewall" Jackson.

24. Diaries, June 18 and 20, 1863.

25. R. Lane, *Roots of Violence in Black Philadelphia,* 19.

26. Diaries, July 31, 1863.

27. Diaries, September 14, 1863.

28. The regiments were the Third, Sixth, Eighth, Twenty-second, Twenty-fourth, Twenty-fifth, Thirty-second, Forty-first, Forty-third, Forty-fifth, and 127th.

29. Julie Winch also notes that this was a compliment that Frederick Douglass, who was often in conflict with the Philadelphia black leadership, reluctantly bestowed upon the city. "Leaders," 6.

30. Ibid., 1.

31. Hershberg, "Free Blacks," 368.

32. Burgess, "Gender Roles," 393.

33. Before slavery was legally applied to *only* black people, chattel slavery was taking place in the colonies, when poor white indentured servants were held in servitude in perpetuity. Giddings, *When and Where I Enter*, 33–35.

34. Berlin, *Generations*, 6–9.

35. A. Davis, "Rape, Racism," 51; Giddings, *When and Where I Enter*, 36–37; Keetley and Pettigrew, *Public Women, Public Words*, 157; Darlene Clark Hine notes that this law ran counter to English law, which allowed a child's status to derive from his or her father. Hine, et al., *African-American History*, 79.

36. In 1967 the Kerner Commission released the "Report of the National Advisory Commission on Civil Disorders," writing that the "nation is moving towards two societies, one black, one white—separate and unequal." I would argue that the creation of two societies happened during the plantation generation, roughly three hundred years before the Kerner Commission, when white America linked color with social status and social conditions.

37. Although there is a lot of dispute about the origins of the word *race*, many researchers claim that William Dunbar may have first used it in a 1508 poem where he refers to the "*bakbyttaris of sindry racis*" (backbiters of sundry races). Smedley et al., *Unequal Treatment*, 490; Ashcroft, "Language and Race," 37–38.

38. In contrast to this theory, Berlin asserts that it was during this generation that the enslaved people began to construct their heretofore unknown African identity. Berlin, *Generations of Captivity*, 67.

39. Bennett, *Before the Mayflower* (1984), 51.

40. Also during this time, the founding fathers of black America, the eight men who founded the Free African Society (FAS), helped to usher in a movement of "self-creation and self-definition." By 1791 the FAS had been dissolved as Absalom Jones went on to head the St. Thomas African Episcopal Church and Richard Allen founded the African Methodist Episcopal Church. Newman, *Freedom's Port*, 62–73.

41. Berlin, *Generations of Captivity*, 111; Sterling, *Speak Out*, 239–45; L. Alexander, *African or American*.

42. Berlin, *Generations of Captivity,* 214.

43. For more information, see Franklin and Schweninger, *Runaway Slaves*.

44. D. Newman, "Black Women," 277.

45. Edward Turner adds that the Philadelphia slaves were happy to be a part of their masters' households as they were treated kindly, with moderation, and as a part of the family. In taking to task Turner's claims, it is important to note that he draws this conclusion from the work of Acrelius, a Swedish man who commented on Philadelphia in 1759, and Hector St. John Crevecoeur, a white American farmer. Moreover, Turner's book was published in 1910, approximately twenty years before the WPA interviews, and forty to fifty

years before research on the slavery was completed from the perspective of the enslaved and not the owners. Turner, *Negro in Pennsylvania*, 38–39.

46. Newman, "Black Women," 282–83.

47. Du Bois, *Philadelphia Negro*, 10–12; Turner, *Negro in Pennsylvania*, 24–25; Thayer, "Town into City," 85.

48. Newman, "Black Women," 280.

49. Bronner, "Village into Town," 85.

50. Horton and Horton, *In Hope of Liberty*, 83.

51. Du Bois, *Philadelphia Negro*, 14–19.

52. Bennett, *Before the Mayflower* (1984), 78–80; Benjamin Chew was a lawyer who represented the interests of the William Penn family in Pennsylvania and was appointed chief justice. Although he supported England during the Revolution, after the Revolutionary War he was appointed to Pennsylvania's court of appeals. He was also the father of Harriet Chew, wife of Charles Carroll of Carrollton.

53. W. Douglass, *Preamble of the Free African Society*.

54. Berlin, *Generations of Captivity*, 111.

55. Bennett, *Before the Mayflower* (1984), 80.

56. On August 22, 1793, Dr. Benjamin Rush, a noted physician and signer of the Declaration of Independence, informed Mayor Clarkson that much to his dismay the 1762 yellow fever epidemic had returned. In less than five months, the disease had swept through the city, killing close to five thousand men, women, and children. The final numbers failed to include black people, the very young, and the anonymous poor. Though many physicians treated patients, none could agree on a cure, which ranged from bleeding and purging to using medicinal herbs and restorative liquids. Richard Miller, "Federal City," 185; Turner, *Negro in Pennsylvania*, 187–88; For more on the yellow fever epidemic from Richard Allen's perspective, see *Life, Experience, and Gospel Labours*.

57. Turner, *The Negro in Pennsylvania*, 89–90.

58. Martin, "Banneker Literary Institute," 304.

59. Du Bois, *Philadelphia Negro*, 25–30.

60. Weigley, "The Border City in Civil War," 386.

61. Turner, *Negro in Pennsylvania*, 186–87.

62. Du Bois, *Philadelphia Negro*, 30–31, 36, 15–17, 83–87.

63. Geffen, "Industrial Development," 352.

64. Du Bois, *Philadelphia Negro*, 310–20.

65. R. Lane, *Roots of Violence*, 60.

66. Hershberg and Williams, "Mulattoes and Blacks," 398–400.

67. Weigley, "The Border City in Civil War," 376–80.

68. Hershberg, "Free Blacks in Antebellum Philadelphia," 377–78.

69. Hershberg and Williams, "Mulattoes and Blacks," 404–6.

70. Sterling, *We Are Your Sisters*, 190–91.

71. The Fortens were descendants of sailmaker James Forten, who was worth over $100,000 in the 1830s; the DuSables descended from Jean Baptiste Pointe DuSable, who led the westward movement and founded Chicago; the Halls were descendants of Prince Hall, the founder of the first black Masonic Temple; and the Cuffees descended from businessman and shipowner Paul Cuffee, who in 1810 was one of the wealthiest men in the country.

72. Bennett, *Before the Mayflower* (1984), 82.
73. Armstrong, "A Mental and Moral Feast," 78–79.

Chapter 5: A World of Women

1. Motz, "Folk Expression," 134.
2. McCarthy, "Pocketful of Days," 295.
3. Gannett, *Gender*, 130; McCarthy, "Pocketful of Days," 285.
4. Gannett, *Gender*, 131–32.
5. Culley, "I Look at Me," 15, 19.
6. Bunkers and Huff, "Issues in Studying Women's Diaries," 5.
7. Gannett, *Gender*, 21, 50–52; Laurel Thatcher Ulrich adds that, regardless of the fact that the terms *journal* and *diary* have become gendered and despite some differences in journal writing and diary keeping, the term *diary* actually "encompasses many modes of expression from religious meditation to account keeping" and, as such, can be viewed as neither an exclusively male nor female space. Ulrich, "Of Pens and Needles," 203. Geneva Cobb-Moore adds that diary writing is usually dismissed as a "nonmasculine pattern of fragmentary and sporadic writing." Cobb-Moore, "When Meanings Meet," 140.
8. Brereton, "Gendered Testimonies," 147.
9. Diaries, November 9 and November 2, 1863; May 20, 1864; December 21, 1865
10. Gannett, *Gender*, 130–31; Smith-Rosenberg, "Female World," 168, 172.
11. King James Version, Proverbs 31:10–31; Smith-Rosenberg, "Female World," 172; Welter, "Cult of True Womanhood."
12. Armstrong, "A Mental and Moral Feast," 79.
13. Smith-Rosenberg, "Female World," 174.
14. Diaries, January 14, 1865; April 26, 1864; February 10, 1865.
15. Diaries, January 7 and 9, 1863.
16. James McCune Smith was the first African American in the U.S. to practice medicine and to run a pharmacy; James Forten Jr. was Charlotte Forten's brother.
17. Armstrong, "A Mental and Moral Feast," 80–82, 85–86.
18. Diaries, January 2, 1863.
19. Lejeune, "How Do Diaries End?," 105–8.
20. The article goes on to list the characteristics of a public diary, which include the addition of different written forms and techniques, and the ability to act as both the author and a character. Bloom, "I Write for Myself and Strangers," 25–27.
21. Diaries, February 18, 1863, February 18, 1864, and February 18, 1865.
22. Ibid., January 2, 1864.
23. Smith-Rosenberg, "Puberty to Menopause," 58–59.
24. Diaries, March 29, 1863.
25. Ibid., September 23, June 24, October 11, and October 16, 1863.
26. After her divorce from Dunbar, Nelson married Dr. Henry Arthur Callis, M.D., one of the founders of the Alpha Phi Alpha fraternity (founded in 1906, on the campus of Cornell University, Alpha is the oldest black Inter-Collegiate Greek-Lettered fraternity); and later after they divorced, she married Robert Nelson, a journalist and the Pennsylvania state athletic commissioner.

27. Stevenson, *Journals*; Hull, *Give Us Each Day*; Decosta-Willis, *Memphis Diary*; McMurray, *To Keep the Waters*; Ione, *Pride of Family*.

28. Salvatore, *We All Got History*.

29. Perry, Rev. of *Give Us Each Day*, 175; Salvatore, *We All Got History*, 22.

30. McMurray, *To Keep the Waters*, 40–41.

31. In 1883, at the age of twenty, Wells sued a railroad company for ejecting her from a first-class coach. This case and the ensuing publicity was the springboard for Wells's foray into journalism. By the 1890s Wells was such a well-known figure that, according to Linda McMurray, she was the only black person who received more press attention than abolitionist Frederick Douglass. McMurray, *To Keep the Waters*, xiii–xiv.

32. Ibid., 35.

33. Dr. William C. Jason, the second president of the State College for Colored Students (now Delaware State College), once wrote that Nelson, "deals in art and literary grace, doth as a princess reign . . . Her name is Alice and her hair is red, for convention not a hoot does she care; but you may bet your life, when all is said, She's got the goods—let those who doubt, beware." Gibson, "Mighty Oaks"; Hull, *Works of Alice Dunbar-Nelson*, lvii–lviii, xxxiii.

34. The interest in recording meteorological events was happening across the country, as both white and black men, including George Washington and Thomas Jefferson, participated in this "utilitarian premise." Although Webber answered this call, he did not send his recordings to Espy. Salvatore, *We All Got History*, 37–39.

35. Du Bois, *Philadelphia Negro*, 310–20.

36. Salvatore, *We All Got History*, 19.

37. Decosta-Willis, *Memphis Diary*, ix–xiii.

38. Cobb-Moore, [Is this Forten quoted in Cobb-Moore?] "When Meanings Meet"; 140–43, 151. Sterling, *We Are Your Sisters*, 282–84; additionally Forten spent a majority of her leisure time horseback riding and exploring with David Thorpe, a young white plantation superintendent from Rhode Island. Thomas, Rev. of *The Journal of Charlotte L. Forten*, 342.

39. Cobb-Moore, "When Meanings Meet," 142–43.

40. Diaries, December 22, 1865.

41. Blockson, *Pennsylvania's Black History*, 271–73; Salvatore, *We All Got History*, 42.

42. Salvatore, *We All Got History*, 10–11. In addition to the diaries of Forten, Nelson, Webber, and Wells, which are comparable to the diaries of Emilie Davis, it is also important to mention three other important primary historical sources that have not been transcribed or published: the diary of Mary Virginia Montgomery, an enslaved woman whose family was owned by Jefferson Davis's older brother, Joseph, and who grew up as part of the Virginia elite; the diary of Frances "Frank" Rollin, a writer and one of the well-known South Carolina Rollin sisters, whose diary was heavily excerpted by her great-granddaughter in the book *Pride of Family: Four Generations of American Women of Color*; and the diary of Laura Hamilton, a young mother and housewife from Mercer County, Ohio—all significant and important stories that should be transcribed in their entirety and made available to the public.

Chapter 6: A World Expanded

1. Diaries, September 18, 1863.

2. Lapsansky, "Discipline to the Mind," 86.

3. Diaries, April 30 and May 4, 1864.

4. Ibid., October 3 and October 5, 1863.

5. Gambler looked specifically at white women of Native and Irish origins confined to the urban Northeast and Midwest; Gambler, "A Gendered Enterprise," 188–217.

6. Connolly, "Disappearance," 31, 34.

7. Diaries, July 12 and 19, 1864.

8. Ibid., May 6 and June 5, 1863.

9. Ibid., January 10 and February 4, 1863; March 19, 1864.

10. Ibid., December 24–December 31, 1863.

11. Ibid., August 31, 1863.

12. Ibid., September 8, 1863.

13. Diaries, September 23, October 16, and October 18, 1863; February 12, 1864.

14. Lapsansky, "Discipline to the Mind": 88.

15. Diaries, January 15, 1863.

16. Salvatore, *We All Got History*, 69–72.

17. Diaries, March 23, 1865.

18. Ibid., April 24, 1865.

19. Gambler, "Tarnished Labor": 186–88.

20. Diaries, January 9, March 9, and May 15, 1863.

21. Diaries, December 9 and 23, 1864, and January 16, 1865.

22. Diaries, March 9, 1863.

23. Ibid., February 7, 1864.

24. Ibid., September 1, 1863–November 4, 1863.

25. Ibid., January 24–30, 1864.

26. Ibid., April 14, 1865; Biddle and Dubin, *Tasting Freedom*, 321.

27. Diaries, April 15, 17, 20, 22, and 23, 1865.

28. Ibid., November 10, December 20, and December 22, 1865.

Epilogue

1. Trustees' Meeting Notes, First African Presbyterian Church, March 1914.

2. Diaries, March 26, 1863; July 3, 1863; December 9, 1864; December 25, 1865; February 5, 1865; March 3, 1865; March 24, 1865; and July 23, 1865.

3. Ibid., April 17, October 28, December 20, and December 22, 1865.

4. Ibid., Memoranda section, 1865.

5. Hull, "Researching Alice Dunbar-Nelson," 314.

6. Emilie and George may have had a sixth child, Julia, born in 1881.

Who's Who

1. Quarles, *Black Abolitionists*, 4.

2. Founded in 1921 in Harlem, New York, by Harry Swan, Black Swan Records was named in Greenfield's honor. W. E. B. Du Bois was both a stockholder and a member of the board of directors. The company went bankrupt in 1923 and was acquired by Paramount Records in 1924.

BIBLIOGRAPHY

Primary Sources

A Day in 1808 at Homewood: Charity's Story. Archives of the Homewood Museum. Baltimore, Md.

Allen, Richard. *The Life, Experience, and Gospel Labours of the Rt. Rev. Richard Allen. To Which is Annexed the Rise and Progress of the African Methodist Episcopal Church in the U.S. of America. Containing a Narrative of the Yellow Fever in the Year of Our Lord 1793: With an Address to the People of Colour in the U.S.* Philadelphia: Martin and Boden, Printers, 1833. http://docsouth.unc.edu/neh/allen/menu.html c2004 (accessed July 20, 2013).

Bacon, Benjamin C. *Statistics of the Colored People of Philadelphia.* Philadelphia: Pennsylvania Society for Promoting the Abolition of Slavery, 1859.

Basker, James G., Sandra M. Tremholm, Justine Ahlstrom, and Jerry Kelly. *"This Government Can Not Endure Permanently, Half Slave, Half Free": Lincoln and the "House Divided."* Gilder Lehrman Institute American History, 1st ed. 2005.

Brooks, Chas H. *The Official History and Manual of the Grand United Order of Odd Fellows in America, A Chronological Treatise of the Origin, Government, and Principles of the Order; the duties of the various officers in every branch of Odd Fellowship with Directions for laying cornerstones, holding thanksgiving services, dedicated lodges, cemetaries [sic], churches, halls, and other public edifices; forms of petitions, reports, change, appeals, & c., & c.* Philadelphia, 1902.

Catto, William T. *A Semi-Centenary Discourse, Delivered in the First African Presbyterian Church, Philadelphia, on the Fourth Sabbath of May, 1857: With a History of the Church from Its First Organization.* Philadelphia: Joseph M. Wilson, 1857. http://quod.lib.umich .edu/cgi/t/text/text-idx?c=moa;idno=AGU9813.0001.001 (accessed July 20, 2013).

Archives of *The Christian Recorder.* 1863, 1864, 1865, 1866.

Committee to Recruit Colored Troops. "Men of Color, to Arms! Now or Never!" Broadside petition. Archives of the Library Company of Philadelphia. http://www.librarycompany .org/steptowardfreedom/section3.htm (accessed July 20, 2013).

Davis, J. C. *An Appeal from the Colored Men of Philadelphia to the President of the United States.* Forwarded to Washington. Philadelphia: August 1862. https://play.google.com/ store/books/details?id=NPhxAAAAMAAJ&rdid=bookNPhxAAAAMAAJ&rdot=1 (accessed July 20, 2013)

Decosta-Willis, Miriam, ed. *The Memphis Diary of Ida B. Wells: An Intimate Portrait of the Activist as a Young Woman.* With a foreword by Mary Helen Washington. Boston: Beacon, 1995.

Diaries of Emilie Davis, 1863–1865. Archives of the Historical Society of Pennsylvania. Philadelphia, Pa.

"Letter from Elizabeth Cady Stanton." In *In Memoriam: Frederick Douglass*, edited by Helen Douglass, 44–45. Philadelphia: J.C. Yorston & Co., 1897. http://antislavery.eserver.org/

legacies/frederick-douglass-elizabeth-cady-stanton/frederick-douglass-elizabeth-cady
-stanton-xhtml.html (accessed July 20, 2013).

Douglass, William. *Preamble of the Free African Society. Annals of the First African Church in the United States of America Now Styled the African Episcopal Church of St. Thomas, Philadelphia*. Philadelphia: King and Baird Printers, 1862. http://www.pbs.org/wgbh/aia/part3/3h465t.html (accessed July 20, 2013).

Foner, Philip S., ed. Adapted and abridged by Yuval Taylor. *Frederick Douglass Selected Speeches and Writing* s. Chicago: Lawrence Hill Books, 1999.

Gibbs, Jonathan. *1868 Florida Constitution.*

———. *The Great Commission Press Copy—Presbyterian Historical Society.* October 22, 1856. Black Abolitionist Archives, Doc. No. 18062.

———. *Weekly Anglo-African.* March 16, 1861. Black Abolitionist Archives, Doc. No. 23752 (b).

Hull, Gloria T., ed. *The Works of Alice Dunbar-Nelson.* Vol. 2. New York: Oxford University Press, 1988.

Jones, Absalom, and Richard Allen. *A Narrative of the Proceedings of the Black People, During the Late Awful Calamity in Philadelphia in the Year 1793 and a Refutation of Some Censures: Thrown Upon Them in Some Late Publications.* Philadelphia: William W. Woodward at Franklin's Head, 1793.

Lerner, Gerda, ed. *Black Women in White America: A Documentary History.* New York: Vintage Books, 1973.

McElroy's Philadelphia City Directory for 1860: Containing the Names of the Inhabitants, Their Occupations, Places of Business, and Dwelling Houses; Also a List of the Streets, Lanes, Alleys, the City Offices, Public Institutions, Banks, Etc. Philadelphia, 1860.

McElroy's Philadelphia City Directory for 1861. Containing the Names of the Inhabitants, Their Occupations, Places of Business, and Dwelling Houses; Also a List of the Streets, Lanes, Alleys, the City Offices, Public Institutions, Banks, Etc. Philadelphia, 1861.

McElroy's Philadelphia City Directory for 1862. Containing the Names of the Inhabitants, Their Occupations, Places of Business, and Dwelling Houses; Also a List of the Streets, Lanes, Alleys, the City Offices, Public Institutions, Banks, Etc. Philadelphia, 1862.

McElroy's Philadelphia City Directory for 1863. Containing the Names of the Inhabitants, Their Occupations, Places of Business, and Dwelling Houses; Also a List of the Streets, Lanes, Alleys, the City Offices, Public Institutions, Banks, Etc. Philadelphia, 1863.

McElroy's Philadelphia City Directory for 1864. Containing the Names of the Inhabitants, Their Occupations, Places of Business, and Dwelling Houses; Also a List of the Streets, Lanes, Alleys, the City Offices, Public Institutions, Banks, Etc. Philadelphia, 1864.

"Memorable Days: The Emilie Davis Diaires." Villanova University. http://davisdiaries.villanova.edu (Accessed 20 July 2013).

Moore, John Hammond, ed. *A Plantation Mistress on the Eve of the Civil War: The Diary of Keziah Goodwyn Hopkins Brevard, 1860–1861.* Columbia: University of South Carolina Press, 1993.

Newman, Richard, Patrick Rael, and Philip Lapsansky, eds. *Pamphlets of Protest: An Anthology of Early African-American Protest Literature, 1790–1860.* New York: Routledge, 2001.

O. V. Catto. *Board of Managers, Institute for Colored Youth Minutes, 1855–1866.* Transcribed from records of the Institute for Colored Youth. Archives of Swarthmore College: Friends Historical Library, Swarthmore, Pa.

Philadelphia, Pennsylvania City Death Certificates, 1803–1915.

Report of the National Advisory Commission on Civil Disorders, http://www.eisenhower-foundation.org/docs/kerner.pdf (accessed July 22, 2013).

Report oft The Ladies' Union Association of Philadelphia (PA) Public Ledger, 19 March 1863, p. 1, col. 2. *Formed July 20th, 1863, For the Purpose of Administering Exclusively to the Wants of the Sick and Wounded Colored Soldiers.* Philadelphia: G. T. Stockdale, Printer, 1867.

Smith, Amanda Berry. *An Autobiography: The Story of the Lord's Dealings With Mrs. Amanda Smith, The Colored Evangelist Containing An Account of Her Life Work of Faith, and Her Travels In America, England, Ireland, Scotland, India, and Africa, as an Independent Missionary.* Chicago: Meyer and Brother, Publishers, 1893. http://docsouth.unc.edu/neh/smitham/smith.html (accessed July 20, 2013).

Sterling, Dorothy, ed. *Speak Out in Thunder Tones: Letter and Other Writings by Black Northerners, 1787–1865.* Garden City: Da Capo Press, 1998.

———, ed. *We Are Your Sisters: Black Women in the Nineteenth Century.* New York: W. W. Norton & Company, 1998.

Still, William. *The Underground Rail Road: A Record of Facts, Authentic Narratives, Letters, etc. Narrating the Hardships Hair-breadth Escapes and Death Struggles of the Slaves in their efforts for Freedom, as related by themselves and others, or witnessed by the author; together with sketches of some of the largest stockholders, and most liberal aiders and advisors of the road.* Philadelphia: Porter and Coales, Publishers, 1872.

U.S. Census records for Pottsville Northwest Ward, Schuylkill, Pennsylvania. 1850, 1860, and 1870.

U.S. Census records for Ward 5, Southern Division, Philadelphia, Pennsylvania. 1860.

U.S. Census records for Ward 13, Southern Division, Philadelphia, Pennsylvania. 1860.

U.S. Census records for Philadelphia, Pennsylvania. 1880.

Wood, Peter. Interview on *The Africans in America* Web site. http://www.pbs.org/wgbh/aia/part1/1i3000.html (accessed July 20, 2013).

Secondary Sources

Alexander, Adele Logan. *Ambiguous Lives: Free Women of Color in Rural Georgia, 1789–1879.* Fayetteville: University of Arkansas Press, 1991.

Alexander, Leslie M. *African or American?: Black Identity and Political Activism in New York City, 1784–1861.* Chicago: University of Illinois Press, 2008.

Amar, Akhil Reed. *America's Constitution.* New York: Random House, 2005.

Amos, Valerie, and Pratibha Parmar. "Challenging Imperial Feminism." In *Feminism and 'Race,'* edited by Kum-Kum Bhavnani, 17–32. New York: Oxford University Press, 2001.

Andrews, William L., and Mitch Kachun, eds. *The Curse of Caste; or The Slave Bride. Rediscovered African American Novel by Julia C. Collins.* New York: Oxford University Press, 2006.

Ang, Ien. "I'm a Feminist but . . . 'Other' Women and Postnational Feminism." In *Feminism and 'Race,'* edited by Kum-Kum Bhavnani, 394–409. New York: Oxford University Press, 2001.

Armstrong, Erica. "A Mental and Moral Feast: Reading, Writing and Sentimentality in Black Philadelphia." *Journal of Women's History* 16, no. 1 (2004): 78–102.

Ashcroft, Bill. "Language and Race." In *The Language, Ethnicity and Race Reader,* edited by Roxy Harris and Ben Rampton, 37–53. New York: Routledge, 2003.

Baltzell, E. Digby. *Philadelphia Gentleman: The Making of a National Upper Class.* New York: Free Press, 1958.

Bambara, Toni Cade. *The Black Woman: An Anthology.* New York: Washington Square Press, 2005.

Barker, Gordon S. *The Imperfect Revolution: Anthony Burns and the Landscape of Race in Antebellum America.* Kent: Kent State University Press, 2010.

Basker, James G. *Amazing Grace.* London: Yale University Press, 2002.

Baugh, John. *Beyond Ebonics: Linguistic Pride and Racial Prejudice.* New York: Oxford University Press, 2000.

———. *Black Street Speech: Its History, Structure and Survival.* Austin: University of Texas Press, 1983.

———. "It Ain't about Race: Some Lingering (Linguistic) Consequences of the African Slave Trade and Their Relevance to Your Personal Historical Hardship Index." *Du Bois Review* 3, no. 1 (2006): 145–59.

Bennett, Lerone, Jr. *Before the Mayflower: A History of Black America, The Classic Account of the Struggles and Triumphs of Black Americans.* 5th ed. New York: Penguin Books, 1984; 8th ed. Chicago: Johnson Publishing, 2007.

———. *Forced into Glory: Abraham Lincoln's White Dream.* Chicago: Johnson Publishing, 1999.

Berkin, Carol. "African American Women in Colonial Society." In *Women's America: Refocusing the Past,* edited by Linda K. Kerber and Jane Sherron De Hart, 59–66. New York: Oxford University Press, 2004.

Berlin, Ira. *Generations of Captivity: A History of African-American Slaves.* Cambridge: Belknap Press of Harvard University Press, 2003.

———. *Many Thousands Gone: The First Two Centuries of Slavery in North America.* Cambridge: Belknap Press, 1998.

———. "North of Slavery: Black People in Slaveholding Republic." In *Conference on Yale, New Haven, and American Slavery.* Yale University, September 2002.

———. *Slaves without Masters: The Free Negro in the Antebellum South.* New York: Oxford University Press, 1974.

Berlin, Ira, Marc Favreau, and Steven F. Miller, eds. *Remembering Slavery: African Americans Talk about Their Personal Experiences of Slavery and Freedom.* New York: New Press, 1998.

Berlin, Ira, Barbara Fields, Steven V. Miller, Joseph P. Reidy, and Leslie S. Rowland. *Free at Last: A Documentary History of Slavery, Freedom, and the Civil War.* New York: New Press, 1992.

Biddle, Daniel R., and Murray Dubin. *Tasting Freedom: Octavius Catto and the Battle for Equality in Civil War America.* Philadelphia: Temple University Press, 2010.

Billington, Ray Allen, ed. *The Journal of Charlotte Forten: A Free Negro in the Slave Era.* 2nd ed. New York: Collier Books, 1967.

Binder, Frederick. "Pennsylvania Negro Regiments in the Civil War." *Journal of Negro History* 37, no. 4 (1952): 383–417.

Blassingame, John. "Before the Ghetto: The Making of the Black Community in Savannah, Georgia." *Journal of Social History* 6, no. 4 (1973): 463–88.

———. *The Slave Community: Plantation Life in the Antebellum South.* 2nd ed. New York: Oxford University Press, 1979.

———. *The Underground Railroad.* New York: Prentice Hall, 1987.

———. "Using the Testimony of Ex-Slaves: Approaches and Problems." *Journal of Southern History* 41, no. 4 (1975): 473–92.

Blight, David W. *American Oracle: The Civil War in the Civil Rights Era.* Cambridge: Belknap Press of Harvard University Press, 2011.

———. *A Slave No More: Two Men Who Escaped to Freedom, Including Their Own Narratives of Emancipation.* Orlando: Harcourt, 2007.

Blockson, Charles L. *Pennsylvania's Black History.* Edited by Louise Stone. Philadelphia: Portfolio's Associates, 1975.

Bloom, Lynn Z. "'I Write for Myself and Strangers': Private Diaries as Public Documents." In *Inscribing the Daily: Critical Essays on Women's Diaries,* edited by Suzanne L Bunkers and Cynthia Ann Huff, 23–27. Amherst: University of Massachusetts Press, 1996.

Bonfiglio, Thomas Paul. *Race and the Rise of Standard America.* New York: Mouton de Gruyter, 2002.

Borome, Joseph A. "The Vigilant Committee of Philadelphia." *Pennsylvania Magazine,* Historical Society of Pennsylvania, 1968.

Boyer, Arthur Truman, comp. *Brief History Sketch of the First African Presbyterian Church of Philadelphia, Pa. Along with Rev. Wm. Catto's History and Discourse, from 1807–1940.* Philadelphia, 1944.

Brereton, Bridget. "Gendered Testimonies: Autobiographies, Diaries and Letters by Women as Sources for Caribbean History." *Feminist Review* 59, no. 1, special issue, "Rethinking Caribbean Difference" (1998): 143–63.

Bronner, Edwin B. "Village into Town, 1701–1746." 2nd ed. In *Philadelphia: A 300 Year History,* edited by Russell F. Weigley, 33–67. New York: W. W. Norton, 1982.

Brown, William Wells. *The Black Man, His Antecedents, His Genius, and His Achievements.* 2nd ed. New York: Thomas Hamilton, 1863; reprint, New York: Johnson Reprint, 1968.

———. *Clotel; or the President's Daughter: A Narrative of Slave Life in the U.S. By William Wells Brown, A Fugitive Slave, Author of "Three Years in Europe," With a Sketch of the Author's Life,* reprint ed. with an introduction and notes by Maria Giulia Fabi. New York: Penguin Books, 2004; Great Britain: Partridge and Oakley, 1853.

Bunkers, Suzanne L. and Cynthia Ann Huff. "Issues in Studying Women's Diaries: A Theoretical and Critical Introduction." In *Inscribing the Daily: Critical Essays on Women's Diaries,* edited by Suzanne L Bunkers and Cynthia Ann Huff, 1–20. Amherst: University of Massachusetts Press, 1996.

Burgess, Norma. "Gender Roles Revisited: The Development of the (Woman's Place) Among African American Women in The U.S." *Journal of Black Studies* 24, no. 4 (1994): 391–401.

Burt, Nathaniel. *The Perennial Philadelphians: The Anatomy of an America Aristocracy.* Boston: Little, Brown and Company, 1963.

Buss, Helen M. "A Feminist Revision of New Historicism to Give Fuller Readings of Women's Private Writing." In *Inscribing the Daily: Critical Essays on Women's Diaries,* edited by Suzanne L Bunkers and Cynthia Ann Huff, 86–103. Amherst: University of Massachusetts Press, 1996.

———. "Women's Historical Novels." In *Feminism and 'Race,'* edited by Kum-Kum Bhavnani, 220–32. New York: Oxford University Press, 2001.

Carby, Hazel. *Reconstructing Womanhood: The Emergence of the Afro-American Woman Novelist.* New York: Oxford University Press, 1987.

Casway, Jerrod. "Octavius Catto and the Pythians of Philadelphia." In *Pennsylvania Legacies* 7, no. 1, (2007).

Christian, Charles M. *Black Saga: The African American Experience.* Boston: Houghton Mifflin, 1995.

Clark-Lewis, Elizabeth. *Living In, Living Out: African American Domestics in Washington, D.C., 1910–1940,* reprinted. Washington, D.C.: Smithsonian Book, 1994.

Cobb-Moore, Geneva. "When Meanings Meet: The Journals of Charlotte Forten Grimke." In *Inscribing the Daily: Critical Essays on Women's Diaries,* edited by Suzanne L Bunkers and Cynthia Ann Huff, 139–55. Amherst: University of Massachusetts Press, 1996.

Collins, Patricia Hill. *Black Feminist Thought: Knowledge, Consciousness, and the Politics of Empowerment.* Boston: Unwin Hyman, 1990.

———. *Fighting Words: Black Women and the Search for Justice.* Minneapolis: University of Minnesota Press, 1998.

———. "The Social Construction of Black Feminist Thought." In *Feminism and 'Race,'* edited by Kum-Kum Bhavnani, 184–202. New York: Oxford University Press, 2001.

Connolly, Marguerite. "The Disappearance of the Domestic Sewing Machine, 1890–1925." *Winterthur Portfolio* 34, no. 1 (1999): 31–48.

Conyers, Charline Howard. *A Living Legend: The History of Cheyney University.* Cheyney, Penn.: Cheyney University Press, 1990.

Cross, William E. "The Negro-to-Black Conversion Experience." *Black World* 20, no. 1 (1971): 13–27.

Crowe, Charles, "Slavery, Ideology, and 'Cliometrics.'" *Technology and Culture* 17, no. 2 (1976): 271–85.

Culley, Margo. "'I Look at Me': Self as Subject in the Diaries of American Women." *Women's Studies Quarterly* 3 (1989): 15–22.

Dagbovie, Pero Gaglo. "Black Women Historians from the Late 19th Century to the Dawning of the Civil Rights Movement." *Journal of African American History* 89, no. 3 (2004): 241–61.

Dannett, Sylvia G. L. *Profile of Negro Womanhood.* New York: American Book–Stratford Press, 1964.

David, Eltis. *The Rise of African Slavery in the Americas.* New York: Cambridge University Press, 2000.

Davis, Angela. "Rape, Racism, and the Myth of the Black Racist." In *Feminism and 'Race,'* edited by Kum-Kum Bhavnani, 50–64. New York: Oxford University Press, 2001.

————. *Women, Race and Class.* New York: Vintage Books, 1981.

Davis, David Brion. "Looking at Slavery from Broader Perspectives." *American Historical Review* 105, no. 2 (2000): 1–15.

Dawson, Kevin. "Enslaved Swimmers and Divers in the Atlantic World." *Journal of American History* 92, no. 4 (2008): 1–30.

Dehler, Kathleen. "Where Women Reveal Themselves." *English Journal* 78, no. 7 (1989): 53–54.

Dickson, Bruce D., Jr., *Black American Writing from the Nadir: The Evolution of a Literary Tradition, 1877–1915.* Baton Rouge: Louisiana State University Press, 1989.

Douglass, Frederick. *Autobiographies.* New York: Library Classics of the United States, 1994.

————. *The Life and Times of Frederick Douglass,* Mineola: Dover Publications, 2003.

Du Bois, Ellen Carol, and Lynn Dumenil. *Through Women's Eyes: An American History with Documents.* Boston: Bedford/St. Martin's, 2005.

Du Bois, W. E. B. *Black Reconstruction in America 1860–1880.* With an introduction by David Levering Lewis. 1st Free Press ed. New York: Free Press, 1998.

————. "The Black Vote of Philadelphia." In *Black Politics in Philadelphia,* edited by Miriam Ershkowitz and Joseph Zikmund II, 31–39. New York: Basic Books, 1973.

————. *The Philadelphia Negro.* Reprint ed. with an introduction by Elijah Anderson. Philadelphia: University of Pennsylvania Press, 1996.

————. "Social Planning for the Negro, Past and Present." *Journal of Negro Education* 5, no. 1 (1936): 110–25.

Du Bois, W. E. B., Carter G. Woodson, and Mary White Ovington. "Reviews of American Negro Slavery." In *Ulrich Bonnell Phillips: A Southern Historian and His Critics,* edited by John David Smith and John C. Inscoe, 83–90. Westport: Greenwood Press, 1990.

duCille, Ann. "The Occult of True Black Womanhood: Critical Demeanor and Black Feminist Studies." In *Feminism and 'Race,'* edited by Kum-Kum Bhavnani, 232–60. New York: Oxford University Press, 2001.

"History of the Lead Pencil." Early Office Museum Web site. http://www.officemuseum.com/pencil_history.htm (accessed July 21, 2013).

Fairclough, Norman. *Discourse and Social Change.* Cambridge, U.K.: Polity Press; Malden: Blackwell Publishing, 1992.

Fish, Cheryl. *Black and White Women's Travel Narratives: Antebellum Explorations.* Gainesville: University Press of Florida, 2004.

Foner, Eric. *Our Lincoln: New Perspectives on Lincoln and His World.* New York: W.W. Norton & Company, 2009.

————. *Who Owns History?: Rethinking the Past in a Changing World.* New York: Hill and Wang, 2002.

Ford, Lacy. "Reconfiguring the Old South: 'Solving' the Problem of Slavery, 1787–1838." *Journal of American History* 95, no. 1 (2008): 95–122.

Fordham, Signithia. *Blacked Out: Dilemmas of Race, Identity, and Success at Capital High.* Chicago: University of Chicago Press, 1996.

Fought, Carmen. *Language and Ethnicity: Key Topics in Sociolinguistics.* New York: Cambridge University Press, 2006.

Franklin, Frazier, E. Rev. of *American Negro Slave Revolts,* by Herbert Aptheker. *American Journal of Sociology,* no. 4 (1944): 374–75.

Franklin, John Hope. *The Emancipation Proclamation.* Garden City: Doubleday, 1963.

———. *The Free Negro in North Carolina, 1790–1860.* Chapel Hill: University of North Carolina Press, 1943.

Franklin, John Hope, and Alfred Moss Jr. *From Slavery to Freedom: A History of African Americans.* 8th ed. New York: Alfred A. Knopf, 2004.

Franklin, John Hope, and Loren Schweninger. *Runaway Slaves: Rebels on the Plantation.* New York: Oxford University Press, 1999.

Fraser, Nancy. "Rethinking the Public Sphere: A Contribution to the Critique of Actually Existing Democracy." In *Habermas and the Public Sphere,* edited by Craig Calhoun, 56–80. Cambridge: MIT Press, 1992.

Fuller, Margaret. *Summer on the Lakes, in 1814.* Reprint ed. Urbana: University of Illinois Press, 1991.

Furstenberg, Frank, Jr. Theodore Hershberg, and John Modell. "The Origins of the Female-Headed Black Family: The Impact of the Urban Experience." *Journal of Interdisciplinary History 6,* no. 2 (1975): 211–233.

Gac, Scott. *Singing for Freedom: The Hutchinson Family Singers and the Nineteenth-Century Culture of Reform.* New Haven: Yale University Press, 2007.

Gallman, J. Matthew. *Mastering Wartime: A Social History of Philadelphia during the Civil War.* Philadelphia: University of Pennsylvania Press, 1990

Gambler, Wendy. "A Gendered Enterprise: Placing Nineteenth-Century Businesswomen in History." *Business History Review 72,* no. 2 (1998): 188–217.

———. "'Reduced to Science': Gender, Technology, and Power in the American Dressmaking Trade, 1860–1910." *Technology and Culture 36,* no. 3 (1995): 455–82.

———. "Tarnished Labor: The Home, the Market, and the Boardinghouse in Antebellum America." *Journal of the Early Republic 22,* no. 2 (2002): 177–204.

———. *The Female Economy: The Millinery and Dressmaking Trades 1860–1930.* Urbana and Chicago: University of Illinois Press, 1997.

Gannett, Cinthia. *Gender and the Journal: Diaries and Academic Discourse.* Albany: State University of New York Press, 1992.

Garcia, Jesus, Donna M. Ogle, C. Frederick Risinger, Joyce Stevos, and Winthrop D. Jordan. *Creating America: A History of the U.S..* Evanston: McDougal Littell, 2001.

Gaspar, David Barry, and Darlene Clark Hine. Editors' preface to *More Than Chattel: Black Women and Slavery in the Americas.* Indianapolis: Indiana University Press, 1996.

Gates, Henry Louis, Jr. *Life upon these Shores: Looking at African American History 1513–2008.* New York: Alfred A. Knopf, 2011.

Gates, Henry Louis, Jr., and Evelyn Higginbotham, eds. *The African-American National Biography.* New York: Oxford University Press, 2008.

Geffen, Elizabeth M. "Industrial Development and Social Crises, 1841–1854." 2nd ed. In *Philadelphia: A 300-Year History,* edited by Russell F. Weigley, Nicholas B. Wainwright, and Edwin Wolf, 307–62. New York: W. W. Norton, 1982.

Genovese, Eugene. *From Rebellion to Revolution: Afro-American Slave Revolts in the Making of the Modern World.* Baton Rouge: Louisiana State University Press, 1979.

———. *Roll Jordan Roll: The World the Slaves Made.* New York: Pantheon Books, 1974.

Gerzina, Gretchen Holbrook. *Mr. and Mrs. Prince: How an Extraordinary Eighteenth-Century Family Moved Out of Slavery and into Legend*. New York: Amistad, 2008.

Gibson, Judith Y. "Mighty Oaks: Five Black Educators," In *A History of African Americans of Delaware and Maryland's Eastern Shore*, edited by Carole Marks. University of Delaware, 1997.

Giddings, Paula. *When and Where I Enter: The Impact of Black Women on Race and Sex in America*. New York: Bantam Books, 1984.

Giesberg, Judith. *Army at Home: Women and the Civil War on the Northern Home Front*. Chapel Hill: University of North Carolina Press, 2009.

Gilbert, Olive. *Narrative of Sojourner Truth; a Bondswoman of Olden Time, Emancipated by the New York Legislature in the Early Part of the Present Century with a History of her Labors and Correspondence, Drawn from Her Book of Life*. Battle Creek: Published for the Author, 1878. Reprint ed. with introduction by Margaret Washington. New York: Vintage Books, 1993.

Gilmore, Al-Tony, ed. *Revisiting Blassingame's The Slave Community: The Scholars Respond*. Santa Barbara: ABC-CLIO Praeger, 1978.

Gilmore, Glenda Elizabeth. *Gender and Jim Crow: Women and Politics of White Supremacy in North Carolina, 1896–1920*. Chapel Hill: University of North Carolina Press, 1996.

Green, Lisa J. *African American English: A Linguistic Introduction*. Cambridge, U.K.: Cambridge University Press, 2002.

Griffin, Farah Jasmine, ed. *Beloved Sisters and Loving Friends: Letters from Rebecca Primus of Royal Oak, Maryland, and Addie Brown of Hartford, Connecticut, 1854–1868*. New York: One World/Ballantine, 2001.

Gross, Ariela. "Beyond Black and White: Cultural Approaches to Race and Slavery." *Columbia Law Review* 101, no. 3 (2001): 640–90.

Guelzo, Allen C. *Lincoln's Emancipation Proclamation: The End of Slavery in America*. New York: Simon and Schuster, 2004.

Guterman, Stanley S. Rev. of *The Debate over Slavery: Stanley Elkins and His Critics*, by Ann J. Lane. *Contemporary Sociology* 1, no. 6 (1972): 528–29.

Gutman, Herbert. *The Black Family in Slavery and Freedom, 1750–1925*. New York: Pantheon Books, 1976.

Habermas, Jurgen. "The Public Sphere: An Encyclopedia Article." Translated by Sara Lennox and Frank Lennox. *German Critique* 57, no. 3 (1974): 49–55.

Hambrick-Stowe, Charles E. "The Spiritual Pilgrimage of Sarah Osborn (1714–1796)." *Church History* 61, no. 4 (1992): 408–21.

Hargrave, Edythe. "How I Feel as a Negro at a White College." *Journal of Negro Education* 11, no. 4 (1942): 484–86.

Harley, Sharon, and Rosalyn Tergborg-Penn, eds. *The Afro-American Woman: Struggles and Identities*. Port Washington, NY: Kennikat Press, 1978.

Harris, Leslie. *In the Shadow of Slavery: African Americans in New York City, 1626–1863*. Chicago: University of Chicago Press, 2003.

Hershberg, Theodore, ed. "Free Blacks in Antebellum Philadelphia: A Study of Ex-Slaves, Freeborn and Socioeconomic Decline." In *Philadelphia: Work, Space, Family, and Group Experience in the Nineteenth Century*, edited by Theodore Hershberg, 368–92. New York: Oxford University Press, 1981.

Hershberg, Theodore, Alan N. Burstein, Eugene P. Ericksem, Stephanie W. Greenberg, and William L. Yancey. "A Tale of Three Cities: Blacks, Immigrants, and Opportunity in Philadelphia, 1850–1880, 1930, 1970." In *Philadelphia: Work, Space, Family, and Group Experience in the Nineteenth Century,* edited by Theodore Hershberg, 461–91. New York: Oxford University Press, 1981.

Hershberg, Theodore, and Stephanie W. Greenberg. "Industrial Location and Ethnic Residential Patterns in an Industrializing City: Philadelphia, 1880." In *Philadelphia: Work, Space, Family, and Group Experience in the Nineteenth Century,* edited by Theodore Hershberg, 204–33. New York: Oxford University Press, 1981.

Hershberg, Theodore, Harold E. Cox, Dale Light Jr., and Richard R. Greenfield. "The 'Journey to Work': An Empirical Investigation of Work, Residence, and Transportation, Philadelphia, 1850 and 1880." In *Philadelphia: Work, Space, Family, and Group Experience in the Nineteenth Century: Essays Toward an Interdisciplinary History of the City,* edited by Theodore Hershberg, 128–173. New York: Oxford University Press, 1981

Hershberg, Theodore, and Henry Williams. "Mulattoes and Blacks: Intragroup Color Differences and Social Stratification in Nineteenth-Century Philadelphia." In *Philadelphia: Work, Space, Family, and Group Experience in the Nineteenth Century,* edited by Theodore Hershberg, 392–434. New York: Oxford University Press, 1981.

Hesse-Biber, Sharlene, Christina Gilmartin, and Robin Lyndberg. *Feminist Approaches to Theory and Methodology.* New York: Oxford University Press, 1999.

Higginbotham, Evelyn Brooks. "African-American Women's History and the Metalanguage of Race." *Signs* 17, no. 2 (1992): 251–74.

———. "Beyond the Sound of Silence: Afro-American Women's History." *Gender and History* 1, no. 1 (1989): 50–67.

Higginson, Thomas Wentworth. *Army Life in a Black Regiment.* Boston: Beacon Press, 1962.

Hinder, Frederick M. "Pennsylvania Negro Regiments in the Civil War." *Journal of Negro History* 37, no. 4 (October 1952): 383–417.

Hine, Darlene. "Rape and the Inner Lives of Black Women." In *Women's America: Refocusing the Past,* edited by Linda K. Kerber and Jane Sherron De Hart, 299–302. New York: Oxford University Press, 2004.

Hine, Darlene, William C. Hine, and Stanley Harrold. *African-American History.* Upper Saddle River: Prentice Hall, 2006.

Hine, Darlene, and Kathleen Thompson. *A Shining Thread of Hope.* Brooklyn: Bantam Books, 1998.

Hine, Darlene Clark, ed., *Black Women in America: An Historical Encyclopedia.* Bloomington: Indiana University Press, 1993.

———. *Black Women in American History: From Colonial Times through Nineteenth Century* Vol. 1. Brooklyn: Carlson Publishing, 1990.

———, ed. *Black Women in the U.S. 1619–1989.* Brooklyn: Carlson Publishing, 1990.

———. *Hine Sight: Black Women and the Re-Construction of American History.* Brooklyn: Carlson Publishing, 1994.

———, ed. "Lifting the Veil, Shattering the Silence: Black Women's History in Slavery and Freedom." In *The State of Afro-American History: Past, Present and Future,* edited by Darlene Clark Hine, 223–49. Baton Rouge: Louisiana State University Press, 1986.

————. "Now That We Know Who We Are." *Public Historian* 19, no. 1 (1997): 41–43.

————, ed. *The State of Afro-American History: Past, Present and Future*. Baton Rouge: Louisiana State University Press, 1986.

"A History of the First African Presbyterian Church of Philadelphia, n.p." May 13, 2003: 1–8.

Holzer, Harold. "Emancipating Lincoln: The Proclamation in Text, Context, and Memory." Cambridge: Harvard University Press, 2012

hooks, bell. *Ain't I a Woman*. Boston: South End Press, 1981.

————. "Black Women: Shaping Feminist Theory." In *Feminism and 'Race,'* edited by Kum-Kum Bhavnani, 33–39. New York: Oxford University Press, 2001.

————. *Teaching to Transgress: Education as the Practice of Freedom*. New York: Routledge, 1994.

Horton, James Oliver, and Lois E. Horton. *Hard Road to Freedom: The Story of African America: Volume I: African Roots Through the Civil War*. New Brunswick: Rutgers University Press, 2002.

————. *In Hope of Liberty: Culture, Community, and Protest among Northern Free Blacks, 1700–1860*. New York: Oxford University Press, 1997.

Huff, Cynthia A. "Textual Boundaries: Space in Nineteenth-Century Women's Manuscript Diaries." In *Inscribing the Daily: Critical Essays on Women's Diaries,* edited by Suzanne L. Bunkers and Cynthia Ann Huff, 123–38. Amherst: University of Massachusetts Press, 1996.

Hull, Gloria T., ed. *Give Us Each Day: The Diary of Alice Dunbar-Nelson*. New York: W. W. Norton, 1984.

————. "Researching Alice Dunbar-Nelson: A Personal and Literary Perspective." *Feminist Studies* 6, no. 1 (1980): 314–20.

Hull, Gloria T., Patricia Scott and Barbara Smith, ed. *But Some of Us Are Brave: All the Women are White, All the Blacks are Men: Black Women's Studies*. New York: The Feminist Press at CUNY, 1993.

Hunter, Tera W. *To 'Joy My Freedom Southern Black Women's Lives and Labors after the Civil War*. Cambridge: Harvard University Press, 1997.

Ione, Carole. *Pride of Family; Four Generations of American Women of Color*. New York: Harlem Moon Classics, 2004.

"The Impeachment of Andrew Johnson." *Harper's Weekly,* June 10, 1865, 355. http://www.andrewjohnson.com/04AJFirstYear/ii-1.htm (accessed August 28, 2012).

Jacobs, Harriet. *Incidents in the Life of a Slave Girl: Written by Herself,* edited by Jean Fagin Yellin. Cambridge: Harvard University Press, 1987.

Johnson, Anna. *Handbags: the Power of the Purse*. New York: Workman Publishing Company, 2002.

Johnson, David Alan. *Decided on the Battlefield: Grant, Sherman, Lincoln and the Election of 1864*. Amherst: Prometheus Books, 2012.

Jones, Jacqueline. *Labor of Love, Labor of Sorrow: Black Women, Work and the Family from Slavery to the Present*. New York: Basic Books, 1985.

————. "(My Mother Was a Woman), Black Women, Work, and the Family under Slavery." *Feminist Studies* 8, no. 2 (1982): 235–69.

————. "Race and Gender in Modern America." *Review in American History* 26, no. 1 (1998): 220–38.

Jordan, Winthrop D. *White over Black: American Attitudes toward the Negro, 1550–1812.* Baltimore: Penguin Books, 1969.

Kagle, Steven E. "Rewriting Her Life: Fictionalization and the Use of Fictional Models in Early American Women's Diaries." In *Inscribing the Daily: Critical Essays on Women's Diaries,* edited by Suzanne L. Bunkers and Cynthia Ann Huff, 38–55. Amherst: University of Massachusetts Press, 1996.

Kaplan, Amy. "Manifest Domesticity." In *The Futures of American Studies,* edited by Donald E. Pease and Robyn Weigman, 117. Durham: Duke University Press, 2002.

Katz, William Loren. *Breaking the Chains: African-American Slave Resistance.* New York: Ethrac Publications, 1990.

Kautzsch, Alexander. *The Historical Evolution of Earlier African American English: An Empirical Comparison of Early Sources.* New York: Mouton de Gruyter, 2002.

Keckley, Elizabeth. *Behind the Scenes by Elizabeth Keckley, Formerly a Slave, but More Recently a Modiste and Friend to Mrs. Abraham Lincoln, or Thirty Years a Slave and Four Years in the White House.* With an introduction by James Olney. New York: Oxford University Press, 1998.

Keetley, Dawn, and John Pettigrew, eds. *Public Women, Public Words: A Documentary History of American Feminism.* Vol. 3 *1960.* 1st paperback ed., New York: Rowman and Littlefield, 2005.

Kelley, Mary. "Reading Women/Women Reading: The Making of Learned Women in Antebellum America." *Journal of American History* 83, no. 2 (1996), 401–24.

Kennedy, Randall L. "Who Can Say 'Nigger'? and Other Considerations." *Journal of Blacks in Higher Education,* no. 26 (1999–2000): 86–96.

King, Wilma. "Eliza Johnson Potter: Traveler, Entrepreneur, and Social Critic." In *Ordinary Women, Extraordinary Lives: Women in America History,* edited by Kriste Lindenmeyer, 91–104. Wilmington: Scholarly Resources, 2000.

————. "Out of Bounds: Emancipated and Enslaved Women in Antebellum America." In *Beyond Bondage: Free Women of Color in the Americas,* edited by David Barry Gasper and Darlene Clark Hine, 128. Urbana: University of Illinois Press, 2004.

Labov, William. *Language in the Inner City: Studies in the Black English Vernacular.* Philadelphia: University of Pennsylvania Press, 1972.

Lane, Ann J. Rev. of *Revisiting Blassingame's 'The Slave Community': The Scholars Respond,* by Al-Tony Gilmore. *American Historical Review* 84, no. 5 (1979): 1476–77.

Lane, Roger. *Roots of Violence in Black Philadelphia: 1860–1900.* Cambridge: Harvard University Press, 1986.

————. *William Dorsey's Philadelphia and Ours: On the Past and Future of the Black City in America.* New York: Oxford University Press, 1991.

Lapsansky, Emma Jones. "'Discipline to the Mind': Philadelphia's Banneker Institute, 1854–1872." *Pennsylvania Magazine of History and Biography* 117, nos. 1/2 (1993): 83–102.

————. "Friends, Wives, and Striving: Networks and Community Values among Nineteenth-Century Philadelphian Afroamerican Elites." *Pennsylvania Magazine of History and Biography* 108, no. 1 (January 1984): 3–24.

————. *Neighborhoods in Transition: William Penn's Dream and Urban Reality*. New York: Garland Publishing, 1994.

Larson, Nella. *Passing*. New York: Alfred A. Knopf, 1929.

Lasser, Carol. Rev. of *The Great Silent Army of Abolitionism: Ordinary Women in the Antislavery Movement*, by Julie Roy Jeffrey. *The Journal of American History* 86, no. 4, (2000): 1776–1777.

Lasser, Carol. Rev. of *Mary Ann Shadd Cary: The Black Press and Protest in the Nineteenth Century*, by Jane Rhodes. *The Journal of American History* 86, no. 4, (2000): 1776–1777.

Lazreg, Marnia. "Decolonizing Feminism." In *Feminism and 'Race,'* ed. Kum-Kum Bhavnani, 281–93. New York: Oxford University Press, 2001.

Lebsock, Suzanne. *The Free Women of Petersburg: Status and Culture in a Southern Town, 1784–1860*. New York: W. W. Norton, 1985.

Lejeune, Philippe. "How Do Diaries End?" *Biography* 24, no. 1 (2001): 99–111.

Lester, Julius. *To Be a Slave*. New York: Scholastic, 1968.

Levine, Peter. "Draft Evasion in the North during the Civil War, 1863–1865." *Journal of American History* 67, no. 4. (1981): 816–34.

Lindenmeyer, Kriste, ed. *Ordinary Women, Extraordinary Lives: Women in America History*. Wilmington: Scholarly Resources, 2000.

Litwack, Leon F. *North of Slavery: The Negro in the Free States, 1790–1860*. Chicago: University of Chicago Press, 1961.

Loewan, James W. "Slave Narratives and Sociology." *Contemporary Sociology* 11, no. 4 (1982): 380–84.

Loewenberg, Bert James, and Ruth Bogin. *Black Women in Nineteenth-Century American Life: Their Words, Their Thoughts, Their Feelings*. University Park: Pennsylvania State University Press, 1976.

Logan, Rayford W., and Michael R. Winston. *Directory of American Negro Biography*. New York: W. W. Norton, 1982.

Logan, Shirley Wilson. *We Are Coming: The Persuasive Discourse of Nineteenth-Century Black Women*. Carbondale: Southern Illinois University Press, 1999.

Lorde, Audre. "The Master's Tools Will Never Dismantle the Master's House." In *Feminism and 'Race,'* edited by Kum-Kum Bhavnani, 89–92. New York: Oxford University Press, 2001.

————. "Poetry is Not a Luxury." In *Sister Outsider: Essays and Speeches*. New York: Crossing Press, 1984.

————. *Zami Sister Outsider Undersong*. New York: Quality Paperback Book Club, 1993.

Majors, Monroe A. *Noted Negro Women: Their Triumphs and Activities*. Chicago: Donahue and Henneberry Printers, Binders and Engravers, 1893. Reprint ed. Salem: Ayer, 1986.

Mallinson, Christine. "The Dynamic Construction of Race, Class, and Gender through Linguistic Practice among Women in a Black Appalachian Community." Ph.D. diss., North Carolina State University, 2006.

Marshall, Kenneth E. *Manhood Enslaved: Bondmen in Eighteenth- and Early Nineteenth-Century New Jersey*. Rochester, N.Y.: University of Rochester Press, 2011.

Martin, Tony "The Banneker Literary Institute of Philadelphia: African American Intellectual Activism before the War of the Slaveholders' Rebellion." *Journal of African American History* 87 (2002): 302–22.

Martinez, J. Michael. *Coming Forth to Carry Me Home: Race in America from Abolitionism to Jim Crow*. Lanham: Rowman and Littlefield, 2012.

Marwick, Arthur. "Two Approaches to Historical Study: The Metaphysical (Including 'Postmodernism') and the Historical." *Journal of Contemporary History* 30, no. 1 (1995): 5–35.

Mataka, Laini. "Ornithology." In *In Search of Color Everywhere: A Collection of African-American Poetry*, edited by E. Ethelbert Miller, 47. New York: Stewart, Tabori and Chang, 1994.

McCarthy, Molly. "A Pocketful of Days: Pocket Diaries and Daily Record Keeping among the Nineteenth-Century New England Women." *New England Quarterly* 73, no. 2 (2000): 274–96.

McDowell, Deborah E. *The Changing Same: Black Women's Literature, Criticism, and Theory*. Bloomington: Indiana University Press, 1995.

McMurray, Linda O. *To Keep the Waters Troubled: The Life of Ida B. Wells*. New York: Oxford University Press, 1998.

McWhorter, John. *Word on the Street: Debunking the Myth of a 'Pure' Standard English*. New York: Basic Books, 1998.

Mease, James. *The Picture of Philadelphia, Giving An Account of Its Origin, Increase and Improvements in Arts, Sciences, Manufacturers, Commerce and Revenue. With a Compendious View of its Societies, Literary, Benevolent, Patriotic, & Religious. Its Police-The Public Buildings—The Prison and Penitentiary System-Institutions, Monied and Civil—Museum*. Philadelphia: E. and T. Kite, 1811. Reprinted, New York: Arno Press, 1970.

Measuring Worth, "Purchasing Power Calculator." http://www.measuringworth.com/uscompare/relativevalue.php (accessed July 20, 2013).

Megginson, W. J. *African American Life in South Carolina's Upper Piedmont 1780–1900*. Columbia: University of South Carolina Press, 2006.

Miller, Richard. "The Federal City, 1783–1800." In *Philadelphia: Work, Space, Family, and Group Experience in the Nineteenth Century, Essays toward an Interdisciplinary History of the City*, edited by Theodore Hershberg, 155–207. New York: Oxford University Press, 1981.

Mills, Tiya. *Ties That Bind: The Story of an Afro-Cherokee Family in Slavery and Freedom*. Berkeley: University of California Press, 2005.

Minow, Martha. "Repossession: Of History, Poverty, and Dissent." *Michigan Law Review* 91, no. 6 (1993): 1204–12.

Moffat, Mary Jane, and Charlotte Painter, eds. *Revelations: Diaries of Women*. New York: Random House, 1974.

Morgan, Jennifer. "State of the Field: Slavery." *Organization of American Historians* (2008): 1–6. http://lectures.oah.org/lecturers/lecturer.html?id=378 (accessed June 28, 2008).

Motz, Marilyn Ferris. "Folk Expression of Time and Place: 19th-Century Midwestern Rural Diaries." *Journal of American Folklore* 100, no. 396 (1987): 131–47.

———. "The Private Alibi: Literacy and Community in the Diaries of Two Nineteenth-Century American Women." In *Inscribing the Daily: Critical Essays on Women's Diaries*, edited by Suzanne L Bunkers and Cynthia Ann Huff, 189–206. Amherst: University of Massachusetts Press, 1996.

Nash, Gary. *First City: Philadelphia and the Forging of Historical Memory*. Philadelphia: University of Pennsylvania Press, 2002.

———. *Forging Freedom: The Formation of Philadelphia's Black Community, 1720–1840.* Cambridge: Harvard University Press, 1988.

Nash, Gary, and Jean R. Soderlund. *Freedom by Degrees.* New York: Oxford University Press, 1991.

Nathans, Sydney. *To Free a Family: The Journey of Mary Walker.* Cambridge, Mass.: Harvard University Press, 2012.

Neunendorf, Kimberly A. *The Content Analysis Guidebook.* Thousand Oaks: Sage Publications, 2002.

Newman, Debra L. "Black Women in the Era of the American Revolution in Pennsylvania." *Journal of Negro History* 61, no. 3 (1976): 276–89.

Newman, Richard S. *Freedom's Port: Bishop Richard Allen, the AME Church, and the Black Founding Fathers.* New York: New York University Press, 2008.

Newquist, Colleen. "Books in Education Article." *Education World,* (1997). http://www.educationworld.com/a_books/books002.shtml (accessed July 20, 2013).

Nichols, Charles. *Many Thousand Gone: The Ex-Slaves Account of their Bondage and Freedom.* Leiden, Netherlands: E. J. Brill, 1963.

Nobles, Jeanne L. *Beautiful, Also, Are the Souls of My Black Sisters: A History of the Black Woman in America.* New York: Prentice Hall, 1978.

Norton, Mary Beth. "Searchers against Assembles: Gender Distinctions in Seventeenth-Century America." In *Women's America: Refocusing the Past,* edited by Linda K. Kerber and Jane Sherron De Hart, 69–78. New York: Oxford University Press, 2004.

"Obituary of Nathan Bedford Forrest." *New York Times,* October 30, 1877. http://www.nytimes.com/learning/general/onthisday/bday/0713.html (accessed July 20, 2013).

Ogbu, John U. "Beyond Language: Ebonics, Proper English, and Identity in a Black-American Speech Community." *American Educational Research Journal* 36, no. 2 (1999): 147–84.

Palmer, Phyllis Marynick. "White Women/Black Women: The Dualism of Female Identity and Experience in the United States" *Feminist Studies* 9, no. 1 (1983): 151–70.

Parker-Terhune, Carol. "Coping in Isolation: The Experiences of Black Women in White Communities." *Journal of Black Studies* 38 (2008): 547–64.

Perkin, Joan. *History Today* 52, no. 12 (2002): 35–41.

Perry, Patsy B. Rev. of *Give Us Each Day: The Diary of Alice Dunbar-Nelson,* by Gloria T. Hull. *Signs* 12, no. 1 (1986): 175.

Peterson, Carla L. *Doers of the World: African-American Women Speakers and Writers in the North (1830–1880).* New York: Oxford University Press, 1995.

Phillips, Christopher. *Freedom's Port: The African American Community of Baltimore, 1790–1860.* Chicago: University of Illinois Press, 1997.

Phillips, Ulrich Bonnell. *American Negro Slavery.* With a forward by Eugene D. Genovese. 1st paperback ed. Baton Rouge: Louisiana State University Press, 1960.

Prince, Nancy. *A Black Woman's Odyssey though Russia and Jamaica: The Narrative of Nancy Prince (1850).* Princeton: Markus Wiener Publishers, 1989.

Pryor, Elizabeth Brown. *Reading the Man: A Portrait of Robert E. Lee through His Private Letters.* New York: Viking Penguin, 2007.

Quarles, Benjamin. *Black Abolitionists* Reprint ed. New York: Da Capo Press, 1991.

———. *The Negro in the Making of America.* 3rd ed. New York: Collier Books, 1987.

Rankin-Hill, Lesley M. *A Biohistory of 19th-Century Afro-Americans.* Westport: Bergin and Garvey, 1997.

Rawick, George. Vol. 1. *From Sunup to Sundown.* Westport: Greenwood Press, 1972.

Reagon, Bernice Johnson. "Ella's Song." *Sweet Honey in the Rock: Selections 1976–1988.* Flying Fish Records, 1997, compact disc.

Reed, Annette Gordon. *Thomas Jefferson and Sally Hemings: An American Controversy.* Charlottesville: University of Virginia Press, 1998.

Reiland, Rabaka. *W. E. B. Du Bois and the Problems of the Twenty-First Century.* Lanham: Lexington Books, 2007: 137–85.

Ritterhouse, Jennifer. Rev. of *How Race Is Made: Slavery, Segregation, and the Senses,* by Mark M. Smith. *Journal of American History* 93, no. 4 (2007): 1–2.

Robertson, Claire. "Africa into the Americas: Slavery and Women, the Family, and the Gender Division of Labor." In *More Than Chattel: Black Women and Slavery in the Americas,* edited by David Barry Gaspar and Darlene Clark Hine. Bloomington: Indiana University Press, 1996: 3–40.

Robertson, James. *The Untold Civil War: Exploring the Human Side of War.* Edited by Neil Kagan. Washington, D.C.: National Geographic Society, 2011.

Rollin, Frank [Frances], *Life and Public Services of Martin R. Delany.* Boston: Lee and Shepard, 1868.

Royster, Jacqueline Jones. *Traces of a Stream: Literacy and Social Change among African American Women.* Pittsburgh: University of Pittsburgh Press, 2000.

Rusan, Francille. "'This Past Was Waiting for Me When I Came': The Contextualization of Black Women's History." *Feminist Studies* 22, no. 2 (1996): 345–61.

Salvatore, Nick. *We All Got History: The Memory Books of Amos Webber.* New York: Times Books, 1996.

Samuels, Shirley. *The Culture of Sentiment: Race, Gender, and Sentimentality in Nineteenth-Century America.* New York: Oxford University Press, 1992.

Schneider, Dorothy, and Carl J. Schneider. *An Eyewitness History of Slavery in America: From Colonial Times to the Civil War.* New York: Checkmark Books, 2001.

Schneider, Edgar, and Michael Montgomery. "On the Trail of Early Nonstandard Grammar: An Electronic Corpus of Southern U.S. Antebellum Overseers' Letters." *American Speech* 76, no. 4 (2001): 388–410.

Schomburg Library of 19th Century Black Women Writers. Oxford: Oxford University Press, 1988.

Scott, Joan W. "Gender: A Useful Category of Historical Analysis." *American Historical Review* 91, no. 5 (1986): 1053–75.

Scott, Michelle R. "The Realm of a Blues Empress: Blues Culture and Bessie Smith in Black Chattanooga, Tennessee, 1880–1923." Ph.D. diss., Cornell University, 2002.

Scott, Rebecca J. "The Atlantic World and the Road to *Plessy v. Ferguson.*" *Journal of American History* 94, no. 3 (2007): 726–33.

Seacole, Mary. *The Wonderful Adventures of Mrs. Seacole in Many Lands.* Bristol, England, 1857.

Seels, Jody M., and Barbara A. Seels. "Civil War Photography and Its Impact from 1863–1993." In *Visuals Literacy in the Digital Age: Selected Readings from the Annual Conference of the International Visual Literacy Association* 25 (1993). Rochester, N.Y.

Shaw, Stephanie J. "Using the WPA Ex-Slave Narratives to Study the Impact of the Great Depression." *Journal of Southern History* 69, no. 3 (2003): 623–58.

Shipler, David K. *A Country of Strangers: Blacks and Whites in America.* New York: Borzoi, 1997.

Silcox, Harry C. "Nineteenth Century Philadelphia Black Militant: Octavius v. Catto (1839–1871)." In *African Americans in Pennsylvania: Shifting Historical Perspectives,* edited by Joe William Trotter and Eric Ledell Smith, 53–76. University Park: Pennsylvania State University Press, 1997.

Sinha, Manisha. "Allies for Emancipation? Black Abolitionists and Abraham Lincoln." *History Now America History Online.* 2008. https://www.gilderlehrman.org/history-by-era/african-americans-and-emancipation/essays/allies-for-emancipation-black-abolitionists (accessed July 20, 2013).

Smedley, Brian D., Adrienne Y. Stith, and Alan Ray Nelson, eds. *Unequal Treatment: Confronting Racial and Ethnic Disparities in Health Care.* Washington, D.C.: National Academies Press, 2003.

Smith, Anna Bustill. "The Bustill Family." *Journal of Negro History* 10, no. 4 (1925): 638–44.

Smith, John David, and John C. Inscoe, eds. *Ulrich Bonnell Phillips: A Southern Historian and His Critics.* Westport: Greenwood Press, 1990.

Smith-Rosenberg, Carroll. "The Female World of Love and Ritual: Relations between Women in Nineteenth-Century America." In *Women's America: Refocusing the Past,* edited by Linda K. Kerber and Jane Sherron De Hart, 168–82. New York: Oxford University Press, 2004.

———. "The Cycle of Femininity in Nineteenth-Century America." *Feminist Studies* 1, no ¾. Special Double Issue: Women's History (1973), 58–72.

Southall, Geneva Handy. *Blind Tom, The Black Pianist-Composer: Continually Enslaved.* Lanham: Scarecrow Press, 2002.

Spelman, Elizabeth V. "Gender & Race: The Ampersand Problem in Feminist Thought." In *Feminism and 'Race,'* edited by Kum-Kum Bhavnani, 74–88. New York: Oxford University Press, 2001.

Stampp, Kenneth M. *The Peculiar Institution: Slavery in the Ante-Bellum South.* New York: Vintage Books, 1956.

Stanley, Amy Dru. "Instead of Waiting for the Thirteenth Amendment: The War Power, Slave Marriage, and Inviolate Human Rights." In *American Historical Review* 115, no. 3 (June 2012): 732–65.

Stauffer, John. *Giants: The Parallel Lives of Frederick Douglass and Abraham Lincoln.* New York: Hachette, 2009.

Steckel, Richard H. "Women, Work, and Health under Plantation Slavery in the U.S." In *More Than Chattel: Black Women and Slavery in the Americas,* edited by David Barry Gaspar and Darlene Clark Hine, 43–60. Bloomington: Indiana University Press, 1996.

Stevenson, Brenda, ed. *The Journals of Charlotte Forten Grimké.* New York: Oxford University Press, 1988.

Sumler-Lewis, Janice. "The Forten-Purvis Women of Philadelphia and the American Anti-Slavery Crusade." *Journal of Negro History* 66, no. 4 (1981–82): 281–88.

Sweet Honey in the Rock. "Beatitudes." *Live at Carnegie Hall.* Flying Fish Records, 1988, compact disc.

Tate, Gayle T. "Free Black Resistance in the Antebellum Era, 1830 to 1860." *Journal of Black Studies* 28, no. 6 (1998): 764–82.

Taylor, Frank Hamilton. *Philadelphia in the Civil War 1861–1865.* Philadelphia: Dunlap Printing, 1913. http://ia700408.us.archive.org/11/items/cu31924028861842/cu31924028861842 .pdf (accessed June 19, 2012).

Taylor, Nikki M. *Frontiers of Freedom: Cincinnati's Black Community 1802–1868.* Athens: Ohio University Press, 2005.

Taylor, Quintard. "(1863) Rev. Jonathan C. Gibbs, 'Freedom's Joyful Day.'" In *An Online Reference Guide to African American History.* http://www.blackpast.org/?q=1863-rev-jonathan -c-gibbs-freedoms-joyful-day (accessed July 20, 2013).

Temple, Christel L. "Rescuing the Literary in Black Studies." *Journal of Black Studies* 36 (2006): 764–785.

Temple, Christel N. "The cosmology of Afrocentric womanism." *The Western Journal of Black Studies* 36, no. 1 (2012): 23+. *Academic OneFile.* Web (accessed July 21, 2013).

Terborg-Penn, Rosalyn. "Teaching the History of Black Women: A Bibliographic Essay." *History Teacher* 13, no. 2 (1980): 245–50.

Thayer, Theodore. "Town into City, 1746–1765." 2nd 3 ed. In Philadelphia: A 300-Year History, edited by Russell F. Weigley, 68–108. New York: W. W. Norton, 1982.

Thomas, Charles Walker. Rev. of *The Journal of Charlotte L. Forten,* by Ray Allen Billington. *Journal of Negro History* 38, no. 3 (1953): 341–43.

Thompson, Julius E. "In My Mind's Eye." In *Trouble the Water: 250 Years of African-American Poetry,* edited by Jerry W. Ward Jr., 496–99. New York: Penguin Books, 1997.

Tillery, Tyrone. "The Inevitability of the Douglass-Garrison Conflict." *Phylon (1960–)* 37, no. 2 (2nd Qtr., 1976): 137–149.

Trotter, William, Jr., and Eric Ledell Smith, eds. *African Americans in Pennsylvania: Shifting Historical Perspectives.* University Park: Pennsylvania State University Press, 1997.

Tucker, Spencer C. *A Short History of the Civil War at Sea.* Wilmington: Scholarly Resources, 2002.

Turner, Edward Raymond. *The Negro in Pennsylvania: Slavery—Servitude Freedom, 1639–1861.* New York: Arno Press and New York Times, 1969.

Ulrich, Laurel Thatcher. *A Midwife's Tale: The Life of Martha Ballard, Based on her Diary, 1785–1812.* New York: Vintage Books, 1991.

———. "Of Pens and Needles: Sources in Early American Women's History." *Journal of American History* 77, no. 1 (1990): 200–207.

———. *Good Wives: Image and Reality in the Lives of Women in Northern New England 1650–1750.* 1st paperback ed. New York: Oxford University Press, 1983.

———. "The Ways of Her Household." In *Women's America: Refocusing the Past,* edited by Linda K. Kerber and Jane Sherron De Hart, 45–54. New York: Oxford University Press, 2004

van D., G. G. Rev. of *American Negro Slave Revolts,* by Herbert Aptheker. *English Historical Review* 63, no. 247 (1948): 283.

van Sertima, Ivan. *They Came before Columbus: The African Presence in Ancient America.* New York: Random House, 1976.

Wade, Richard C., ed. *Negroes in American Life: Selected Readings.* Boston: Houghton Mifflin, 1970.

Walker, Alice. *In Search of My Mother's Garden.* Orlando: Harcourt Books, 1983.

Walters Shelton B. *We Have This Ministry: A History of First African Presbyterian Church, Philadelphia, Pennsylvania, The Mother Church of African American Presbyterians.* Philadelphia: Gloucester Memorial and Historical Society, 1994.

Warren, Wendy Anne. "The Cause of Her Grief: The Rape of a Slave in Early New England." *Journal of American History* 93, no. 4 (2007): 1031–49.

Weigley, Russell F. "The Border City in Civil War, 1854–1865." In *Philadelphia: A 300-Year History,* 2nd ed., edited by Russell F. Weigley, Nicholas B. Wainwright, and Edwin Wolf, 363–416. New York: W. W. Norton, 1982.

Welter, Barbara. "The Cult of True Womanhood." *American Quarterly* 18, no. 2 (1996): 151–74.

White, Deborah Gray. *Ar'n't I a Woman?: Female Slaves in the Plantation South.* New York: W. W. Norton, 1985.

———. "Mining the Forgotten: Manuscript Sources for Black Women's History." *Journal of American History* 74, no. 1 (1987): 237–42.

Whitehead, Kaye Wise. "The Impact of the Civil Rights Movement on American Policies, Laws and Procedures." In *The National Visionary Leadership Project's Online Civil Rights Movement,* edited by John Hope Franklin, Renee Poussaint, Camille Cosby, and Percy Sutton, 2006. http://www.visionaryproject.org/teacher (accessed June 24, 2008).

———. *Reconstructing Memories: A Case Study of Emilie Davis, a 19th Century Freeborn Colored Woman.* Ph.D. diss., University of Maryland, Baltimore County, 2009.

———. "Reconstructing the Life of a Colored Woman: The Pocket Diaries of Emilie F. Davis." *Pennsylvania Magazine of History and Biography* 135, no. 4 (2011): 561–64.

———. "'Rise in the Scale of Being': Jonathan Clarkson Gibbs, Philadelphia Ministry, and Florida Politics." In *Before Obama: A Reappraisal of Black Reconstruction Era Politicians,* edited by Matthew Lynch, 330–59. Santa Barbara: ABC-CLIO

———. "'They Both Got History': Using Diary Entries to Analyze the Written Language and Historical Significance of Free Black Philadelphia." *LLC Review* (2009): 48–61.

———. "We Are Your Sisters: Comparing the Lives of Free and Enslaved Black Women in the 19th Century." In *Teaching American History Online,* 2005. http://www.umbc.edu/che (accessed June 24, 2008).

Wilson, Harriet. *Our Nig; or, Sketches From the Life of a Free Black, In a Two-Story White House, North. Showing That Slavery's Shadows Fall Even There.* With an introduction and notes by Henry Louis Gates Jr. New York: Random House, 1983.

Winch, Julie. *Philadelphia's Black Elite.* Philadelphia: Temple University Press, 1998.

———, ed. *The Elite of Our People: Joseph Willson's Sketches of Black Upper-Class Life in Antebellum Philadelphia.* University Park: Pennsylvania State University Press, 2000.

———. "The Leaders of Philadelphia's Black Community, 1787–1848." Ph.D. diss., Bryn Mawr College, 1982.

Woodson, Carter G. *The Mind of the Negro as Reflected in Letters Written during the Crisis.* New York: Negro Universities Press, 1969.

Wright, Richard R., Jr. *The Negro in Pennsylvania: A Study in Economic History.* New York: Arno Press and the New York Times, 1969.

Wyatt-Brown, Bertram. Rev. of *Roll Jordan Roll: The World the Slaves Made,* by Eugene D. Genovese. *Journal of Southern History* 41, no. 2 (1975): 240–42.

Yee, Shirley J. *Black Women Abolitionists: A Study in Activism, 1828–1860.* Knoxville: University of Tennessee Press, 1992.

Yetman, Norman R. Rev. of *Slave Testimony: Two Centuries of Letters, Speeches, Interviews, and Autobiographies,* by John Blassingame. *Journal of Negro History* 68, no. 2 (1983): 218–20.

————, ed. *When I Was a Slave: Memoirs from the Slave Narrative Collection.* Minneola: Dover Publications, 2002.

Young, Lola. "'Race,' Identity and Cultural Criticism." In *Feminism and 'Race,'* edited by Kum-Kum Bhavnani, 171–83. New York: Oxford University Press, 2001.

Young, Verhsawn Ashanti. "Your Average Nigga." *College Composition and Communication* 55, no. 4 (2004): 693–715.

Zboray, Ronald J., and Mary Saracino Zboray. "Books, Reading, and the World of Goods in Antebellum New England." *American Quarterly* 48, no. 4 (1996): 587–622.

INDEX

The abbreviation EFD in subheadings refers to Emilie Frances Davis. Italic page numbers refer to illustrations.